Praise for

The Real Warren Buffett

*"James O'Loughlin's new book is a timely and insightful account
of the career and achievements of the head of Berkshire
Hathaway, Buffett's investment business.
Above all Buffett is revealed as a thoughtful long-term
investor, or 'capital allocator' as he calls it, who rejects fads and
fashions, and who will not be taken in by the latest big thing.
As this intelligently written and neatly set out book shows, it is a
formula that has proved amazingly successful, and rewarding, for
four decades."*
Stefan Stern, Accounting & Business

*"Buffett, the second richest man in the US, is known as the
world's master stock picker, but that alone does not account for
how he has grown his investment vehicle Berkshire Hathaway at
a compound rate of 25 per cent a year for 37 years.
O'Loughlin digs into the deeper business story: how Buffett uses
capital and get his managers to 'think like owners.' He has
uncovered a simple model of clever management that many
companies can follow with profit. The model is based on a few
unswerving principles...
Buy and hold, as a stock analyst would say."*
Carol Kennedy, Director

The Real
Warren Buffett

*To Sarah—my strength,
in her sickness and in her health.
And Harry and Niamh—my hope and my joy.*

The Real
Warren Buffett

Managing Capital,
Leading People

James O'Loughlin

NICHOLAS BREALEY
PUBLISHING

LONDON

This updated paperback edition first published by
Nicholas Brealey Publishing in 2004

3–5 Spafield Street   PO Box 700
Clerkenwell, London   Yarmouth
EC1R 4QB, UK   Maine 04096, USA
Tel: +44 (0)20 7239 0360   Tel: (888) BREALEY
Fax: +44 (0)20 7239 0370   Fax: (207) 846 5181
                http://www.nbrealey-books.com

First published in hardback in 2002
Reprinted in 2003

ISBN 1-85788-332-2

British Library Cataloguing in Publication Data
A catalogue record for this book is available from the British Library.

LCCN 2002114498

Printed in Finland by WS Bookwell.

Contents

Preface

At the death of writing this book, and before settling on its final version, I handed the manuscript to a good friend of mine for one last sanity check. David Crowther, the man with the quickest brain I know, duly digested the work and downloaded his observations, one of which was the realization: "My God, Jim. Buffett just knows it all."

And that's precisely why I wrote this book.

In my career as a fund manager and equity strategist, the more I read of the theory of investment and the more I progressed to learn about the challenges facing managements in the creation of value—in organizational theory, complexity theory, behavioral psychology, *whatever*—the more Buffett's insights into these disciplines leapt out at me from his letters to the shareholders of Berkshire Hathaway.

Whatever I was learning, he already knew. Whatever I was struggling to synthesize into a framework, he had already embedded in a model. What I was just beginning to comprehend, he had already made work.

In this respect, I realized, Warren Buffett did know it all—even though he didn't always get it right. In order to appreciate this fact, all I had to do was know where to look and then I was able to read his letters differently.

It is in the spirit of my discovery that I present this illumination of Buffett's model for managing capital and leading people. My intention is to share my experience with a wider audience. Buffett has this model because he has undergone what I argue is an explosion of cognition. Writing about it has enriched me in a similar way: I have had my own explosion and I now view the world through a different lens. If I have done my job, then by the end of this book you will too.

James O'Loughlin
Birkenhead, Cheshire
August 2002

Acknowledgments

So many people have contributed to the writing of this book, it is difficult to know where to start.

Thanks must initially go to Warren Buffett for his kind permission to quote from his letters to the shareholders of Berkshire Hathaway, for his compliments on this work, and for his well wishes.

The use of further quotes from the *Outstanding Investor Digest* (OID), which provides, among other things, a write-up of Berkshire Hathaway's annual meeting, has also improved the book enormously.* My thanks go to Henry Emerson for allowing me to quote from this publication and to Clara Cabrera who facilitated the process. It was Duncan Clark, ex-managing director at Brown Brothers Harriman in London, who first alerted me to the writings of Charlie Munger, and therefore to the service provided by the OID. Both have proven invaluable. It comes as no surprise that Buffett recommends Henry's publication to investors everywhere. I only hope I can extend that readership to include a few managers.

This book would not have been possible save for the efforts of all those who have gone before me in writing about Warren Buffett. In this regard, I found the works of Andrew Kilpatrick and Roger Lowenstein particularly valuable and would commend their reading to anyone with an interest in this subject. Andrew Kilpatrick's *Of*

---

*Quotes used in this text from the *Outstanding Investor Digest* are not to be reproduced without permission from the Outstanding Investor Digest Inc., 295 Greenwich Street, Box 282, New York, NY 1007, tel. 212 025 3885, www.OID.com.

Permanent Value represents a vast repository of information on Buffett and Roger Lowenstein's *Buffett: The Making of an American Capitalist* is a must for any serious student of Buffett. The writings of Robert Hagstrom, particularly *The Warren Buffett Portfolio* and *Latticework*, have also proven enlightening.

It was Mike Mauboussin, managing director and chief US investment strategist at Credit Suisse First Boston and co-author with Alfred Rappaport of *Expectations Investing*, who lit the spark to this fire. At a meeting in London Mike was kind enough to scribble the names of a handful of books that I should read on the back of a business card. From there, I went to the nearest bookstore and bumped into Stephen Pinker's *How the Mind Works*, which was not on Mike's list but is a text that I now know he would have recommended. All else followed. Thank you, Michael.

My colleagues at the C.I.S. have provided support, advice, and insights.* Thanks to Linda Desforges and Mark McBride on the US desk in this regard. And a further thank-you to Neal Foundly, pension fund manager, Chris Hirst, chief investment manager, and John Franks, deputy chief investment manager, for taking the time to read, edit, and improve the manuscript. Neal Foundly's input was profoundly reassuring, Chris's backing most welcome, and John Franks' editorial input invaluable.

On that note, I'm also grateful to all those who took part in the feedback process, which did much to shape the book near its completion: Duncan Clark, James Becker of Pereire Todd in London, Frank McCann, also of the C.I.S., Rupert Carnegie, director of global research and strategy at Henderson, Mark Thomas of PA Consulting, who leads the shareholder value work in PA's Management Group, Chris Mack, executive director, Goldman Sachs International, and Dr.

---

*The views expressed in this book are my own and should not be interpreted as necessarily representing those of the C.I.S. or of my colleagues.

Gulnur Muradoglu, Cass Business School, London, all contributed meaningfully to this task.

My particular thanks with regard to feedback go to Hersh Shefrin, Arnold Wood, Bob Olsen, and Nick Chater, details of whom appear at the beginning of this book. Aside from Nick, who was a recent professional acquaintance, none of these people knew me before I approached them to ask if they would take a look at my manuscript. Each gave unselfishly of their time and their encouragement of the project was heartening—as was their willingness to give it their public endorsement.

Thanks also to Edgar Peters, author of several highly readable books and chief investment strategist for Panagora Asset Management, for his early encouragement of this project and his advice to a budding author, to Alice Schroeder at Morgan Stanley for her insights into the insurance industry, to Denis Hilton, Professor of Social Psychology at the University of Toulouse, for sending me his lecture notes, and to Dave Crowther for his feedback, insights, and encouragements and for all those early dialogs we had as colleagues.

This book is unrecognizable compared to the original version that I sent to my publisher Nick Brealey. I am eternally grateful to Nick that, on receipt of that package in 1999, he reacted in the way of the small boy when his father presented him with a pile of manure on Christmas Day. With a cry of "There's got to be a horse in there somewhere!" he jumped right in and started to dig.

Nick's digging has, I hope, paid off. His editorial contribution has done a great deal to extract a book from a manuscript and now, as I put the finishing touches to the creation that he has done much to influence, I finally feel able to forgive him the "torture" that he put me through. I only hope that he feels able to reciprocate.

I also take my hat off to Sally Lansdell, my editor, who displayed considerable understanding of the text in its editing. She has improved the book's readability enormously, was a joy to work with, and pulled out all the stops when necessary. Any residual errors and oversights are completely my own and I absolve anybody who has had a hand in this book from responsibility for any of its shortcomings.

Lastly, my wife Sarah has been unstinting in her efforts to free up my time to work on this book, particularly at the weekends. Sarah has been my biggest fan, my most vocal cheerleader, and a willing reader of every word I have written. Her support throughout has been immense, matched only by the patience of Harry and Niamh, my children, who each typed at least one word of this book. I could not have done it without their understanding and I love them dearly.

1

The Real Warren Buffett

We're only responsible for two functions... First, it's our job to keep able people who are already rich motivated to keep working at things... they don't need to do for financial reasons. It's that simple. Secondly, we have to allocate capital.

Warren Buffett[1]

During his 37-year tenure as chairman and chief executive of Berkshire Hathaway, Warren Buffett has grown the market value of this company at a compound growth rate of over 25% *per year*.

The consequences of compound growth of such long duration can be difficult to imagine. So let's put Buffett's record into a perspective that can be more easily visualized. At birth, my son measured 60cm in length. If he were to grow at the same rate as Buffett has managed to grow the value of Berkshire Hathaway, by the time *he* is 37 he will be taller than the Empire State Building!

Thus, anyone who had the foresight to invest $10,000 in Berkshire Hathaway when Buffett took charge of the company in 1965 would have seen the value of this stake grow to over $40 million today. Indeed, had anyone invested the same sum with Buffett when he began his professional investing career with the Buffett Partnership nine years earlier, and reinvested in the stock of Berkshire Hathaway when the Partnership was wound up, it would now be worth a staggering $270 million—or something like *$500 million* before fees.[2]

By comparison, $10,000 invested in 1965 in the S&P 500, a basket of stocks broadly representative of the largest corporations in America, would today be worth only $144,000—a 9m pygmy to Buffett's towering colossus.

Buffett has not delivered this performance by being a stock picker. He has done it by being a CEO: by leading people and by managing capital.

Nor was he born to such excellence. He had to learn it. In his early years he made mistakes—plenty of them. He still makes mistakes now. In the 1970s and 1980s, however, Buffett underwent an explosion of cognition in which his model of leadership and capital management emerged.

This is the model that has sustained Berkshire Hathaway's performance as an operating company, as opposed to the investment vehicle it once was. This is the model that has elevated Buffett above all other CEOs. It is also the model that is made available in this book.

Capital markets offer a sophisticated arena in which to emulate Warren Buffett, who, with a personal fortune of $37 billion, is currently the second richest man in America behind Bill Gates. They also offer a thousand opportunities to make the mistakes that will ground your compound returns in the average and stunt your growth. Buffett was, and is, able to identify opportunity. He has been, and is, able to circumvent most errors of decision making, and to learn from those that he does make. He has combined this into a form of leadership that allows him free expression of his talent. And he has endowed managers within Berkshire Hathaway who also allocate capital with the ability to do so on a similarly informed basis.

Warren Buffett appreciates the challenges of attempting to act like an owner of an enterprise when functioning as its manager. He has discovered the difficulties of getting Berkshire's subsidiary managers to act like owners too.

He has learned the necessity of working with people who have the right mindset. He has uncovered what this is and how to identify it. He has also learned how difficult it is to change behavior in people made of the wrong stuff. Importantly, he has discovered how to attract the one to join Berkshire and how to discourage the other. And he has found a way of fostering enduring loyalty among those who do work for him, of eliciting their compliance with the objectives he sets for Berkshire Hathaway, and of drawing out lasting commitments from his managers to the principles he espouses as a leader.

Buffett has found the instrument of leadership in his own personality: in his belief system, in his attitude toward those who entrust their savings to him, in his honesty, his high-ground ideals, and his fairness. These have become an expression of Berkshire Hathaway's corporate ideals. Above all, Buffett has learned that people management transcends into personal motivation when the rules of behavior that people are expected to follow are implanted from within, rather than set from above; that compliance and diligence are at their height when these rules are set in sympathy with that small voice that exists inside all of us, which tells us *how* to behave.

Buffett has found that managerial control comes from letting go— and he adheres to the same philosophy in his management of capital.

Buffett does not believe that the world in which he operates lends itself to the imposition of his will upon it. It only yields itself to those who are prepared, ahead of time, to take advantage of the opportunities that it inevitably throws up, yet that cannot be reliably predicted.

Buffett wants to reduce subjectivity in capital management decisions to a minimum. Correspondingly, he wants to maximize the objectivity that he brings to bear. In the face of a welter of information that would otherwise threaten to overwhelm him, Buffett filters the universe in which he manages capital down to the important and knowable. He wants to make most of his capital management decisions in this realm and it is on the basis of the enlightenment conveyed by what he calls the Circle of Competence that he wants to make *all* of his capital management decisions.

Oftentimes, this suggests behavior that is deeply unconventional. The emotional consequences of this threaten to distort Buffett's decision-making process and undo his rationality. Therefore, by putting in the groundwork ahead of time, Buffett ensures that every decision he takes in his management of Berkshire's capital is taken from a position of utmost psychological security.

The construction of Buffett's Circle of Competence and the nature of this groundwork are explained at length in this book. The end product allows Buffett to allocate capital *where* he sees fit, *when* he sees fit, and *at the pace* he sees fit. He does so in opportunities that he can qualify as such and is able to evaluate. The accuracy of his cognition is enhanced, his capital management enlightened, and Buffett transports his framework into the art of acting like an owner.

The stock valuation principles that most readers of Warren Buffett crave are in this book. But they have been placed within a framework that makes sense of them for the practitioner. As a professional investor of 20 years' experience, it is only in writing this work that I found this framework. Prior to this, I too explored Buffett's approach to investment with the hope of finding the Holy Grail. I was looking in the wrong place and suffered from illusory competence.

It is only when I recognized that a holistic approach was required that I came to appreciate Warren Buffett's Circle of Competence. Now that I have his framework, I am far closer to Buffett than I ever was when I simply tried to piggyback on his investing style, and I can, at last, put what I know about him into practice as an equity strategist. I have dispelled my illusions.

The financial institution for which I work has found it can do the same. In pursuit of its fiduciary duty of care in the management of other people's money, it is adopting the framework I have described to extend its investment philosophy and enhance its investment process. This book will provide similar lessons for a wider audience—in particular for corporate managers in *their* duty of care to their shareholders.

It will explain what Warren Buffett means by saving on behalf of those who place their savings with a manager and elucidate Buffett's ideals of corporate governance.

The book will illuminate what it means to be an owner; how to use this ideal as an instrument of leadership that *leads*, rather than drags, kicks, pushes, and corrals; how to attract the right people to the organization; how to effect acquisitions in this regard that do not fail; and how to devise rules of behavior that drive these principles down through an organization at the operational level.

It will elucidate the role of corporate strategy and describe how Buffett prevents prior commitments from becoming blindfolds.

The book will describe Warren Buffett not as a demigod free from error, but as a mortal with human failings. However, it will also inform managers that mistakes need not be tombstones, rather that they can be stepping stones to better decision making.

It will illustrate the psychology and emotion of decision making in order to improve that function. It will also defuse the psychology and emotion of poor decision making.

The book will prescribe a set of rules that a public company can adopt in order to conduct itself according to Buffett's credo.

It will provide a guide for managers who wish to defy *current* convention and manage in accordance with reality rather than in its defiance. It will explain how Buffett attracts shareholders who think like owners and how he dissuades those who do not; why he is able to embrace volatility in operating results and how he manages the psychological and emotional consequences of this; how he cultivates the bond of trust that exists between him and his shareholders and how he harvests this to deliver unparalleled returns to them.

Most importantly, whether it be in managing people or in managing capital, this book will show managers how to *act* like owners. It is a narrative, but it is also a manual of high-ground corporate governance.

Buffett himself advises people to "pick out a few heroes." "There's nothing like the right ones," he says.[3] It is in the spirit of *this* advice that I offer you the real Warren Buffett. A manager of capital. And a leader of people.

A COMPOUNDING MACHINE

We're like the hedgehog that knows one big thing. If you generate float at 3% per annum and buy businesses that earn 13% per annum with the proceeds of the float, we have actually figured out that that's a pretty good position to be in.

Charlie Munger[4]

In 1965, when Warren Buffett officially took charge of Berkshire Hathaway, it operated in just a single line of business—the manufacture of textiles—and generated revenues of around $600 million.

Today, it is enormously diverse, with interests that stretch from the conduct of insurance to shoe manufacturing, from the production of flight simulators to vacuum cleaners, and much more in between—including investments in quoted shares on the stock market. Measured by its

$60 billion of book value, it is the second largest corporation in America after Exxon Mobil; by its market capitalization of $109 billion, it is the 19th largest in America and 26th in the world. Revenues now amount to over $30 billion and Berkshire employs approximately 112,000 people.

This is a truly massive undertaking. It is also one that Buffett manages out of a small, unassuming office in Omaha, Nebraska, calling on the help of just "13.8"[5] other people.

If Buffett maintains the pace he has set at Berkshire Hathaway, his company will absorb the whole of the US economy within the next 34 years. An interesting concept—not least because, at the age of 72, Buffett says that he plans to retire about 10 years *after* he dies.

Clearly, Berkshire Hathaway is a compounding machine. How is it constructed?

Buffett's long-stated objective has been to grow the value of Berkshire at a rate of 15% per year, measured over the long term. Since Buffett attests "the absolute most that owners of a business, in the aggregate, can get out of it in the end—between now and Judgment Day—is what that business earns over time," he knows that he can only grow Berkshire's value to the extent that the cash that can be taken out of it exceeds the amount put into it.[6] So in order to construct a compounding machine he must do two things.

First, he has to own and operate high-return businesses; that is, those that generate substantially more cash than is required to maintain their respective competitive positions.

Second, he has to find opportunities to reinvest their excess cash at high rates of return so that he can keep the cash machine running. As Buffett says:

> *When returns on capital are ordinary, an earn-more-by-putting-up-more is no great managerial achievement. You can get the same result personally while operating from your rocking chair. Just quadruple the capital you commit to a savings account and you will quadruple your earnings.*[7]

He recognizes that "if retained earnings… are employed in an unproductive manner, the economics of Berkshire will deteriorate very quickly."[8]

His focus in the allocation of capital therefore revolves around this reality. Ideally, he would prefer to find opportunities to reinvest Berkshire's excess capital in existing businesses—so he wants to own businesses with ample opportunities to grow—but, if this is not the case, he has to find others that possess the desired characteristics.

The key to Buffett's ability to compound is his ability to harvest the cash from cash-generative businesses and reinvest this elsewhere. As much as Buffett has to be skillful in the reinvestment of this cash in capital management, crucially, he has to be careful that it continues to be generated long into the future, which is more a challenge of leadership. If ever the harvest failed, Berkshire Hathaway would cease to compound. It would not grow its value at a rate of 25% per annum, nor at 15% either. It would, instead, be average.

Buffett's bank

Berkshire Hathaway's insurance operations are crucial components of Buffett's compounding machine. As a centerpiece to a cash-generating model, these are ideal because insurance companies take cash in *before* they pay it out. Additionally the industry, which is fragmented, offers ample opportunities for individual players to grow.

If an insurance company can price its policies in such a way that it retains more money from them than it pays out as claims, then the cost of its float is zero. Essentially, that makes it an interest-free loan. And if it can do this on a consistent basis, its access to this free loan becomes permanent. This is Warren Buffett's bank.

In the 33 years since he entered the insurance business, Buffett has grown Berkshire's float at a compound annual rate of around 25%. He has given himself the option of reinvesting this either in the insurance industry to produce yet more float, or in instruments that yield returns significantly higher than its cost. And, vitally in this regard, the average cost of Berkshire's float over this period, contrary to the impression that Munger gives above, has been very close to zero.[9]

This is remarkable, and explains why Berkshire's float is the rocket fuel for Buffett's compounding machine.[10] To remain rocket fuel, however, it *has to be* free or, if not, generated at least at low cost. If

Buffett's underwriting were unprofitable, Berkshire's float would tran-
sition from fuel to an expensive and low-margin cargo.

Often, conditions in the insurance industry do not allow Buffett to
reinvest in it with the prospect of generating cheap float. However, he
embraces the volatility in results in his insurance operations and is
happy to invest their float elsewhere—either in the acquisition of *controlling* interests in other companies, or in the acquisition of *stakes* in
companies quoted on the stock market.

When he does the latter, Buffett looks for companies that are also
cash generative, and that present opportunities to reinvest at high
rates of return, although he still has to buy these at prices allowing him
to earn a commensurately high rate of return on his investment.

In spite of the fact that he is more famous for this activity—investing in a highly select, that is, nondiversified, portfolio of stocks, often
in *enormous* size—he does, however, have a preference for outright
purchases. This often requires him to pay a premium for the privilege
of complete control, but with the ownership of the enterprise *comes
the ownership of its cash flow*.

Importantly, if Buffett owns the cash flow, he gets to harvest it and
sow it elsewhere if he so chooses. Indeed, the only stipulation he
makes of the management of the companies that he acquires is that
they send their excess cash—or the money left over after they have
attended to maintaining and growing their businesses—to him in
Omaha. Apart from that, they are left completely to their own devices.
Buffett even allows *them* to define what they mean by "excess cash."

Naturally, in order to compound the value of his investments in the
companies he acquires outright, Buffett also has to price them accordingly. In addition to this, to ensure that they continue to produce a
healthy crop of cash, he has to ensure that they continue to perform
well long after he has acquired them. For the diverse interests that
Buffett has assembled under Berkshire Hathaway, this is an enormous
challenge.

The pace at which Buffett reinvests the cash from his insurance
and other subsidiary companies can vary from the frenetic when prices
are right to the slothful when they are not. He may invest a trickle.
Often he will commit a waterfall—often, and unusually, in a single tar-

get. In between times, he may do nothing, just sit on cash or other low-return assets. The lumpiness that this approach induces in Berkshire's operating results is of no concern to Buffett, but it is also the case that he has no pre-determined idea of *where* he will invest Berkshire's excess cash. He simply allows the price/value equation in those industries that he feels he understands to do this for him.

The nature of Buffett's compounding machine is such that, apart from a 10 cent dividend paid to shareholders in 1969 (he must have gone to the bathroom during the board meeting, he tells me), thus far he has not returned a single cent of the profits that Berkshire generates to its shareholders, either in the form of dividends or share repurchases.[11] Instead, by degree, he has invested 100% of the company's capital back into the enterprise.

A RECIPE FOR FAILURE

One of the greatest tragedies of life is the murder of a beautiful theory by a gang of brutal facts.

Benjamin Franklin

The laws of physics dictate that bumblebees should not be capable of flight. In proportion to their body mass, the surface area of their wings is too small and they beat them too rapidly to generate sufficient thrust to impart the required lift. So in theory, bumblebees should flail rather than fly.

The same is true of Warren Buffett's machine. As found in the base rate probabilities expressed in the field, the *laws of finance* dictate that Berkshire Hathaway should suffer from chronic underperformance.

Taken individually, the base rate probabilities of failure in the ventures in which it is engaged are stacked against it. *Compounded* as they are in Buffett's chosen corporate form, the odds against success are hugely magnified. As a publicly quoted corporate entity, with all that this implies in the way in which management of public companies has come to be practiced, Berkshire Hathaway should never get off the ground.

Clearly, like the bumblebee, it does fly. *And* its performance packs a sting! *This is the enigma of Warren Buffett.*

Consider the empirical evidence:

○ The insurance industry is attractive *in theory only*. In practice, insurance companies, as a rule, *do not* possess the underwriting discipline required to generate low-cost float. And such is the commodity-like nature of this business that slack pricing often ruins the profitability of every player in the game, preventing even disciplined underwriters from reinvesting in the business on a sound basis.

○ Highly diversified firms are notoriously inefficient. At a human level they are difficult to manage and it is not readily apparent which divisions deserve to be funded and which do not—a process in which capital gets dissipated.

○ Putting such a firm together by acquisition is sheer madness. The majority of mergers and acquisitions fail to deliver on the expectations of those who engineer them. Prices paid are generally too high, the integration of the entities involved normally backfires, and capital value is destroyed in the process.

○ Reinvesting 100% of a company's cash in the enterprise is an exercise fraught with risk. In a competitive environment, managements face an enormous challenge to add value over and above that which their shareholders could earn elsewhere, to *all* of the cash their businesses generate. In fact, at the margin, managements generally earn the highest return on cash by giving it back to their shareholders.

○ Leaving managers to their own devices can be dangerous: They habitually attend to their own selfish interests rather than complying with the objectives set by the owners that employ them.

○ Investing in the stock market is a losing proposition. In the sense that it discounts all known information into prices, it is efficient. Therefore, it should not be in the compass of one man to find stocks that do not fully reflect their attractive fundamentals in their valuations. Nor should he be able to do this on a consistent basis.

○ Holding cash and other low-return assets acts as a dead weight when the target returns of a firm are substantially higher.

The fact is, Warren Buffett has chosen as a key component of his machine a business with lousy *ex post* economics. Yet he relies on his insurance companies—which operate in a business typically profligate in the destruction of profitability and therefore prone to the generation of high-cost float—to act as bankers to his machine. He further relies on this industry for the bulk of his reinvestment opportunities, even when its fortunes are hostage to the actions of its dumbest players.

Around these he has wrapped an eclectic mix of subsidiary companies that have very little in common, creating a far-flung empire, the operating performance of which is vital to the returns he makes on his investments in it and in which the proper definition of excess capital is of paramount importance when "conglomerate" is still a dirty word in finance.

Overseeing these disparate entities is a cadre of lieutenants whose efforts Buffett must orient toward a single goal defined by him, and not by their own self-interest. Yet he leaves these people largely to their own devices, exposing the interests of Berkshire Hathaway to the weaknesses of human nature.

Alarmingly, he grows this empire by acquisition when acquisitions fail. It should not be possible for him to get these at prices yielding an appropriate return on his investment and he should not be able to align the interests of his new employees with the objectives of their new parent.

Otherwise he picks stocks, taking very large bets in a game that ordinarily condemns its adherents to mediocrity.

In between times, he sits on cash and other low-return assets until the right opportunity, which could be years in the making, presents itself. This would tax the discipline of any mortal and should seriously impair his ability to compound at 15%.

Buffett eschews managements' "best" use of capital and invests 100% of the cash at his disposal back into the enterprise.

In the process, he refuses to adhere to at least one modern managerial tenet, which is to incentivize key management personnel at Berkshire with stock options. Yet he has experienced no motivational shortfall from this.

Buffett has also flouted three of Wall Street's unwritten laws of corporate governance. He has refused to establish a forecast for

Berkshire's earnings growth; he has not provided its investors with the game plan that might achieve such a forecast; and he has spurned the delivery of the linear stream of results that might illuminate either of these two and on which most CEOs have come to rely in conducting their relationship with the stock market. In theory, Buffett's abrogation of the norms of "investor relations" should constrain the valuation placed on Berkshire Hathaway's shares. In practice, it has been more efficiently priced than any other major, publicly quoted stock in the US, and Buffett's refusal to govern Berkshire according to the demands of Wall Street has failed to put a dent in the superlative total shareholder returns that he has delivered through time.

And he does all of this virtually single-handed, geographically far removed from the business hubs of America.

THE EVOLUTION OF WARREN BUFFETT

Warren E. Buffett had a fascination with investing from early childhood, making his first stock purchase at the age of 11. However, it was not until he discovered the teachings of Benjamin Graham that he took the first step toward becoming the Warren Buffett we know today.

Buffett was just 19 when he first read *The Intelligent Investor*, Graham's seminal text on equity valuation (in which he laid out the revolutionary concept of bringing mathematical discipline to bear on the analysis of a company's stock market valuation). The book had a profound effect on Buffett. Hitherto, he had paid little or no attention to the fundamentals underpinning the value of the shares in which he was dealing. Instead he studied charts of their stock prices, read "all the technical stuff," and listened out for tips,[12] and his results from doing so were distinctly average. "[Prior to reading Graham], I had been investing with my glands instead of my head," he was later to say.[13]

Subsequently, Buffett got to study investment analysis under Graham at Columbia University. After graduating in 1951, he returned to Omaha where he quickly earned himself a reputation as an astute stock picker working for his father's firm of brokers, Buffett-Falk and

Co., and thence back to New York to work for Graham at his investment partnership, Graham-Newman.[14]

For those attuned to Graham's principles, this was the golden era of investing. The "science" that Graham taught was new and the market highly inefficient. Bargains were available in large number if you only knew how to identify them. The young Warren Buffett did.

Beginning in 1951 my performance improved. No, I hadn't changed my diet or taken up exercise. The only new ingredient was Ben's ideas. Quite simply, a few hours spent at the feet of the master proved far more valuable to me than had ten years of supposedly original thinking.[15]

Buffett's personal fortune grew apace over the next five years and, in addition to using some of this money as an initial stake, he was able to attract other investors on the strength of his reputation, so that he could set up an investment vehicle known as the Buffett Partnership.

A metamorphosis

Under the aegis of the Partnership, and in sole control, Buffett began to broaden his canvas. In 1961 he took control of a manufacturer of farm and windmill tools called Dempster Mills Manufacturing and installed himself as chairman. Two years later he was to sell the company, but while in residence Buffett extracted cash from Dempster to fund other investments for the Partnership. A nascent model took its first, faltering steps—faltering because Buffett found managing to be far more difficult than investing.

Thereafter, he entered into the same relationship with Berkshire Hathaway, a manufacturer of textiles based in New England. Only this time, it would be far more durable: Buffett the investor metamorphosed into Buffett the manager *and* investor.

While attempting to fix the business, Buffett rationed Berkshire's use of capital and funneled the excess into more conventional stock market investments and other outright acquisitions. One of these was the float-rich insurance company National Indemnity, which Buffett also used as a source of funds for investing elsewhere; his lasting involvement with the insurance industry had begun.

By now, however, he had picked up a confidant and adviser to his activities. That man was Charlie Munger, a lawyer friend from the West Coast. Munger had little time for the conservative nature of Graham's valuation techniques and, instead, preached that value could be found in a company's enduring earnings potential. Naturally, this meant assessing the ability of management to create enduring value. So Buffett found himself asking the same questions of prospective investments as he did of himself as a manager of Berkshire Hathaway.

Munger's advice would prove timely. Inexorably, as the investment industry became more professional—not least because Graham's teachings were gaining a wider audience—the kind of statistically cheap stocks that Graham advocated buying grew increasingly rare. In order to maintain his comparative advantage over the market, Buffett knew he would have to move on from Graham.

Crucially, however, before we was able to do so, Buffett found himself taking some painful lessons, particularly in his outright purchases. These interim difficulties were also compounded by events elsewhere. Although his overall investment returns were still healthy, the stock market was changing shape. Growth stock investing had become the vogue and Buffett found his investment style out of place. Furthermore, other investment managers were beginning to post stellar results of their own. For the first time in his life, Buffett wasn't knocking the lights out of the index or the competition.

He began to feel pressure. Not pressure to perform as such, but pressure from his partners, who urged him to *change* his approach to investing, to manage the Partnership in a way that pandered to *their* needs and desires.[16] This was an emotional time for Buffett and he became so uncomfortable that, in 1969, he folded his Partnership.

Seminal lessons for Buffett

Disposing of the Partnership's assets, but retaining his holding in and chairmanship of Berkshire Hathaway, Buffett hunkered down. He expanded his interests in the insurance industry by acquisition. He took on more of the managerial responsibilities of an operating manager. And he wrestled with Munger's definition of value versus that of Ben Graham. It was here that the finished article was forged. Clearly, Buffett had to find some other way of sustaining his relative performance. Reflecting on the lessons of experience, he found it.

He found it in the challenge of managing people and managing enterprises. He found it in the exercise of analyzing durable franchises, which contained the same challenges of management. He found it in his own business failures and therefore in comprehending why prospective investments might fail. And he found it in the feedback loop created between the way in which he managed his partners' money and their expectations of him doing so.

In his own mistakes, in his observation of the mistakes of others, in his own experience; there was a common thread running through each. In these, Buffett uncovered the deficiencies of human nature first hand: the emotional and psychological challenges of managing, and investing *in* management.

However, he already combined the functions of manager and investor in the same person. Once again, he found himself ideally placed to take advantage of his schooling. The time had arrived: Warren Buffett was ready to shape Berkshire Hathaway in his own image.

Now, the improbable, compounding, odds-defying model that is Berkshire Hathaway emerged into its adult form. Now, Warren Buffett would emerge as a manager of capital and a leader of people.

BERKSHIRE HATHAWAY: THE VISION

The current gold standard of corporate management is Jack Welch, who retired in 2001 after 17 iconoclastically successful years at the helm of General Electric, one of America's most admired companies.

Welch was an operational manager who rose to the top of GE by overcoming a series of sequentially larger tasks. In his role as chief executive—as befits his legacy—Welch was a process man at heart whose managerial excellence could be described by his remarkable ability to get the teams he assembled under him to pull together and perform. His management style was thus defined by two instruments. These were people—he surrounded himself with, and recruited, only those who were "filled with passion and a desire to get things done"[17]— and memes, the ideas and directives originated and set from on high that Welch managed to spread like a virus through the minds of these people.

In order to spread these memes or viruses of the mind more easily, Welch created what he called a "boundaryless" organization, which cut across divisions and functions within those. He says:

> *I was an outrageous champion of everything we did… Whenever I had an idea or message I wanted to drive into the organization, I could never say it enough.*[18]

No boundary exists between a company and its shareholders, however, and the memes that are spread within organizations cannot be confined to them. "In large part," says Warren Buffett, "companies obtain the shareholder constituency that they seek and deserve."[19]

This is why Welch's overriding objective at GE, which was to be the number one or the number two player in every industry it engaged in, became embodied in the following statement: *"What we have to sell as an enterprise to the equity investor is consistent, above-average earnings growth throughout the economic cycle."*[20]

The soup-mix of Welch's meme generation within GE fueled his vision for achieving this aim. Rather than being reactive to change, Welch anticipated it and then engaged on a personal crusade to adapt the company to his vision.

This meant reinventing America's largest conglomerate at every turn, finding and driving a new meme with each of the four major initiatives defining GE's strategic purpose: Globalization, Services, Six Sigma, and E-business, which, in turn, were designed to deliver on the call for consistent and above-average returns. In order to do this, Welch as chief executive *had* to stay the process/details man he had been as an operational manager. "I got involved in everything my nose could get me involved in," he professed, "from the quality of our X-ray tubes to the introduction of gem-quality diamonds."[21]

That Welch successfully executed his strategy is to be commended. Many who share his objective have failed. Reinventing an organization at every turn, in anticipation of every turn, *and* striving to deliver consistent and above-average returns is a risky strategy and one that Buffett rejects.

The similarities between Jack Welch's management style and Warren Buffett's are evident. In putting together the eclectic mix of companies that comprise Berkshire Hathaway, Buffett has also been extraordinarily careful in choosing with whom to associate, seeking out those managers who "relish the thrill of outstanding performance" and "find all aspects of their business absorbing."[22]

However, there are two modes of leading these types of people after the event, and distinct ways in which to manage the capital that Buffett says is his other function.

With regard to motivation, you can go the hands-off route that Buffett chooses and set managers free. In Buffett's case, this means designing minimum rules of behavior, which tap into a form of motivation that comes from within. This principle of leadership is founded on his confidence in that immutable tenet of human behavior that informs him that trust will be reciprocated with compliance and effort. "I found in running businesses that the best results come from letting high-grade people work unencumbered," he says.[23] It is also a form of leadership that recognizes that, if it is not within the nature of a manager to reciprocate trust, no amount of "management" of the individual will engender the desired behavior.

Or you can adopt Welch's command-and-control style, "by alternately hugging and kicking… setting stretch goals, and relentlessly following up on people to make sure things get done,"[24] which speaks of a distrust of that part of human nature that is selfish and will attend to its own interests if left unattended.

Equally, you can choose a single, high-ground, over-arching meme to direct the enterprise as Buffett does. His leadership of Berkshire Hathaway is premised on the espousal of a single idea that enriches the separate entities comprising his company and that leaps the void between them and their CEO and the company's shareholders. Atop the pyramid in corporate governance and the allocation of capital, that meme is this: *Act like an owner*.

Or you can co-opt multiple, just-in-time memes that resonate with strategies that must be reinvented at every turn *à la* Jack Welch.

Neither solution is free from error. Warren Buffett's abrogation of details and his positive inattention to the minutiae of people management is occasionally costly—as he discovered in the underwriting standards of his largest subsidiary, General Re. Jack Welch's inverse preoccupation with details could be just as costly—causing him to miss warning flags of aberrant behavior at Kidder Peabody, which caused GE considerable losses and Welch personal embarrassment.[25] (He couldn't be everywhere at once.)

Of the two, however, Buffett's is the more robust. When the leadership philosophy of letting go is carried into the capital management function, it is this mindset that provides the returns that Buffett's shareholders expect more assuredly than its alternative, which is to impose one's prescience on the environment and manage the results.

WARREN BUFFETT'S CIRCLE OF COMPETENCE

Risk comes from not knowing what you are doing.

Warren Buffett[26]

To Buffett's mind, the shareholders of a company, as its *owners*, should expect to generate a return on their assets over their and the assets' lifetimes. They do not suffer from myopia. They are willing to pass up the substandard opportunities that may be necessary to deliver *consistent* returns in favor of those rarer opportunities that guarantee the *above-average* variety; at Berkshire Hathaway, Buffett's corporate governance reflects this.

As this ethos manifests itself in Buffett's management of capital, Buffett perceives himself as a fragment of a capital market that functions as a conduit via which society's savings are transformed into the products and services that people want and need. In order to fulfill his role, Buffett has to ensure that only those businesses within Berkshire Hathaway that deserve capital get it, and that less deserving businesses do not needlessly retain capital that could be put to better use elsewhere. In making this judgment he also has to ensure that he weighs his use of capital against all other possible uses—in other companies and industries that he may acquire or invest in, and also his shareholders, who themselves may have a better use for it.

For Buffett this is a simple concept, summarized in the simplicity of his own job description. However, not everyone agrees that this is so. That august body of academic work *The Theory of Finance*, for instance, has it that Warren Buffett is a misguided individual.

It says that the million eyeballs of the capital market itself are better at deciding which businesses deserve funding than the eyes of one man, and that those eyeballs are better at policing managements' use of capital via the pricing of companies in the stock market. And it says that these functions are so important that they *must* be left to the all-seeing market.

After all, as the empirical evidence attests, it is *efficient*.

Perhaps not surprisingly, given the perverse nature of a model in which Buffett has set himself up as a one-man, two-eyeballed, capital market (three eyes if you include Charlie Munger who has sight in only one), Warren Buffett has his own ideas:

> *Observing correctly that the market was frequently efficient, they [the proponents of finance theory] went on to conclude incorrectly that it was always efficient. The difference between these propositions is night and day.*[27]

In his own evolution as manager and investor, Buffett struggled with, and witnessed, too many basic errors made in the allocation of capital to believe that it was the efficient mechanism described by the academics. While they were right in theory, they were dead wrong in practice. And nothing Buffett has seen since has changed this opinion.

Thus, where Warren Buffett differs from Jack Welch in his management of people, he also differs from Welch in his management of capital. Just as Buffett exhibits an informed, pragmatic acceptance of the facts of life in the one and lets go, he does the same in the other: "We simply hope that something sensible comes along—and, when it does, we act."[28]

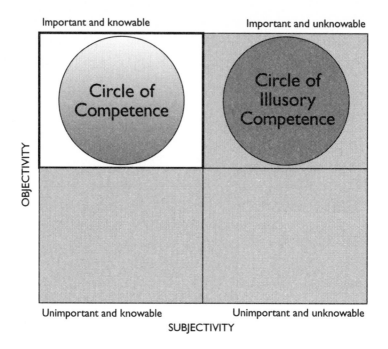

Figure 1 The Circle of Competence

Where Buffett *bends* to the immutable laws of human nature in his leadership of Berkshire's managers, he also *bows* to the realities of making those decisions in the face of uncertainty that are a prerequisite of capital management. And where he works *with* immutable human nature as a leader when he can find it oriented toward the targets he sets for Berkshire, he works *with* the complexity of Berkshire's operating environment as a capital manager. Where Welch shot for consistency, his shareholders full-square behind this principle—indeed, reliant on it in their evaluation of GE—Buffett embraces uncertainty and aims for above-average results over the long haul.

Buffett does not know when, where, or how opportunity will present itself in this regard. But he does know that it will, how to identify it when it does, which requires an ability to evaluate opportunity, and how to place himself in a position to capitalize on it. He knows these things because he manages Berkshire's capital within his Circle of Competence (Figure 1).

By confining his capital management to the important and knowable, Warren Buffett places himself in control. Buffett has identified the immutable economic and behavioral laws that apply in this sphere. He is intimately familiar with the rules by which humans make decisions under conditions of uncertainty. He has defined his Circle of Competence with rigor and honesty. He has a fix on where its boundaries lie. He can identify the origin of his errors and therefore amend his decision rules after the event. His decision making is enlightened.

Buffett's Circle of Competence conveys objectivity on him. It grants him the ability to make forecasts with a degree of accuracy that allows him to judge the price/value equation. In the process, it endows him with the luxury of choosing opportunity from a wide-ranging menu, the comfort of biding his time until opportunity presents itself, and the discipline not to squander his capital in the meantime. At the same time, he feels completely free to manage capital in this way.

Buffett's Circle of Competence creates the bond of trust that exists between him and his shareholders. It liberates him to defy convention. The control that it conveys on him also conveys the *feeling* of control. When emotions must be kept in balance, this is important. And Buffett has backed this up with a number of structural additions to the circle that ensure his psychological and emotional security. Doing this allows him to act like an owner.

Buffett holds to the decision rules supporting his circle with religious zeal. Its framework contains the ingredients of efficient capital management. They are the distillation of logic. And no manager would disagree that this is so.

Yet there are few who are able to emulate him in this regard. Not because they do not want to; ideally they would. Nor because they are ignorant, because plainly they are not. Rather, it is because of the insidious nature of decision making under conditions of uncertainty.

While the model is made available to anyone, its inverse—the Circle of Illusory Competence—is to be avoided. In this extension of Buffett's representation of the universe, capital will be managed in an inverse fashion to that to which he adheres. Subjectivity will reign. Emotions will be in the vanguard. And those who inhabit such a Circle of Illusory Competence will come to "know" the important but *unknowable*.

The consequences of operating under such an illusion can be easily guessed. They are not so easy to avoid. Because of the way our minds work when we labor within a Circle of Illusory Competence, it is difficult to learn from disappointment.

In the process of *his* personal development as a manager and an investor, Warren Buffett underwent an explosion of cognition in which the distinction between these two circles became apparent. His Circle of Competence is infused with insight into the common errors that can be made when making decisions under conditions of uncertainty. He is familiar with these because he made many of them himself. The mistakes he has not made, he has witnessed in others.

In the presence of human failure, Buffett rewired his own brain, defusing the psychology of illusory competence, cementing that of genuine competence. Thereafter, he designed a model for the allocation of capital that would allow him adhere to its tenets.

This is Buffett's "hidden" secret.

THE REAL WARREN BUFFETT

It is in the appreciation of the living sculpture that is Berkshire Hathaway that we find the real Warren Buffett.

Yet here's the curiosity. Most people, when they think of Buffett, think of him as simply an investor. That is sad—and also inevitable.

The steady increase in the intrinsic value of Berkshire's nonquoted, subsidiary companies is far less salient than Buffett's high-profile successes in the stock market and the wisdom that he brings to bear on the subject of picking stocks. More importantly, the steady cash flow that he harvests from his subsidiary companies—the devil of a leadership job—is even less transparent.

It is therefore not surprising that the books that have been written on Warren Buffett thus far have largely restricted themselves to trying to unlock the secret of his stock market wizardry. In doing so, they have, in one way or another, rephrased what he has taught us on this subject, and they have explained clearly the principles to which he adheres.

The paucity of this approach, however, does Buffett, *and* those who would seek to learn from him, a major disservice. These books have missed the point. The real Warren Buffett is far more than simply an investor. And the success of Berkshire Hathaway is predicated on far more than his stock-picking prowess.

The question that demands answering is not: "What is the secret of Warren Buffett's success in investing?" It's much bigger than that.

The question is: "How does Warren Buffett transform a model that should fail into one that clearly excels?"

In spite of the tenets of finance theory, it is not Berkshire's board of directors that regulates this model and governs its success. It is fortunate that this is the case. As an institution, the board of directors has evolved in order to represent the interests of disparate investors, but it has proven ineffectual in this regard, even when it does measure up to the supposed requirements of a rational deliberating body, which are to be small in size, diverse in background and experience, and independent. "The CEO's boss is a Board of Directors that seldom measures itself," observes Buffett.[29] Nor is it the stock market that performs the governance function, which is equally fortunate since it regularly fails the test of disciplining the capital allocation process. The board "is infrequently held to account for substandard corporate performance," observes Buffett,[30] noting also that "the pleasant but vacuous director need never worry about job security."[31] Warren Buffett holds sole responsibility for the transformation and stewardship of an unlikely model into an incomparable success story.

Rather than gravitate toward the prescribed ideal of running a corporation, Buffett has chosen the practical working solution. Pre-empting Alan Greenspan's declaration that "the state of corporate governance to a very large extent reflects the character of the CEO,"[32] Buffett has opted for integrity. "CEOs want to be respected and believed," he says. "They will be—and should be—only when they deserve to be." They "don't need 'independent' directors, oversight committees or auditors absolutely free of conflicts of interest. They simply need to do what's right."[33]

❖❖❖

The plan of this book is as follows.

Part I: *People Leader* begins in Chapter 2 with a description of

Buffett's early struggle with the challenges of management, the lessons learned, and the explosion of cognition that would illuminate both his model for leading and his model for managing capital: his vision of acting like an owner in Berkshire Hathaway's corporate governance. Chapter 3 explains how Buffett puts his vision into practice where it counts—in the motivation of those he wishes to comply with it. The fundamentals of Buffett's decentralized management style will be delineated, and the emphasis he places on careful managerial selection explained. Chapter 4 proceeds to discuss how Buffett effects successful acquisitions and elicits buy-in to Berkshire's owner-oriented ethos from managers who are new to the firm. Thereafter, Chapter 5 reveals Buffett's principles in practice in the insurance industry, elucidating the human challenges of deploying capital at the operational level and the leadership that underpins Buffett's abilities to overcome these.

Part II: *Capital Manager* reflects on the aura that has come to surround Warren Buffett. A picture is painted in Chapter 6 of a man who is not immune to failure, as some might think—a man who does make mistakes, who manages change reactively, and who effects change in personnel proactively. Chapter 7 goes on to explain why Buffett's mistakes have not put a dent in Berkshire's success and why he is able to learn from them. It details Buffett's Circle of Competence and walks the reader through the essentials of its construction. It also shows how Buffett combines this with other structural features of his approach to ensure that he enjoys the psychological and emotional security required to take the decisions that count in sustaining Berkshire Hathaway's performance.

Part III: *To Act Like an Owner* presents readers with a user's manual for translating Buffett's model for managing capital into a framework for acting like an owner. Chapter 8, listing the key features of the model in action, serves as a guide to managers of publicly quoted companies in the conduct of the firm. Chapter 9 explains why Buffett has embraced the Circle of Competence. By illustrating the Circle of Illusory Competence, the inverse of Buffett's approach is illuminated. It serves as a guide to managers of publicly quoted companies as to where the pitfalls lie in conducting a relationship with shareholders and the wider stock market.

Chapter 10 concludes with some thoughts about the future of Berkshire Hathaway and the challenges it will face with, or without, Warren Buffett at the helm.

Part I
People Leader

2

Berkshire Hathaway and the Institutional Imperative

The directors of [joint stock] companies, however, being the managers rather of other people's money than of their own, it cannot be well expected, that they should watch over it with the same anxious vigilance [as owners]... Negligence and profusion, therefore, must always prevail, more or less, in the management of the affairs of such a company.

Adam Smith[1]

I'm not adapted for football, I'm not adapted for violin playing. I happen to be in something that pays off huge in this society... if I had been born some time ago I would have been some animal's lunch.

Warren Buffett[2]

In the early 1960s, after having spent the best part of 20 years as a highly successful stock picker, Warren Buffett developed a vision of his future role—as the manager of an enterprise—that was unique when he had it, and remains unique today.

The vision was this: In the management of that enterprise, to act like its owner.

In order to do this Buffett would have to define his role as manager as one who would choose, from the universe of opportunities that lay within his core competence, the application of capital that would earn its highest return while, at the same time, incorporating the least risk, just as his shareholders surely would if the money was in their hands. Alternatively, if he could not achieve a return in excess of what they could earn on it elsewhere, he would return it to them.

That meant he could not characterize himself, as most chief executives do, as a manufacturer of textiles, candies, insurance policies, widgets, or whatever. Henceforth, he would be an *allocator of capital*.

There could be no other way. Thereafter, he would also have to ensure that the managers who worked for him in Berkshire Hathaway's subsidiary companies fell in with this philosophy.

It sounds simple, but it's not.

It is simple because, at Berkshire Hathaway, Warren Buffett is both owner and manager, which means that his interests as one are perfectly aligned with his interests as the other.

It's not so simple, however, in the sense that Buffett treats even the smallest of Berkshire's shareholders as an equal partner in the enterprise, so that he manages the company on their behalf as much as his.

It's also not so simple because, even though Buffett owns Berkshire's subsidiary companies, he gives his managers enormous autonomy. Therefore, he stands in relation to them as his shareholders do to him—they manage their companies on *his* behalf.

However, chiefly it's not so simple because, ever since the Industrial Revolution when the separation of the ownership of the enterprise by its disparate shareholders from its control by management became widespread, one question has been left unanswered: How is it possible to get the managers to act *like* owners?

Adam Smith summarized the issue as early as 1776. Given the deficiencies of human nature, he was fatalistic in believing that the problem of aligning the interests of the two parties would ever be resolved, and firmly believed that managers would attend to their own interests more diligently than those of the owners on whose behalf they worked.

He was right.

Nothing in the modern era of corporate governance would suggest that this issue has been resolved. Not by most, anyway. And until he had acquired a few lessons himself on the nature of man, not by Warren Buffett either. For Buffett's determination to act like an owner faltered as soon as he donned the mantle of manager. In this guise he encountered what he calls his "most surprising discovery"—a force that, hitherto, had been invisible to him and that he came to term "the institutional imperative."[3]

THE INSTITUTIONAL IMPERATIVE

Churchill once said, "You shape your houses and then they shape you."
Warren Buffett[4]

By way of example, Buffett described the workings of the institutional imperative as follows:

(1) As if governed by Newton's First Law of Motion, an institution will resist any change in its current direction; (2) Just as work expands to fill the available time, corporate projects or acquisitions will materialize to soak up additional funds; (3) Any business craving of the leader, however foolish, will be quickly supported by detailed rate of return and strategic studies prepared by his troops; and (4) The behavior of peer companies, whether they are expanding, acquiring, setting executive compensation or whatever, will be mindlessly imitated.[5]

He adds:

In business school I was given no hint of the imperative's existence, and I did not intuitively understand it when I entered the business world. I thought then that decent, intelligent, and experienced managers would automatically make rational business decisions. But I learned over time that it isn't so. Instead, rationality frequently wilts when the institutional imperative comes into play.[6]

Buffett came to a conclusion as momentous for his future management of Berkshire Hathaway as that of Jack Welch's seminal revelation at GE, which was to make the company the number one or number two player in every industry in which it was active.[7] "Institutional dynamics," said Buffett, "not venality or stupidity, set businesses on these courses, which are too often misguided."[8]

That the imperative took Buffett by surprise can be explained by the fact that, while he had been a remarkably successful stock picker, during this period he had paid little attention to the business fundamentals in which the imperative might be expected to manifest itself. His holding period was too short.

If Buffett were to retain his competitive advantage and continue to outperform both the index and his competitors, he realized that he would have to change his approach. But this would not be as simple as choosing to dominate the industries in which Berkshire engaged. The imperative has no respect for size or market position.

To attain sustainable advantage, Buffett would have to acknowledge the imperative in himself. He would have to realize that renting stocks only compounded the problem of the imperative. He would have to open his eyes to the concept of value creation on an ongoing basis and see that the imperative was an obstacle to this: in the company he managed, in those he acquired, and in those in which he invested. And he would have to take this into account in all those activities.

Buffett had a head start in the early years before he became a manager but, given what he had learned, it was not one that was sustainable. He had to find something far more durable.

He did. He recognized the imperative. He specified its mechanism as a problem of human nature. And he finally put himself in a position where he could bridge the void between the manager of an enterprise and its owner and act like the capital allocator that all owners want their managers to be.

A HEAD START FOR WARREN BUFFETT

As a young man Buffett was drawn to the world of investing during a time when stock markets were the habitat of insiders. Share price movements were often rigged and what we now commonly understand as valuation analysis did not exist.

When Benjamin Graham began to expound the theory of valuation and stock selection in the late 1920s and early 1930s—firmly establishing the mathematical notion of value—this started to change, however.

As we have seen, at the age of 19, when he read Graham's *The Intelligent Investor*, Warren Buffett was staggered by its revelations.[9] In

1950 he enrolled on a course at Columbia University in which Graham taught security analysis. Buffett quickly adopted Graham as hero and, after he was recruited to Graham's own investment firm, as mentor too. Years later he was able to comment that "Ben had more influence on me than any person except my father."[10]

In a period where few cared to look at valuation, this was a golden era for those who did. Schooled in the principles that Graham had taught him, Buffett voraciously scanned the data available on companies.

A peculiar mental felicity with numbers set him apart in this regard. Childhood friends Bob Russell and Don Danley recall throwing series of two-digit numbers at him to multiply and lists of cities for which he had to supply the populations. Buffett fired back the answers just as quickly.[11] At Graham-Newman, where Ben Graham himself was legendary for his ability to process data in his head, Buffett astounded his colleagues by being better and faster.

His total recall of facts and figures enabled him to memorize the statistical profile of every company he analyzed; and the speed of his brain enabled him to analyze them *all*. An almost impossible task for anyone else, this allowed him to follow stocks assiduously, track their appropriate valuations, and pounce on them when they became cheap—*while they were still cheap.*[12]

Buffett's education with Graham as mentor capitalized on this natural advantage and it soon began to pay off. Between 1951 when he graduated from Graham's class and 1956 when he returned home to Omaha after having worked in Graham's partnership, Buffett's personal fortune grew from $9,800 to $140,000, a compound annual growth rate of around 70%![13]

He did this by buying stocks that most people found unpalatable. Indeed, during a brief stint at his father's firm of brokers, Buffett-Falk and Co., the young Buffett encountered a great deal of resistance to his ideas.

Oftentimes, these stocks appeared so darn cheap that people believed there must be something wrong with them. Even Buffett felt at times that the valuations looked too good to be true.[14] And yet he pressed on regardless—continuing to sell his ideas as a broker, still salting them away as an investor. Persistent in the face of doubt.

Supremely confident in his own, very often contrarian opinion. Holding complete trust in a methodology that was relatively new.

The combination of Buffett's resolute self-belief and his calculator brain was irresistible. Prior to reading and studying under Graham, Buffett's track record was, by his own admission, just average. Now it appeared as though he was born to invest. "I think it was in his genes," said his younger sister, Roberta.[15] Ideally suited to the task, Warren Buffett (quite literally) had a head start.

An allocator of capital was born

Thereafter, attracting investors on the back of his growing reputation and using some of the money he had amassed, Buffett set up the three pools of funds that were later to be amalgamated into the Buffett Partnership. He was sole manager, with total discretion. The year was 1956 and Buffett was just 26 years old. This was the first step on the road that was to transform him.

In 1961, Buffett bought a majority stake in Dempster Mills Manufacturing for the Partnership. Statistically this was a cheap stock, straight out of Graham's playbook. It was also a company in which Buffett eventually installed himself as chairman. Even though Ben Graham had not been averse to taking influential roles in the companies in which he invested, this was a revolutionary step for a fund manager.

Except that Warren Buffett did not conceive himself to be a fund manager. In Dempster he saw a company that was investing too heavily in low-return businesses. If as chairman he could redress this, he could free up some of the money earmarked for the manufacture of windmill tools and farm equipment. He could then channel this into alternative investments yielding higher returns, assets that the owners of the business would choose if they could only get the management to return them their capital.

An allocator of capital was born; just how Buffett happened on this insight is covered in the next chapter. But this strange, hybrid creature was also nearly strangled at birth. Buffett's initial foray in the new role did not work out.

Up against the imperative

Buffett made a handsome return on his money, but only after he had drafted in a new manager to deal with problems that were "too tough" for Buffett to solve, that is to put the squeeze on existing personnel, so that they complied with objectives set by him, their owner and chairman, rather than pursuing their own welfare as managers of the enterprise.[16] Attempts to do so himself, on his regular visits to the company, had failed to achieve the necessary reduction in overheads and inventory in a company whose manufacturing line did not allow for fat.

Brief as it was (he sold his stake in 1963), this was Buffett's first brush with the institutional imperative and his discovery was that having the vision was one thing, but there was a world of difference between being a short-term investor and a manager who was intent on acting like an owner. Bridging the gulf between owning and managing—*motivating managers to behave like owners*—was an essential element in his new guise, Buffett found. And aligning the interests of these people with his was no easy task, hence the sale of his stake.

A year earlier he had begun buying up shares in another company for the Partnership: Berkshire Hathaway, a manufacturer of textiles based in New England. By 1965, he had built this up to a sufficient size to allow him to take charge of its operations. (Only later would he become the company's chairman.)

There were alarming similarities between Berkshire and Dempster. Buffett's initial investment was premised on statistical cheapness. In addition, they both struggled in low-return industries, and thereafter his status as interested investor developed into one as active owner (the first hint of the entrapment that the imperative had in store for him). However, there was also a material difference between them.

At Berkshire, Buffett was very careful to retain an operating manager who was made of the right stuff—who possessed the personal qualities that Buffett could work with, as opposed to being an individual he would have to manage. That man was Ken Chace. Buffett admired Chace. He trusted the motivation that ran to Chace's core, which was to comply with the objectives set for the organization. Buffett's association with this man of integrity was the precursor in motivational design for all of his subsequent associations with the managers of his myriad subsidiary companies.

At the helm of yet another company whose management had previously acted out of its own self-interest to the detriment of its shareholders, but one that was now compliant with his wishes, Buffett resolved not to compound the problem of operating in a difficult industry by going deeper into it. Instead of reinvesting in his textile operations, he would only do sufficient to keep them ticking over—at a rate that would allow him to harvest a crop of cash from them to invest elsewhere at higher returns. Now, with the diligent Chace at his side, Buffett's model of acting like an owner was put on a much sounder footing. Once again, he was allocating capital.

In his role as manager, he determined how much capital would be retained in the manufacture of textiles. In his role as owner, he conducted the managerial relationship with Chace by directing his activities. And in his role as investor, in effect, he deployed the cash extracted from the company in order to earn higher returns elsewhere. "It's really the interaction of capital employed, the return on that capital, and the future capital generated," says Buffett.[17] However, as simple as this notion reads, things did not quite go to plan.

Buffett appeared to have solved the man management problem. Ken Chace *did* attend to his wishes in his management of the operations. As owner, therefore, he was able to let go and yet still control the company. Crucially, however, in the other aspects of allocating capital as manager and investor, he still found himself making mistakes.

ENTANGLED IN TEXTILES

I knew it was a tough business… I was either more arrogant or innocent then. We learned a lot of lessons, but I wish we could have learned them somewhere else.

Warren Buffett[18]

From the outset of taking charge at Berkshire Hathaway, Buffett struggled with its operations. There was simply no letup in the pressures that had assailed the company under its original owner, Seabury Stanton, who had clung doggedly to the textile industry through adversity.

Buffett was to learn, first hand, why Stanton had acted in this fashion. In spite of his resolve, and irrespective of the return on capital employed in the business, his engagement in Berkshire Hathaway seemed to grow of its own volition.

He bought into the company on a purely bargain basis and came close to selling his stake in 1964 after Stanton made repeated offers to buy back his stock—except that he refused to do so because he thought the old man was cheating him on the price. According to Munger, "they were three-eighths of a point apart" on the deal and "it was an absolute accident that Berkshire became his vehicle."[19] *Yet 20 years later, after first contemplating closing his textile business in the mid-1970s—precisely because of its low returns—Buffett was still entangled in it.*

In the interim, the threat to his ambition to grow the value of what became the wider enterprise was plain. Unless Buffett could maintain Berkshire's textile operations in a state that would at least produce the required rate of return, or, more seriously, if it began to *consume* capital, this would impede his ambition to compound his returns. If this happened he would be far better served by investing in a business that would produce a higher, more secure yield, *now*.

Indeed, the problem was evident as early as 1969 when he warned his Partners about his low expectations of the business.[20] But he was agonizingly slow to do something about it, and the opportunity cost of not doing so, for Buffett and the other owners of his company, was substantial.

In the interim, Buffett was *mostly* disciplined in paring down the textile business. However, he still found himself, against his better judgment, making investments in it that never earned their required rate of return.

In 1978, for instance, Buffett reported to his shareholders that "your chairman made the decision a few years ago to purchase Waumbec Mills in Manchester, New Hampshire, thereby expanding our textile commitment." Although "by any statistical test, the purchase price was an extraordinary bargain… the purchase was a mistake. While we labored mightily, new problems arose as fast as old problems were tamed."[21]

Nevertheless, Buffett cast around for reasons in support of this decision. One of these was the expectation of synergistic benefits. "Although a mistake, the Waumbec acquisition has not been a disaster. Certain portions of the operation are proving to be valuable additions to our decorator line."[22]

In fact, it *was* a disaster. The synergies, such as they were, were not sufficient to justify throwing good money after bad.

The curse of the imperative: Entrapment

Buffett's problem was that he had already made a *commitment* to the business. It was this prior conclusion that ensnared him.

Try as he might to maintain his perspective, to harvest and sow elsewhere without plowing anything back into textiles, Buffett found that he could not. Once begun, his commitment to the business stayed in motion. Just as Stanton had done before him, although in a slightly different manner, Warren Buffett had become a victim of the institutional imperative. Inexorably increasing his commitment to the textile industry, planting obstacles to his retreat as he went, the dynamics of the imperative had trapped him.

Whereas Stanton's commitment to Berkshire Hathaway was rooted in his conception of himself as a "textiles man" whose job was to grow the business—not an unusual definition of self for a manager— Buffett saw himself as a compassionate *businessman* who cared deeply about and prized most highly the personal relationships that came with this. He was a man who wished to reciprocate the effort and loyalty shown to him by the managers and other employees who complied with his wishes as owner of the firm they looked after. Once in this business, however, the path of least resistance was to stay and make a go of it.

Nevertheless, by 1985, when the accumulated results were so bad and the outlook so clear that he could no longer delude himself to the contrary, Buffett was forced to explain to his shareholders why he had taken the painful decision to close the textile operations. By now, he had spent about one-third of his life in the business. He wrote:

I should emphasize that Ken and Gary [the management team] have been resourceful, energetic, and imaginative in attempting to make our textile operation a success. Trying to achieve sustainable profitability, they reworked product lines, machinery configurations and distribution arrangements.[23]

He admitted that he had, in effect, been lying to himself:

In the end nothing worked and I should be faulted for not quitting sooner... 250 textile mills have closed since 1980. Their owners were not privy to any information that was unknown to me: they simply processed it more objectively. I ignored Comte's advice— "the intellect should be the servant of the heart, but not its slave"— and I believed what I preferred to believe [emphasis added].[24]

In the allocation of capital, when the commitments made to businesses go wrong, a particular danger arises. Those who bear a high degree of responsibility for initiating them have a tendency to commit greater funding to these projects in subsequent rounds of budgeting than do those who are not burdened by responsibility for the mistake, who are not part of the dynamic.[25]

While new brooms sweep clean, incumbents go in deeper. They resolve to escalate their commitment to a game that still might deliver a chance of making good on their mistake; a reprieve for lying to themselves. Says Charlie Munger:

You've made an enormous commitment to something. You've poured effort and money in. And the more that you put in, the more that the whole consistency principle makes you think: "Now it has to work. If I just put in a little more then it'll work..." People go broke that way because they can't afford to stop, rethink and say... "I don't have to pursue this thing as an obsession."[26]

In Stanton's case, the consistency principle urged him to make a return on his investments. In Buffett's case, it was to preserve his perception of himself. This is entrapment.

Both responses are instinctive in managing an enterprise. They are also what distinguish managing from allocating capital. Using the case of Burlington Industries as an example, in 1985 (not without coincidence, the year he closed the textile business) Buffett was able to present an excellent analysis of the consequences:

> *In 1964 Burlington had sales of $1.2 billion... [and] made the decision to stick to the textile business. During the 1964–85 period, the company made capital expenditures of about $3 billion... more than $200-per-share on that $60 stock. A very large part of the expenditures, I am sure, was devoted to cost improvement and expansion. Given Burlington's basic commitment to stay in textiles, I would also surmise that the company's capital decisions were quite rational.*
>
> *Nevertheless, Burlington has lost sales volume in real dollars and has far lower return on sales and equity now than 20 years ago... the stock now sells... just a little over its $60 price in 1964. Meanwhile the CPI has more than tripled. Therefore, each share commands about one-third the purchasing power it did at the end of 1964.... This devastating outcome for shareholders indicates what can happen when much brainpower and energy are applied to a faulty premise.*[27]

Warren Buffett was able to pinpoint so clearly where the management of Burlington had gone wrong because, by this time, he had finally come to admit where *he* had gone wrong with Berkshire Hathaway. He had been acting in the same way, although to a far lesser extent. He had to—the dynamics of the situation had overtaken him.

Clearly, from the point of view of its owners, Burlington's commitment to the textile industry was a mistake. Equally clearly, that commitment manifested the dynamics of the institutional imperative. It did so in the same way that it had trapped Warren Buffett. Even though logic suggested the opposite, it made Buffett afraid to admit the failure of his strategy, afraid to be inconsistent with a prior commitment (which became part of his definition of self), and afraid to face up to his self-deception.

The wakeup call for Buffett was this: An unseen force, the institutional imperative absorbed energy from those around it, tapping into basic human nature to do so.

CIGAR BUTT INVESTING

A cigar butt found on the street that has only one puff left in it may not offer much of a smoke, but the bargain purchase will make that puff all profit.

Warren Buffett[28]

Buffett suggests it was either arrogance or innocence that blinded him to the existence of the imperative. To an outside observer, it seems that the latter was more likely to have been the cause. Prior to taking over at Berkshire Hathaway, rather than buying and holding stocks for the long term Buffett had *rented* them. And if his problem in his textiles operations was that, rather than confronting his fear, he chose to run from it—trampling over logic as he did so—this problem was compounded by the fact that he had stuck with the teachings of Ben Graham for too long.

While Graham paid deference to the role played by the future earning power of a business in its stock market valuation, he appraised companies far more in relation to the valuation of the assets on their balance sheets than their ability to create value on an ongoing basis. Buffett's early career was premised on this technique: identifying companies that were statistically cheap compared to the value in their tangible assets, whose prices would rise once other investors caught on to this discrepancy. He refers to this as "cigar butt investing."

However, the problem with this type of investing is that whether the managers of the underlying companies that Buffett rented acted like allocators of capital or not was essentially irrelevant to the highly lucrative game in which he was engaged. He bought stocks when they were oversold and had gotten too cheap, and then simply waited for others to realize this fact. When they did so, and the prices rose to fair value, he bade farewell, serenely oblivious to any dynamics that may have been unfolding within the stocks.

Cigar butt investing relied on Buffett's ability to analyze a still photograph of valuation. Managing an enterprise, in contrast, requires the capacity to produce, direct, and *act* in a streaming video—and one whose storyline is populated by other, *human* actors playing out animated roles in scenes of strategic decision making, facing the behavioral challenges that these presented and that Buffett was facing, and had faced with Dempster Mills.

Perforce, cigar butt investing did not prepare Warren Buffett for the job of anticipating the imperative and/or managing it. *And* it predisposed him to escalating his commitment by choosing to own and operate these companies rather than simply renting their stocks, a classic description of entrapment.

Years later, in 1977, Buffett illustrated the drawbacks of his stunted approach to investment analysis:

> *Berkshire Fine Spinning Associates and Hathaway Manufacturing were merged in 1955 to form Berkshire Hathaway Inc. In 1948... they had earnings after tax of almost $18 million and employed 10,000 people... In the business world of that period they were an economic powerhouse... But, in the decade following the 1955 merger aggregate sales of $595 million produced an aggregate loss for Berkshire Hathaway of $10 million. By 1964 the operation had been reduced to two mills and net worth had shrunk to $22 million, from $53 million at the time of the merger. So much for single year snapshots as adequate portrayals of a business.*[29]

In time he came to admit the error of his ways to his shareholders:

> *It must be noted that your Chairman, always a quick study, required only 20 years to recognize how important it was to buy good businesses. In the interim, I searched for "bargains"—and had the misfortune to find some. My punishment was an education in*

the economics of short-line farm implement manufacturers, third-place department stores, and New England textile manufacturers.

He continued:

Keynes identified my problem: "The difficulty lies not in the new ideas but in escaping from the same old ones." My escape was long delayed, in part because most of what I had been taught by the same teacher had been (and continues to be) so extraordinarily valuable. [30]

But the pain of admitting the discord in the fact that the teachings of his hero were not complete, and that both he and Graham had been, if anything, naïve in their assessment of value, would have been intense: enough to distract Buffett from the recognition that value creation can be a durable, ongoing process and could be found in companies that are not necessarily balance-sheet cheap.

Evidently, by 1977 when he told the snapshot story Buffett was learning. But he had still not quite got it. The institutional imperative, which inadvertently he had accurately described (had he but known it), was still invisible to him, and its mechanism—of preferring what he preferred to believe and failing to escape from this—was also not within his comprehension. It stemmed not from "venality or stupidity," as he would call it, but from a lack of understanding of human nature and awareness of this in himself.

Now that he was a manager, if he was to sustain the performance he had enjoyed as an investor, Buffett would have to recognize these faults for what they were and correct for them.

That is not to say that Berkshire Hathaway, the wider enterprise, was struggling; it wasn't. Buffett's biggest mistakes during this period were what he calls his errors of omission: his failure to buy, and retain, outstanding franchise stocks when they were truly cheap in the great bear markets of the 1970s. This would have compounded Berkshire's value at a materially higher rate. Nevertheless, he was funneling the excess cash from other investments—principally National Indemnity—into other cheap stocks and, as these subsequently appreciated in value, Berkshire's value rose with them. In comparison, he counts his mistakes of commission, getting stuck in textiles being the major one, as "relatively few" in number.[31]

Tellingly, when he exited this period, he was no longer investing in the kind of stocks or owning the kinds of companies with which he had hitherto been preoccupied. Nor was he managing Berkshire Hathaway in the same fashion. Something had happened to change him.

Buffett spent much of the 1970s buying up insurance companies and investing their float in the stock market. During that period, he occupied both an executive and operational role, managing Berkshire and working as an underwriter of its risks. In 1982, he handed the operational role over to Mike Goldberg and rescinded his underwriting responsibilities. He was now a full-time chief executive of an insurance company. An advert appeared in his letters to his shareholders that sought to attract those who had businesses for sale. The following year, Buffett published an *Owner's Manual*, which set the tone for the relationship he wanted to establish with Berkshire's shareholders and the objectives to which he wanted his managers to adhere. Berkshire embarked on an acquisition spree that embraced its most famous wholly owned subsidiaries, most of which Buffett would find outside the insurance industry.

The conglomerate emerged. But this was no ordinary conglomerate and Buffett was no ordinary leader. The evidence from that burst of activity and behavioral *change*, rare for Buffett, is that he had gained an insight into how his brain worked. He was *able* to pinpoint his prior mistakes and come up with a novel blueprint for Berkshire Hathaway, so somehow he did become dramatically self-aware.

Perhaps there were clues all along that he had this capacity within himself, and it was merely waiting for a catalyst. Evidence that this is so comes from his folding of the Buffett Partnership in 1969.

A triumph of self-awareness: The folding of the Partnership

Between 1956 and 1969, the value of the Partnership's assets had grown at a compound annual rate of 29.5%, compared with 7.4% for the Dow Jones index.[32] However, the late 1960s was the *go-go* era of investing. Growth stocks had been discovered. Stocks were going to the moon (Go! Go!). And investment managers were hitching their fortunes to them.

Not least because the behavior of the index is not always logical, Buffett knew that he would not be able to outperform it every year, and now this risk presented itself more than ever. With that in mind, in 1967 he reduced his target of beating the Dow from ten percentage points annually to five percentage points (or by growing the value of existing assets under management by 9% per annum, whichever was the larger).[33]

As the "madness" proceeded, Buffett became increasingly uncomfortable—because the pressure from his partners was becoming palpable. These people had grown accustomed to Buffett comfortably outperforming both the index and other fund managers. Now they were faced with the prospect of standing on the sidelines while other investors made out like crazy. They were still doing well in an absolute sense, but it felt as if they were losing out. And it was this aversion to losses that drove them to try to persuade Buffett to pitch in with the go-go investors. Nevertheless, falling back on that resoluteness that had defined him as an investor, Buffett told them:

I will not abandon a previous approach whose logic I understand even though it may mean forgoing large, and apparently easy, profits to embrace an approach which I don't fully understand, have not practiced successfully and which, possibly, could lead to substantial permanent loss of capital.[34]

So he folded the Partnership—a stunning move for a man who straddled the stock market like a colossus. But running with the herd, and using a methodology that was foreign to him and, more importantly, lacked any logic in which he had trust, was too much to contemplate. By confronting it—listening to the voice of logic and taking the consequences—he eliminated it.

Crucially, whether or not he recognized his internal discord as a naturally occurring condition that could distort the lens through which he viewed reality, Buffett was already examining his own behavior:

Elementary self-analysis tells me that I will not be capable of less than all-out effort to achieve a publicly proclaimed goal to people who have entrusted capital to me.[35]

There's a hint here that Buffett, even though he could not speak its name, was aware of the psychological power of prior commitments. He had already lowered his target, reducing his commitment. But he still knew that, in order to stay faithful to his partners and himself, he would have to run flat out to keep up with the market and his peers if he stayed in the game. Inevitably, in a stock market in which valuations had broken anchor from what he perceived as value, this would be dangerous. So he stepped away.

THE MUNGER FACTOR

Charlie shoved me in the right direction of not just buying bargains, as Ben Graham had taught me... It took a powerful force to move me from on from Graham's limiting views. It was the power of Charlie's mind.

Warren Buffett[36]

It is safe to say that Warren Buffett had a proclivity for introspection that cast light on the workings of his mind and the drivers of his behavior in certain aspects of his activity, even at this stage of his career. However, *it did not illuminate the whole*.

He could spot the pitfalls of continuing the Partnership, but he could not use this insight to inform him of the psychologically similar pitfalls of sticking with Berkshire Hathaway and/or cigar butt investing, or of the mechanism of the institutional imperative. This is because Buffett lacked a framework for his introspection—a system of analysis that would link one to the other, that would make sense of the totality of his behavior.

Enter the man with that framework: one Charles T. Munger.

Eight years his senior, Charlie Munger is no less an extraordinary character than Warren Buffett. His contribution to the success of

Berkshire Hathaway has been immeasurable. To some, Munger comes across as an abrasive individual: opinionated, pompous, and arrogant. Of his decision to move from Omaha to California, he says that he would probably have done better financially had he stayed and hooked up earlier with business luminaries like Buffett and Peter Kiewit, *but* he adds, "They might have done better, too."[37] His friend Rick Guerin says: "He has a habit of saying, 'I'm right and you're smart enough to figure it out sooner or later'… and the fact is that most of the time he is right."[38]

It was being so self-assured, however, that allowed Munger to unstick Buffett from his commitment to Ben Graham. Buffett and Munger first met in 1959 and soon after struck up an informal working relationship. Thus, as Buffett struggled with Berkshire Hathaway and to "escape" from Graham, the teachings of his "West Coast philosopher" friend were working away in the background.[39]

Today, except for the principle of requiring a margin of safety in the valuation of a company before investing in it, Buffett has completely abandoned his mentor's method of valuing stocks. Instead, he looks for value in enduring franchises—value that companies create, for instance, by dint of their ingenuity, service, brand, marketing, managerial competence, inherent profitability, and ability to exploit growth opportunities. Above all, he looks for value in their capacity to act like owners, the totality of which requires reference to the capital they employ on their balance sheets, but the products of which cannot necessarily be guessed by reference to that.

Buffett is under no illusion that it was Munger who wrought this wholesale transformation within him. Munger had very little time for Graham's ideas. He wanted to invest in good businesses, and defined "good" in relation to the abbreviated list of characteristics outlined above.

As the stock market grew increasingly efficient, Buffett's and Graham's cigar butts became increasingly rare. With Berkshire growing in size, those that did get tossed into the street did not possess sufficient puff to make a difference to the company's overall performance. Serendipitously, Buffett came under Munger's influence just at the right time—in more ways than one, as it happened.

By necessity, Munger's approach meant analyzing the factors shaping the future economics of a company: the orientation of management with respect to the company's shareholders, their quality and corporate culture, for instance, and the competitive characteristics of the industry—in fact, the very same kettle of fish that Buffet faced as a *manager*.

Charlie Munger is in the habit of inverting problems. He tends to ask what might go *wrong*, rather than what might go *right*, and concentrates his efforts on determining where mistakes might be made— particularly in the (mis)management of otherwise impregnable franchises.

Munger infected Buffett with the same habit and eventually this would pay off. By analyzing his own mistakes, recognizing those of others, and relating these to the challenge contained in managing Berkshire Hathaway as a streaming video, Buffett's explosion of cognition would come.

The final ingredient was Charlie Munger's framework of mental models.

Munger's mental models

Neurophysiologist William Calvin tells us that "a particularly intelligent person often seems 'quick' and capable of juggling many ideas at once."[40] This is Charlie Munger. On their first meeting Buffett was struck by Munger's intelligence. Indeed, later he was to comment that "Charlie, even though he had no particular training in it, instinctively understood investment about as well as anybody I'd ever met."[41]

Munger is hooked on knowledge, driven in its pursuit. "When I learn something new that I think is important, and maybe even useful to boot to me or to others, that is what really turns me on," he says.[42] But for Munger *wisdom*—the application of knowledge—goes beyond its mere accumulation.

He reads widely, across many disciplines, well beyond the realms of theories of finance, searching for the "why?" of everything. However, he does not use a scatter-gun approach in this. Munger organizes his knowledge around a framework of mental models that define the disciplines he studies. It is through the use of these models that he distills the wisdom from his knowledge. He says on the subject of wisdom:

> *The first rule is that you can't really know anything if you just remember isolated facts and try and bang 'em back. If the facts don't hang together on a latticework of theory, you don't have them in a usable form.*[43]

Munger constructs his latticework of theory out of models drawn from the fields of mathematics, biology, chemistry, physics, economics, probability theory, evolutionary theory, and behavioral psychology—to name a few of the principal ones. (In total they number 100 or so, although a handful carry most of the freight.) He uses these as a *filter* through which he passes his observations of the world around him, and he interprets everything in their light.

Each analytical problem, hypothesis, all information pertaining to an issue, any experience, or data, *everything* is dissected for rules, laws, relationships, illuminations, or rejections that may reside in one or more of these models. They furnish a representation of his universe, ordering, cleansing, and enhancing his cognition. *For Munger, this filtering is the process that transforms knowledge into wisdom.*

This is why he had that instinct for investment that revealed itself in his first meeting with Buffett, even though it was a novel subject to him. As Buffett talked, Munger would have been running his comments through his models. Principles, rules, and relationships that are key to the investment process would have jumped out as salient: anything consonant with his representation of the world ripped from the noise of the conversation. Out of this, by inferring rules drawn from his framework, Munger would have built a rudimentary theory of finance on the fly—enough to impress Warren Buffett in the space of a single conversation, and that's enough to be very impressive.

Hence, says Buffett: "Charlie's got the best 30-second mind in the world."[44]

The behavioral psychology of the institutional imperative

Of the models that he uses, Munger rates psychology as the most valuable, and he carries in his head around 20 psychological principles that he feels are important for understanding how humans tick.

For Munger, the lesson from psychology is:

Your brain has a shortage of circuitry and so forth—and it's taking all kinds of little automatic shortcuts.... So when circumstances combine in certain ways [that cause a] cognitive dysfunction—you're a patsy.[45]

In other words, humans are wired to incorporate biases, rules of thumb, and emotions into their decision making. These do not always produce sound results, particularly if you are unaware of the way in which they work. *Thus Charlie Munger accurately describes the underlying dynamic of the institutional imperative.*

The institutional imperative grows out of the existence of a cognitive dysfunction wherein humans adhere to an ancient logic that has everything to do with survival and self-interest, but very little to do with allocating capital efficiently. Within this ancient logic is contained the fear of being inconsistent with a prior commitment, the fear of departing from a prior definition of self, and the discord attached to admitting failure—because in the struggle to survive, behaving in this fashion kept you in the game with still a chance of ultimate success, which was measured by the replication of your genes.

Once he recognized the limitations of his own cognitive apparatus—but more prevalently its limitations in others—Warren Buffett's vision of capital allocation was infused with insight. He already had the facts:

○ As a manager, you can't just tell people what to do and expect them to do it. You have to find some other way, some other form of leadership. They have to be motivated personally to do it.
○ Commitments to businesses manifest their own dynamics, divorced from their original conception, aggregated around self-interest.

○ The psychological needs of the people for whom managers work can threaten to change the way companies are managed on their behalf.

○ The streaming video companies in which Buffett would henceforth invest also faced the same problems as he had experienced—in man management, in the dynamics of self-interest and growth versus the interests of the owners, and in dealing with the expectations of shareholders whose motivation was subject to imperatives of their own.

However, now these facts spoke to Buffett with one voice. *At last, he had them in a usable form.*

Once he had the framework, Buffett's cognition exploded out of its fixtures. It conveyed an overwhelming comprehension of the nature of the human condition in the allocation of capital and illuminated the surrender of economic logic in the face of a logic dictated by that condition. The mechanism of the institutional imperative manifested itself.

It's not intelligence that makes the difference, Buffett concluded. It's about *how* you think, how you're wired and, therefore, on what basis you are motivated to make decisions in the allocation of capital. This is why, today, Buffett is happy to admit to the charge that he is lucky, aimed at him by the proponents of the Efficient Market Hypothesis.

Informed by the notion that it should not be in the compass of one man consistently to steal bargains from under the collective nose of thousands of other investors, the academics who gaze on Buffett's record conclude that he has to be a statistical anomaly. "The reason he is rich," says Michael Lewis, author of *Liar's Poker*, neatly summarizing the principle on which their opinion is based, "is simply that random games produce big winners."[46]

With so many practitioners in the field, operating over such a long period of time, the chances are that someone *would* string together a sequence of fabulous years. It just happened to be Warren Buffett. He *is* lucky. End of story. And, notwithstanding the fact that the academics have made the same mistake as most people who look at Buffett's record—mistaking his success as that of simply an investor—Warren Buffett concurs.

However, this is not in the sense that the academics mean. Instead, he says:

I'm lucky. I don't run very fast, but I'm wired in a particular way that I thrive in a big capitalist economy with a lot of action.[47]

Buffett examined his own cognitive apparatus and found it wanting. He identified the mistakes of his wiring. And when he looked up from doing so, he saw these same mistakes repeated on a wholesale basis in the allocation of capital. Therefore, he identified that if this was the locus of poor decisions, his only solution would be to rewire his brain—using Charlie Munger's framework of mental models to do so.

This framework functions by rerouting all information into his brain so that it passes through a filter composed of the 100 or so models that Buffett now employs to make sense of the world *before it gets acted on.*[48] The normal route into the brain—which triggers the short-cut method of analysis and adherence to the imperative—is suppressed. By using this filtering mechanism, in Munger's words, "things gradually fit together in a way that enhances cognition."[49] In governing all of his decisions, all of the time, these filters have become Buffett's new rules of thumb, telling him what information to pay attention to and how to process it.

In contrast to most of those employed in the allocation of capital, Warren Buffett has *adapted*. Professing that "I am a better investor because I am a business man, and a better business man because I am an investor,"[50] and that "I evolved. I didn't go from ape to human... in a nice even manner," he became hardwired for this function.[51]

In so doing, it became clear to him that, if his vision of acting like an owner in the management of an enterprise was to see fruition, he would have to construct an organization in which the institutional imperative could not gain a foothold. He would have to ensure that his own motivation and that of his key employees was guided by the objective of measuring the return on capital employed in the enterprise, comparing this across other available opportunities, and that the feedback loop with his shareholders reinforced rather than negated this.

Just how he achieved this is the subject of the next chapter.

3

Leadership and the Allocation of Capital

Ben Graham taught me 45 years ago that in investing it is not necessary to do extraordinary things to get extraordinary results. In later life, I have been surprised to find that this statement holds true in business management as well.

Warren Buffett[1]

Intelligent control appears as uncontrol or freedom. And for that reason it is genuinely intelligent control. Unintelligent control appears as external domination. And for that reason it is really unintelligent control.

Lao Tzu[2]

The most profound statement that Warren Buffett has made with regard to the edge that Berkshire Hathaway has over other companies does not pertain to how he values stocks. Nor is it contained within a piece of advice about investing.

It is this: "We do have a few advantages, perhaps the greatest being that we *don't* have a strategic plan."[3]

Buffett says that the numbers posted by Berkshire Hathaway

have not come from some master plan we concocted in 1965. In a general way, we knew then what we hoped to accomplish but had no idea what specific opportunities might make it possible. Today we remain similarly unstructured: Over time, we expect to improve [our figures]... but have no road map to tell us how that will come about.[4]

Stephen Schneider of CPS, a company that specializes in this area, points out that strategic plans and leadership are inextricably linked. He defines a strategy as a "process of positioning an organization for future advantage," which requires a deep understanding of the internal and external factors that influence a company. "Leadership," he continues, "is the weapon that provides strategic impact," demanding "the articulation of an argument so compelling that other people see its merits and are prepared to act on it."[5]

Professing not to have a strategic plan is therefore an extraordinary statement for the chairman of any public company to make. According to Schneider's definition of the term, it amounts to an abdication of leadership. The chairman who has no plan has no basis on which to lead.

Equally, he has no road map of the future—and this is sufficient to strike fear into the heart of anyone whose task is to navigate an uncertain terrain and get others to follow him.

All humans, not merely managers and their employees, crave the visibility that strategic plans deliver. Conversely, they loathe uncertainty and will strive to eradicate it. That is why, when human culture advanced to the colonization of new habitats other than the savannah plains where our wiring evolved, instinct told us to map out these areas, find the lay of the land, and familiarize ourselves with the surroundings in order to "remove the terror of a landscape lacking a frame of reference," as Stephen Pinker puts it.[6]

By planting guideposts in an uncertain *future*, strategic plans fulfill this role for the managements of corporations and their employees. They set the direction for the company. Internally, they inform people of their roles, let them know where they are going and how they will get there. Externally, they seek to influence proceedings, shaping the marketplaces in which companies operate, molding them to management's desires by prescient manipulation of supply and demand.

Schneider is right therefore: Strategic plans are indeed the instruments of leadership. They are a mechanism for subjugating the fear contained in uncertainty that we have been wired to abhor. And they do this by asserting control over it. By proclamation, however, Warren Buffett has no such instrument. In the face of uncertainty, he does not seek control—either internally or externally.

He does, of course, have a very clear goal, which is to grow the value of Berkshire Hathaway at a rate of 15% per annum over the long term. But he has no preconceived notion of how he is going to achieve this, and provides no specific route for his employees to follow:

> *At Berkshire, we have no view of the future that dictates what business or industries we will enter... We prefer instead to focus on the economic characteristics of businesses that we wish to own and the personal characteristics of managers with whom we wish to associate—and then hope we get lucky in finding the two in combination.*[7]

To Buffett's mind, the way in which we strive to assert control over the corporate environment, planning, budgeting, forecasting, *managing*—processes, *people*, and results, by decree—simply replaces the fear of uncertainty with other fears. Contained in one place, this emotion squeezes out elsewhere, and finds itself expressed in the fear of not complying with ancient rules of behavior that are the accidental impedimenta of every strategy.

For Warren Buffett, strategic plans are the genesis of the institutional imperative, whereby managers are deprived of and/or lose their perspective as allocators of capital.

Therefore, in order for him to retain his perspective, Buffett has excised the strategic plan from his organization. By so doing, he has been able to restrain its dynamics *before* they get a chance to break into their stride, thereby allowing him to maintain his focus on his vision to act like an owner.

Thus, in respect to both managing the company and managing the managers within it, Buffett lets go of the controls to which most people in his position cling. Strategically, Berkshire Hathaway is effectively inert and in the management of its subsidiaries Buffett does nothing—*it seems*. But the logic of this approach is that neither he, nor the managers who work for him, ever lose sight of the fact that their job is to act like owners.

❖❖❖

HOBBLING THE DYNAMICS OF THE INSTITUTIONAL IMPERATIVE

After 25 years of buying and supervising a great variety of businesses, Charlie and I have not learned how to solve difficult business problems. What we have learned is how to avoid them.
Warren Buffett[8]

I kind of made up my management approach as I went along... but I learned more from Warren, and from his example, than from anyone else.
Chuck Huggins, See's Candies[9]

So in order to minimize the influence of the institutional imperative within Berkshire Hathaway, Buffett hobbles its dynamics. As we have seen, the principal mechanism by which he does this is to remove the strategic plan from his organization. He says:

To earn 15% annually... will require a few big ideas—small ones just won't do. Charlie Munger, my partner in general management, and I do not have any such ideas at present, but our experience has been that they pop up occasionally. (How's that for a strategic plan?)[10]

To those who cling to strategic plans for the reassurance they provide, and to those whose behavior strategic plans orient, this mindset is deeply disturbing. Buffett relinquishes control in the face of uncertainty. He is spectacularly nonspecific in his management of Berkshire. In effect, he favors torpor over activity. He does not clearly articulate to people what they should do. He does not tell them how to get to their goal. He is reactive to the environment, rather than proactive. He does not appear to manage *anything*.

There is no dynamic.

The dynamic of the institutional imperative requires a foundation from which it can proceed to extend its influence, tendril-like, throughout an organization. That foundation is the strategic plan.

The strategic plans of companies establish the commitments to which they feel they must remain consistent. This inclines them to polarize around these plans to the exclusion of other possible uses for their capital and usually, since this is where their self-interest is located, to lurch toward growth. That is why Warren Buffett refuses to make a commitment to any of the businesses in which he has chosen to engage.

Having been ensnared by the dictates of commitment before, he is determined not to let this happen again. Hence he makes this statement:

We're not in the steel business, per se. We're not in the shoe business, per se. We're not in any business, per se. We're big in insurance, but we're not committed to it. We don't have a mindset that says you have to go down this road. So we can take capital and move it into businesses that make sense.[11]

THE ALLOCATION OF CAPITAL BUSINESS VS. THE INSTITUTIONAL IMPERATIVE

After making some expensive mistakes because I ignored the power of the imperative, I have tried to organize and manage Berkshire in ways that minimize its influence.

Warren Buffett[12]

"Taking capital and moving it into businesses that make sense" is the essence of Buffett's *raison d'être*.

His resolve not to commit to any particular functional manifestation of capital allocation guarantees that he never loses sight of the fact that the real business he is in, whether he is writing insurance policies, making candy, or training airline pilots, is the allocation of capital.

That explains why he and Charlie

feel no need to proceed in an ordained direction... but can instead simply decide what makes sense for our owners. In doing that, we always mentally compare any move we are contemplating with

*dozens of other opportunities open to us... Our practice of making
this comparison... is a discipline that managers focused simply on
expansion seldom use.* [13]

And it explains why commitments at Berkshire Hathaway, such as they
are, have no hold over the company: "We can expand the business into
any areas that we like—our scope is not circumscribed by *history, structure, or concept*" [emphasis added]. [14]

If a manager can adopt this perspective, *and maintain it* (perhaps
the most difficult challenge given the way commitments operate), then
the efficiency with which capital is allocated will be materially
enhanced. Unfortunately, this is not a perspective that most (any?)
other chief executives possess. Says Buffett:

*After ten years on the job, a CEO whose company annually retains
earnings equal to 10% of net worth will have been responsible for
the deployment of more than 60% of all the capital at work in the
business.* [15]

However, he continues:

*The heads of many companies are not skilled in capital allocation.
Their inadequacy is not surprising. Most bosses rise to the top
because they have excelled in some area such as marketing, production, engineering, administration—or, sometimes, institutional
politics. Once they become CEOs, they face new responsibilities.
They must now make capital allocation decisions, a critical job
that they may never have tackled and that is not easily mastered.
To stretch the point, it's as if the final step for a highly-talented
musician was not to perform at Carnegie Hall but, instead, to be
named Chairman of the Federal Reserve... [and] in the end,
plenty of unintelligent capital allocation takes place in corporate
America. (That's why you hear so much about "restructuring.")* [16]

Allocating capital is not what these people do. Although capital necessarily forms the DNA of the people, products, marketing, research and

development, and plant and machinery that they manage, it is essentially invisible to them. *Things* are what they touch—processes too. Their managerial function is defined with reference to this to the most important people who check for consistency of behavior with prior definitions of self—*themselves*.

Given that the salaries of managers (not to say their egos) are correlated with size, the risk of bankruptcy negatively so, and the probability of exercising their stock options, if they have them, considerably enhanced if they are able to stick around for long enough, the self-interest of these people finds itself expressed in a resolve to grow. Given their perspective of their role, it's only human nature that this should be the case.

BUFFETT'S INSIGHT: CORPORATE SAVER

At the end of every year about 97% of Berkshire's shares are held by the same investors who owned them at the start of the year. That makes them savers.

Warren Buffett[17]

Having graduated from investor to manager, Warren Buffett took a different route to the top. This meant that his insight into the management function was, and still is, entirely novel.

The task facing Buffett as an investor was to find value within the *universe* of opportunities available, and to buy the one that offers the highest return (risk-adjusted, technically):

The investment shown by the discounted-flows-of-cash calculation to be the cheapest is the one that the investor should purchase—irrespective of whether the business grows or doesn't, displays volatility or smoothness in its earnings, or carries a high price or low price in relation to its current earnings and book value.[18]

As an investor, Buffett became accustomed to dealing with capital as an abstraction—as the discounted stream of cash produced by those assets in which it is embodied. This abstraction is also available to managers, and they are accustomed to evaluating projects on this basis. Buffett's physical separation from operational management, however, granted him an intellectual perspective that does not come naturally to managers who have graduated the Jack Welch way. When Buffett exported this perspective to the same function as Welch *et al.*, he became not a manager, steel executive, or insurance man, but an *allocator of capital*.

Buffett looks on himself as a fragment of a capital market, the job of which is to allocate resources where they can be most efficiently utilized within an economy. Indeed, in a fractal sense, he is a one-man capital market, allocating capital to its point of best use within his area of competence.

As such, Buffett recognizes two characteristics of the capital he manages:

1　It is fungible. It will assuredly become embodied in some form of activity, but Buffett sees the DNA of the form, not its flesh. His concern therefore is not for the form itself but for the replication of each unit of capital that comprises it—and this might be better achieved in some other body host.
2　To the extent that he manages this replication, he does so only on behalf of the company's shareholders (among whom he is counted, of course). As such, his self-interest is not found in writing insurance policies, or in making widgets. Instead, it is in looking after other people's savings—and in as much as they store their wealth with him, he husbands it for them in his allocation of capital at Berkshire.

By investing in Berkshire Hathaway for the long term, its shareholders "are automatically saving even if they spend every dime they personally earn," says Buffett.

> Berkshire "saves" for them by retaining all earnings, thereafter using these savings to purchase businesses and securities. Clearly, the more cheaply we make these buys, the more profitable our owners' indirect savings program will be.[19]

This is what it is to act like an owner in the management of an enterprise.

Most managers have no sense of this perspective. If they have any relationship with the market as allocator of capital, it is one in which they feel they must manage, manipulate, and, in fact, use it to their own advantage. Most often, CEOs consider the market as a nuisance that only complicates their real job, which is to obey the imperative and grow the business. Sometimes they do not consider the capital allocation relationship at all.

Jack Welch's description of what it is to be a CEO, for instance, may be more colorful than Buffett's but lacks his clarity, focus, and sense of wider purpose:

Being a CEO is nuts! A whole jumble of thoughts come to mind: Over the top. Wild. Fun. Outrageous. Crazy. Passion. Perpetual motion. The give-and-take. Meetings into the night. Incredible friendships. Fine wine. Celebrations. Great golf courses. Big decisions in the real game. Crises and pressure. Lots of swings. A few home runs. The thrill of winning. The pain of losing.[20]

The allocation of capital is in here somewhere—in a way. The CEO as corporate saver is most definitely not.

Indeed, comparing Buffett's perception of his role with Welch's is rather like the apocryphal story of the article run by a leading national newspaper when the Cold War was at its height. A journalist asked the president of the US and the leader of the Soviet Union, individually, what they would like for Christmas. Next day, it ran with the front-page headline:

Brezhnev Calls for World Peace this Christmas:
Carter Asks for Basket of Glazed Fruit

It's a vision thing. A perspective thing. It's about putting yourself in context.

This is exactly why Warren Buffett has no strategic plan. In pursuing one, he too would risk losing his perspective in the allocation of capital.

The seductive nature of commitments would ensure that were so. Says Buffett, "We think it's usually poison for a corporate giant's shareholders if it embarks upon new ventures pursuant to some grand vision."[21] Thus, at every point in the capital allocation process Buffett now stops and measures his use of capital in that venture against all other possible uses:

○ Prior commitments to particular ventures are no longer subject to the risk of entrapment.
○ First conclusions are no longer buttressed by the search for reasons in their support, but rather constantly challenged as to whether they stand on their own and relative merits.
○ Walking away from these invokes no discord within him, because they are superseded by a *prior* commitment of a greater calling, which is to allocate capital.

TRANSLATING THE VISION INTO LEADERSHIP

He has a way of motivating you. He trusts you so much that you just want to perform.
        Bill Child, R.C. Willey Home Furnishings[22]

Note Buffett's statement that he and Charlie Munger perform just two tasks at Berkshire Hathaway:

First, it's our job to keep able people who are already rich motivated to keep working at things they… don't need to do for financial reasons… Secondly, we have to allocate capital.[23]

Notice how he puts the motivation of his managers first in order of priority. That's because, in pursuing his objective of acting like an owner, *the strategic impact of Warren Buffett as a leader is to elicit compliance with this objective: to motivate everybody who counts in his organization to think and act in the same way as he does in the allocation of capital.*

Buffett's perspective of the proper function of a manager would count for naught if he could not get the managers of Berkshire

Hathaway subsidiaries to tilt their efforts as diligently as he does in the direction of the owners of the firm.

In striving to do this, Buffett has rejected the strategic plan as an instrument of leadership. But that is not to say that he does not have any instrument at all. He does: the vision contained in his ambition to bridge the gap between the management of the firm and its shareholders.

The articulation of the vision: The *Owner's Manual* as meme

I want employees to ask themselves whether they are willing to have any contemplated act appear on the front page of their local paper the next day, to be read by their spouses, children and friends.

Warren Buffett[24]

The philosophy underpinning this ideal is pervasive in Buffett's behavior at Berkshire Hathaway and in his communication with his shareholders. "Act like an owner" is the meme—the directive from on high—that Warren Buffett spreads throughout his organization. It is in what he says, in what he does, and, as we shall see later, enshrined in the rules of conduct (such as they are) that he prescribes for his managers to follow.

If he specifically distills this meme anywhere in concentrated form, he does so in what he calls the company's *Owner's Manual*. This document—which, interestingly given his entrapment in the textiles industry, did not appear in his annual reports until 1983—has been reprinted in every annual report since then. In it, Buffett articulates the principles that guide his stewardship of other people's money.

Its main principles are the following:

1 "Although our form is corporate, our attitude is partnership. Charlie Munger and I think of our shareholders as owner-partners, and as ourselves as managing partners… We do not view the company itself as the ultimate owner of our business assets but instead view the company as a conduit through which our shareholders own the assets."

2 "We do not measure the economic significance of Berkshire by its size; we measure by per-share progress… The size of our paychecks

or our offices will never be related to the size of Berkshire's balance sheet."

3 "A managerial 'wish list' will not be filled at shareholder expense... We will only do with your money what we would do with our own, weighing fully the values you can obtain by diversifying through direct purchases in the stock market.

4 "We feel noble intentions should be checked periodically against results. We test the wisdom of retaining earnings by assessing whether retention, over time, delivers shareholders at least $1 of market value for each $1 retained."

5 "We will be candid in our reporting to you, emphasizing the pluses and minuses important in appraising business value. Our guideline is to tell you the business facts that we would want to know if our positions were reversed. We owe you no less."

Aimed at explaining Berkshire's "broad principles of operation" to the shareholders of the company, Buffett's *Owner's Manual* furnishes by example the principles to which he expects the managers of his subsidiary companies to adhere.

INTRINSIC MOTIVATION

If we were not paid at all, Charlie and I would be delighted with the cushy jobs we hold.

Warren Buffett[25]

The greatest strength he has—giving you a lot of freedom to run the business the way you want. And that way, you can't pass the responsibility back to him.

Ralph Schey[26]

The *Owner's Manual* is no public relations bullshit mission statement, ghostwritten ideals of the marketing department to which the chief executive "aspires" but against which more often fails. This is the *substance* of the way Buffett behaves, the way he has *striven* to behave in the past, and the way he most assuredly *will* behave in the future.

In managerial terms, it occupies the unassailable high ground of corporate governance, to which other public companies do not even come close. And it establishes Warren Buffett's integrity as corporate saver.

This is important because, as Donald Langevoort notes, "the widespread belief among employees that their firms' integrity policies are insincere is consistent with a view that the belief is manufactured out of convenience."[27] When this is the case, leaders do not get buy-in. If their employees fall into line with the philosophy espoused, they do so because of the presence of control mechanisms encouraging the desired kind of behavior rather than because they believe in what they are doing. However, says Robert Cialdini:

> *One problem with controls… is that when people perceive of themselves performing the desirable monitored behavior, they tend to attribute the behavior not to their own natural preference for it but to the coercive presence of the controls. As a consequence, they come to view themselves as less interested in the desirable conduct for its own sake… and they are more likely to engage in the undesirable action whenever controls cannot detect the conduct.*[28]

When intrinsic motivation—behaving in a particular fashion because you believe it is right—is lost, effort falls and compliance is low. Buffett is looking for the inverse of this system among his managers. He wants them to take *inner responsibility* for their actions.

Rather than telling them how to behave, he would prefer them to pay deference to the authority contained in that still small voice that comes from within. The voice planted there by Buffett whispers the logic of acting like an owner.

Cialdini reports on the effectiveness of this form of motivation.[29] Jonathan Freedman conducted an experiment in which he first instructed a group of boys (individually), on pain of punishment, not to play with a toy robot out of a selection of toys made available for them. Consequently, while he was present, they did not. Six weeks later, however, back in the same room but this time with Freedman absent, most of the boys did play with the robot. Externally imposed rules did not work.

Next, Freedman gathered another group who were also warned against playing with the robot. Only this time Freedman added a reason: "It is wrong to play with the robot." Again, most obeyed the rule. But with this group, six weeks later most were *still* obeying the rule.

The difference was, of course, that the rule now came from the inside—the boys had decided that they would not play with the robot because *they* did not want to. They had taken inner responsibility for their actions and it was not necessary for Freedman or anyone else to be present to police their behavior with outside pressures. They could trust them because they had explained why they did not want the boys to play with the robot. Munger confirms a similar view:

Just as you think better if you array knowledge on a bunch of models that are basically answers to the question why, why, why, *if you always tell people why, they'll understand it better, they'll consider it more important and they'll be more likely to comply.*[30]

Serendipitously, getting his managers to take inner responsibility for their behavior means that in order to police it, Buffett does not have to be present in the managerial sense of the term; they police their own conduct. He then sets up a *virtuous circle* in which his managers' intrinsic motivation is fostered by the very freedom from control that his managerial style requires.

BUFFETT'S DECENTRALIZED MODEL

Our contribution to See's Candies has been limited to leaving it alone. When we bought it, it already had a wonderful culture, a wonderful trademark and a wonderful reputation. Our contribution was not screwing it up. There are a lot of people who would have bought it and would have screwed it up. They would have thought that headquarters knows best.

Charlie Munger[31]

In managing Berkshire Hathaway's subsidiary companies toward an objective of growing the intrinsic value of the whole at a rate of 15% per annum, Warren Buffett does not intervene in the conduct of his managers. There is no formal, tangible mechanism of control at Berkshire Hathaway. Instead, Buffett takes his hands off the reins.

He is there as a sounding board whenever required and supplies advice when requested. Says Chuck Huggins:

> *He's always available, and that's really remarkable. He looks at the successes and the mistakes of all these companies that he deals with directly, as well as those where his contact is not direct, and he's always willing to share whatever lessons there are to be learned.*[32]

Buffett is supportive at all times: "We avoid the attitude of the alumnus whose message to the football coach is *I'm 100% with you—win or tie*," he says.[33] But he never prescribes behavior. In keeping with his philosophy, if a manager comes to him for counsel, Buffett gives his spin on the situation and then leaves that person to decide what action to take.

 He requests only that they "run their companies as if these are the sole asset of their families and will remain so for the next century."[34] As they go about doing this, he assures them that there will be no "show-and-tell presentations in Omaha, no budgets to be approved by head-quarters, no dictums issued about capital expenditures."[35] Indeed, there is no centralized budgeting process to which they are either expected to adhere or to contribute. "In most cases," says Buffett, "the managers of important businesses we have owned for many years have not been to Omaha or even met each other."

"The only item about which you need to check with me," he tells his managers, "are any changes in post-retirement benefits and any unusually large capital expenditures."[36] (Projects of sufficient size to have a meaningful impact on Berkshire's fortunes are those in which Buffett wants to bring his capital allocation skills to bear.)

The principles contained in Buffett's *Owner's Manual* are sufficient to orient his key employees in the right direction—*and no more*. Thereafter, in putting these into effect, he eschews the role of grand designer. He does not specify how these high ideals should be met at the operating level. *Instead, he supplies the barest of rules required to do this.* He sets some loosely defined boundaries for the firm to meet its target, creating enabling conditions only for this to be met, and then lets Berkshire Hathaway find its own form. Crucially, this feeds back into allowing his managers to find *their* own way of complying with Berkshire's overall objective.

The managers of his subsidiary companies, Buffett says, "are truly in charge."[37]

The boids

We are surrounded by evidence of the antithesis of Buffett's managerial model—command and control—and hence of his apparent recklessness in not adhering to it. As Mitch Resnick points out:

> *When we see neat rows of corn in a field, we assume correctly that the corn was planted by the farmer. When we watch a ballet, we assume correctly that the movements of the dancers were planned by a choreographer. When we participate in social systems, such as families and school classrooms, we often find that power and authority are centralized, often excessively so.*[38]

For instance, when we consider the behavior of a colony of ants, or a flock of birds, we tend also to believe that this complex pattern of behavior is the product of centralized control—an ant general or a lead bird. In fact, this behavior is determined by the *interaction* between the agents, each of which behaves according to a simple set of rules.

The science behind this principle traces its roots back to a computer simulation developed in 1987 by Craig Reynolds.[39] The simulation consists of a collection of autonomous agents—the *boids*—in an environment with obstacles. In addition to the basic laws of physics, each boid follows three simple rules:

1 Try to maintain a minimum distance from all other boids and objects.
2 Try to match speed with neighboring boids.

3 Try to move forward to the center of the mass of boids in your neighborhood.

Remarkably, when the simulation is run, the boids exhibit the very life-like behavior of flying in flocks. Their behavior emerges from their interaction. They self-organize. They do not require the existence of a grand plan or a central manager to function efficiently. They produce a symphony without a conductor. *They flock even though there is no rule explicitly telling them to do so.*

This is Warren Buffett's model of management.

MIN SPECS: THE ARTIFICE IN BUFFETT'S DECENTRALIZED APPROACH

It was pointed out by a colonel that GE had plenty of intelligent leaders who would always be clever enough to define their markets so narrowly that they could safely remain No. 1 or No. 2.... for nearly 15 years, I had been hammering away on the need to be No. 1 or No. 2 in every market. Now this class was telling me that one of my most fundamental ideas was holding us back.

Jack Welch[40]

Craig Reynolds showed with his boids that complex behavior can be ordained by simple rules, minimum specifications (*min specs*) of conduct for each agent. In the same way that Reynolds designed three simple rules governing the behavior of the boids, in imposing external rules of behavior for his managers Buffett designs his in minimum form.

The principles contained in the *Owner's Manual* are a recipe for eliciting behavior that is the inverse of the institutional imperative: They set objectives in light of the knowledge that the shareholders of Berkshire Hathaway have alternative uses for their money. The allocation of capital within Berkshire therefore has to meet their return requirements. Nevertheless, with the right rules of behavior in place, Buffett can have complete confidence in setting his managers free to attend to this.

To that end, rather than fall into the same trap as Jack Welch, Buffett has been careful to design rules ensuring that the behavior of his managers self-organizes around the interests of Berkshire Hathaway's owners. Thus, the rules require the following:

1 Remuneration packages are compatible with the principle of taking inner responsibility for behavior.
2 Self-interest is oriented toward return on capital and not growth.
3 The optimum amount of capital is retained within the enterprise, with the excess sent to Buffett.
4 If Berkshire's managers find themselves struggling, they do not throw capital at the problem.

However, in designing these rules, Buffett has gone one better than Reynolds. He has turned to nature and borrowed from the codes it conceived for governing behavior—the wiring inside all our brains. Rather than telling people *how* to behave, Buffett influences the *way* in which they behave by allowing their wiring to do his management for him. Now his rules are truly min specs.

In Warren Buffett's *fly-by-wiring* model, the specifications for managers do not appear as such. The managers' complicity with his objectives is not forced. Their behavior is completely "natural." And it taps into the most powerful motivational force that any human knows—one that comes not from complying with rules imposed by some external body, but from within: the intrinsic motivation that Warren Buffett is looking to nurture inside Berkshire Hathaway.

To the casual observer, it may look as though Buffett interferes very little in the day-to-day management of his subsidiary companies, but in reality he is in constant (ethereal) attendance. *The trick is to mediate in the interaction between the agents and their environment, rather than to control it.*

Min spec 1: Own your own efforts

Buffett is very careful about his incentive schemes, and usually they are the only things he changes in a company when he acquires it. "At

Berkshire," he comments, "we try to be as logical about compensation as about capital allocation."[41]

That's how important this subject is.

First and foremost, therefore, if Buffett is to rely on the intrinsic motivation of his managers to comply with the *Owner's Manual*, he has to establish this as correct behavior and answer the natural human question: "What's in it for me?" He does this with a compensation scheme that rewards "correct" behavior appropriately (and potentially very handsomely). Nevertheless, in accordance with the principle of getting people to take inner responsibility for their actions, the primary driver in his compensation packages is that people should own their efforts. That is why they only get paid in relation to the performance of the part of the organization that they can influence. Says Buffett:

> *Arrangements that pay off in capricious ways, unrelated to a manager's personal accomplishments, may well be welcomed by certain managers... But such arrangements are wasteful to the company and cause the manager to lose focus.*[42]

The origin of that loss of focus can be found when a manager becomes distracted by behavior that is in his best interest. Leaving his colleagues to attend to the greater good, he knows that *they* will deliver the bonus that is tied to overall corporate performance. In this kind of free-rider problem, the catch is, of course, that a manager rarely operates under this illusion alone.

To obviate this tendency, Buffett employs an

> *incentive compensation system that rewards key managers for meeting targets in their own bailiwicks. If See's does well, that does not produce incentive compensation at the News—nor vice versa... In setting compensation, we like to hold out the promise of large carrots, but make sure their delivery is tied directly to results in the area that a manager controls... We believe, further, that such factors as seniority and age should not affect incentive compensation... a 20-year-old who can hit .300 is as valuable to us as 40-year-old performing as well.*[43]

At Berkshire Hathaway, you reap what you sow.

In contrast, at GE Jack Welch took the opposite tack. He scrapped a system similar to Buffett's stating that "if you did well—even if the overall company did poorly—you got yours."[44] His reasoning was sound. A compensation system like Buffett's did not support the behavior he required. "If we wanted every business to be a lab for ideas, we needed to pay people in a way that would reinforce the concept,"[45] he said, and a company-wide bonus scheme "reinforced the idea of sharing among the top 500 people."[46]

However, this was all about managing change, shape shifting the whole company in response to new threats and opportunities. That is why Welch also changed his compensation systems. He said:

> *Static measurements get stale. Market conditions change, new businesses develop, new competitors show up. I always pounded home the question "Are we measuring and rewarding the behavior we want?"*[47]

Buffett has no such worries. If he had to change his compensation system at every turn, then he'd be using the wrong one. A company like Berkshire, which earns over 20% on its equity and reinvests the lot, has the potential to renew itself every four to five years *and there's only one type of behavior that needs to be measured and rewarded when this is the case: that those responsible for reinvestment act like owners.*

Min spec 2: Reward return on capital and put rewards at risk

Having assured his managers that they will receive reward in proportion to their own efforts, Buffett lets them know how he measures that. It is not measured in the growth of their managerial domain, it is by the return on the capital that they tie up in the business.

Buffett will not tell his managers what constitutes the right amount of capital to retain in a business, however. That would be imposition of an external control. Instead, he lets them decide what this is. But, says Buffett:

When capital invested in an operation is significant we… charge managers a high rate for incremental capital they employ and credit them at an equally high rate for capital they release.[48]

Buffett is happy to fund businesses that have the opportunity to grow profitably. "Guess what you get to do today?" he tells new managers. "Start breaking all your banking relationships, because from now on I'm your bank."[49] But he also wants to ensure that if they do need recourse to external financing, it comes from Berkshire and not some other intermediary. Buffett wants to be able to charge them for the true cost of employing that capital, which is the opportunity cost of what it would earn if he deployed it elsewhere. "Easy access to funding," he says, "tends to cause undisciplined decisions."[50]

Thus, a manager's results are only credited in relation to the amount of capital employed to produce them, and a manager's self-interest becomes defined in relation to this metric. It is vital that this is so, because the predictable sustainability of the profitability of Berkshire's noninsurance operations provides a significant competitive advantage to its insurance businesses. Buffett observes:

In managing insurance investments, it is a distinct advantage to know that large amounts of taxable income will consistently recur. Most insurance companies are unable to assume consistent recurrence of significant taxable income. Berkshire insurance companies can make this assumption confidently, due to the large and diverse streams of taxable income flowing from Berkshire's numerous non-insurance subsidiaries.[51]

As a rule, insurance companies have to invest most of the capital supporting their operations in high-grade fixed-income instruments.[52] Warren Buffett can hunt for bigger game and therefore out-earn the industry.

However, as much as rewards for posting high-return-on-capital results are on offer to the managers of Berkshire's subsidiaries, Buffett also puts them at risk. He says:

If Ralph [Schey, for example] can employ incremental funds at good returns, it pays him to do so. His bonus increases when earnings on additional capital exceed a meaningful hurdle charge. But our bonus calculation is symmetrical: If incremental investment yields substandard returns, the shortfall is costly to Ralph as well as Berkshire. The consequence of this two-way arrangement is that it pays Ralph—and pays him well—to send to Omaha any cash he can't advantageously use in his business.[53]

He continues:

It has become fashionable at public companies to describe almost every compensation plan as aligning the interests of management with those of shareholders. In our book, alignment means being a partner in both directions, not just on the upside. Many "alignment" plans flunk this basic test, being artful forms of "heads I win, tails you lose" *[emphasis added].*[54]

At Berkshire, however, managers "truly stand in the shoes of owners."[55]

Putting rewards at risk is an important concept. Once again, it does not seek to impose a rule that defines how much capital to employ, but it does tap into an internal rule of behavior that Buffett can rely on to do his management for him, in this case loss aversion, which is that integral part of human wiring anchoring most contestants on the television show *Who Wants to Be a Millionaire?* to the questions they know they can get right.

Min spec 3: You *will* receive reward in proportion to your effort and skill

In accordance with the principle that managers will receive compensation for performance within their own remit, Buffett also ensures that "performance" is defined appropriately—in this instance by reference to the business cards they have been dealt.

Warren Buffett is not biased in his attribution of talent. When he looks at managerial performance he does not blindly ascribe it to the personal qualities of his managers, rather than the quality of the businesses they happen to be running. Therefore, he does not make the mistake—as the majority do—of rewarding managers in businesses in which excellent results accrue by dint of the fundamentals of the business more highly than those equally skillful managers toiling to eke excellent results out of less attractive businesses. For the latter, who—like the majority—ascribe *their* performance more to the situation they find themselves in, rather than to their own particular talent, this would appear grossly unfair, and the danger is they would start to work in their own interests, rather than for Berkshire Hathaway.

To counteract this, Buffett defines performance

in different ways depending on the underlying economics of the business: in some our managers enjoy tailwinds not of their own making, in others they fight unavoidable headwinds.[56]

Therefore, he tailors each package to fit the degree of difficulty of the enterprise being managed: "the terms of each agreement vary to fit the economic characteristics of the business at issue."[57] This grants him the perspective to be able to recognize and reward, and therefore incentivize, those "excellent managers"[58] who nevertheless "struggle" in difficult environments. Thus at Berkshire managers get paid according to ability, and in the past Buffett has found managers of his less than stellar businesses to be "every bit the equal of managers at our more profitable businesses."[59] Buffett's capacity to distinguish between the individual and the environment means that he does not alienate his managers.

Min spec 4: You don't necessarily lose by standing still

Basing his compensation packages on return on capital and putting bonuses at risk naturally remove a bias to growth from Buffett's managers. Growth is not ruled out (you might be able to raise returns by getting larger), but it is not generally a profitable strategy to pursue, and may well prove costly to both Berkshire and the manager.

However, Buffett reinforces this notion with two other characteristics of his incentive schemes. First, given the role that options play in the growth dynamic (people get paid for sticking around and the best way of doing this is by growing), Warren Buffett does not use options—full stop. At Berkshire Hathaway, nobody is incentivized to grow for the sake of raising the odds that, one day, they may strike it lucky merely by being there.

Secondly, Buffett says, "We never greet good work by raising the bar."[60] In other words, if you are doing a good job with the cards dealt to you in your particular industry, and thereby earn a bonus, next year Buffett will not make it harder for you. Buffett's managers have everything to gain by moving forward at top speed, but nothing to lose by standing still (if standing still is already excellent). The CEO who resets hurdle rates when they are exceeded runs the risk of encouraging managers who have this year's bonus "in the bag" to hold some back for next year, and those who do not to destroy results this year so that a bonus may be earned next, when year-on-year results are measured.

Min spec 5: Send excess cash to Omaha

Once he has established in your mind what excess capital is—it's that which is left over after you have exhausted the possibility of garnering reward from your own efforts and you're afraid it will cause you losses if you hang on to it—Buffett requires that it be forwarded to him.

This is a very simple rule. It is also very powerful.

It is in the deployment of excess capital that Buffett finds most managerial shortcomings. Generally this is because managers define themselves as managers rather than as allocators of capital, and this lays down an open invitation to the institutional imperative. Buffett observes:

> By sending it to us, [managers] don't get diverted by the various enticements that would come their way were they responsible for deploying the cash their businesses throw off.[61]

In other words, by taking control of the allocation of all of Berkshire's excess capital, *Buffett ensures that it is taken from those whose wiring may be prone to the intrusion of the imperative and given to one whose wiring—by adaptation—is not.*

Min spec 6: Guard *against* loss aversion

Nevertheless, what happens to those managers who truly are struggling? Those who are slipping behind even in tasks already recognized as difficult?

Buffett simply reassures these people of their position within Berkshire Hathaway. He is immensely loyal. As we shall see in the next chapter, he has gone to great lengths to get these people on board, and part of the package he offers them is that he is not in the habit of discarding poor-performing businesses so that he can pick up good ones. "Gin rummy managerial behavior (discard your least promising business at each turn) is not our style," he says.[62] Equally, he tells his managers: "I won't close down businesses of sub-normal profitability merely to add a fraction of a point to our corporate rate of return."[63] And, again as we shall see later, he does not judge performance on a short-term basis, already having factored into the purchase price of the businesses he acquires (which supply their own managers) the chance, nay the *expectation*, that success will not be an ever-present constant.

Thus reassured, struggling managers at Berkshire Hathaway who contemplate losses, either materially in their own incentive programs or relatively against prior reference points of performance, are *not* inclined, as most are when in a hole, to up the ante in order to get back to break even. By eradicating this "get-evenitis," as Hersh Shefrin calls it,[64] Buffett ensures that his managers do not succumb to the natural human response when threatened, which is to scramble madly in order to avoid the consequences—in this case by throwing capital at the problem—because, ultimately, in terms of their personal survival, there are none.[65]

Buffett's retort to those in trouble? "You don't have to make it back the way that you lost it."[66]

CROWDING INTRINSIC MOTIVATION *IN*

Contracts cannot guarantee your continued interest; we... simply rely on your word.

Warren Buffett[67]

Having opened up the void between himself as owner and his managers, economists would recommend to Buffett that he elicit their compliance with his objective that they should act like owners too, by appealing to their selfish nature that would otherwise result in them pursuing their own interests.

Buffett knows that when his managers go to work in the morning, they do so as volunteers, able to determine within the guidelines set for them exactly how much of themselves they are willing to invest in the task at hand.[68]

Rather than appealing to their selfishness, Buffett prefers to appeal to their basic instinct to reciprocate his trust and the fairness with which he treats them (contained primarily in his min specs, which are designed above all else to be fair and to be perceived as fair) with diligence, honesty, and effort. In this way he can tap into the willing volunteer that exists in all of them.

Therefore contracts of employment, the device normally used to establish and enforce relationships within most workplaces, do not exist at Berkshire Hathaway. Warren Buffett does not believe in them—largely because he perceives them as a poor, second-best alternative for controlling managers.

By dint of the leeway that managers are given within Berkshire Hathaway, however, legal contracts are replaced with the same social contract that Buffett has engineered between himself and his shareholders (specified in the *Owner's Manual*), which is premised not on Berkshire's shareholders having recourse to the armory of enforcement sanctions available to them as owners of the firm, but on trusting him to do their bidding because he is intrinsically motivated to do so.

The same motivational mechanism that works for Buffett works for those over whom he presides: "Our basic goal as an owner," he says, "is to behave with our managers as we like our owners to behave with us."[69] Therefore, in the same way that he is granted his freedom by his shareholders, he sets his managers free—pursuing a decentralized style of leadership that actively encourages the very separation of control from ownership that is so troubling to many.

Doing this fosters managers' self-esteem, and with freedom to manage their self-determination is enlarged. This gives them a chance to show that they are doing the job because they love to, because they believe in the correctness of acting like owners, and not because Buffett is looking over their shoulders. And this is the mechanism by which intrinsic motivation is *crowded in*: Buffett *can* rely on their word.[70]

In contrast, command systems that crowd out intrinsic motivation set up a vicious circle in which control mechanisms escalate even as compliance falls. Sometimes these can be made to work. At GE, for instance, managers who do not acquiesce are sacked and, over time, the company has self-selected those personality types that thrive in a high-pressure, controlled environment. But systems like this require huge policing efforts on the part of senior management.

Buffett has no such problems. At Berkshire Hathaway, the only control he has left when he abrogates the normal tools of management is one based on trust, fairness, and reciprocity. Paradoxically, this creates loyalty among his managers and obedience to his wishes manifesting themselves in an overwhelming eagerness to please, rather than (which an economist or like-minded corporate manager might expect) a sly keenness to cheat. This should not be surprising. Trust, fairness, and reciprocity form the basis of the same social glue that has carried successful human organizations all the way from the savannah plains of Africa, where it evolved as the *first-best solution* to cooperation, exchange, and progress.

THE PAYOFF: COMPLIANCE

I try to make every shareholder proud. I feel very obligated to try to do that. I don't want to run a company that you read bad things about in the newspaper.

Al Ueltschi, FlightSafety International[71]

As the institutional imperative seeks out the path of least resistance within companies, normally finding this in a manager's interest in growing the business, within Berkshire Hathaway it zeroes in on the loyalty that Buffett shows to those with whom he has entered into a commitment.

Buffett still makes the occasional mistake in this regard. In a letter to his shareholders on November 9, 2001, he had to explain why he had overstayed his welcome in his ill-advised Dexter Shoe acquisition. He informed them:

> *At Dexter, we have sadly and reluctantly ended shoe production in the U.S. and Puerto Rico. We had an outstanding labor force but the ten-for-one wage advantage enjoyed by competitors producing elsewhere in the world finally forced us to act—after our having delayed longer than was rational. I cost you considerable money by my unwillingness to face unpleasant facts when they first became obvious.*[72]

Having corrected for this type of error after his initial foray into Berkshire textiles, Buffett has virtually eliminated the "loyalty problem." By ensuring that he only enters into commitments with people who also manage businesses that can create value on a durable basis, or at worst are likely to earn a minimum rate of return, Buffett's internal conflict, which pits him acting like an owner for his shareholders versus him acting like a compassionate owner for his managers, is noticeable by its rarity.

Nevertheless, in spite of his vow not to abandon businesses for the sake of a marginal contribution to performance, any subsidiary that no longer holds out the prospect of earning its required rate of return will be put on severe capital rations. *Not directly by Buffett, however, but by its own managers, acting out of an instinct borne of adhering to Buffett's min specs.*

Overridingly at Berkshire Hathaway, good money is not thrown after bad. Managers' compensation packages reflect economic reality and Buffett has designed his min specs to ensure that they can still do well, *and feel they are doing well,* by competently managing businesses

that face headwinds. More importantly, they are also intrinsically motivated to act as the owners of Berkshire Hathaway would want them to,
and this kind of motivation transcends material gain.

To show how far this goes, managers who have found in the past
that they have run out of opportunities to deploy their capital at
returns comparable to those available elsewhere have been content—
contrary to normal managerial instinct—to see their domains get
smaller and smaller. At Berkshire, size does not matter—to *anybody*.
Thus, after several years of harvesting cash from the "cornerstone
businesses" of Berkshire Hathaway that existed at its inception after he
closed the Partnership, Warren Buffett was able to report that they had
"(1) survived but earned almost nothing, (2) shriveled in size while
incurring large losses, and (3) shrunk in sales volume to about 5% its
size at the time of our entry."[73] And yet, in his letter to his shareholders
in 2000, Buffett could boast that "in our last 36 years Berkshire has
never had a manager of a significant subsidiary voluntarily leave to join
another business."[74]

That is compliance.

Deep inside Berkshire Hathaway, Buffett has created an environment in which his managers are content to act in the interests of the
company's shareholders, even if this means passing up the temptations
of the institutional imperative—a rare alignment. Going forward, any
capital that cannot be employed profitably within one of Berkshire's
subsidiaries over the long haul will not be consumed by a manager who
acts in his own interests, but will surely find its way into the hands of
someone who can put it to good use. For instance Ralph Schey, the
CEO of one of Berkshire's largest subsidiaries, Scott Fetzer, was able
to distribute $1,030 million to Buffett compared with a net purchase
price of $230 million, during the 15 years of his tenure.[75] And Chuck
Huggins at See's Candies put up earnings of $857 million pre-tax by
1999, on a purchase price of $25 million in 1972, absorbing very little
additional capital in the meantime.[76]

The reciprocal nature of the contract between Warren Buffett and
his employees achieves results such as these. It allows him to set them
free. The company then moves in a direction set by Buffett but guided
by min specs. These are not so much external impositions on behavior

as they are internal—driven intrinsically by their wiring, in harmony with that wiring, and perceived as fair (and they therefore should be reciprocated with effort). In turn, this means that he *can* set his employees free—and this fosters the very intrinsic motivation on which the notion of decentralized management depends. *The result is that the employees of Berkshire Hathaway flock to Warren Buffett even though there is no rule explicitly telling them to do so.*

This is the intelligent control of Lao Tzu. This *is* leadership.

In the next chapter we will find out how the acquisitions that Buffett makes are shaped in such a way as to dovetail seamlessly into this model of leadership, if anything enhancing its effectiveness rather than multiplying its problems as Berkshire Hathaway grows in size and complexity.

4

Making Acquisitions Work

CEOs who recognize their lack of capital-allocation skills (which not all do) will often try to compensate by turning to their staffs, management consultants, or investment bankers. Charlie and I have frequently observed the consequences of such "help." On balance, we feel it is more likely to accentuate the capital-allocation problem than solve it.

Warren Buffett[1]

At Berkshire, our carefully-crafted acquisition strategy is simply to wait for the phone to ring.

Warren Buffett[2]

Ultimately, Warren Buffett does one of two things with the excess cash that his managers send him. He invests it in the stock market or, preferably, he uses it to buy other companies outright, which is no easy task. As he says:

Many managements were apparently overexposed in impressionable childhood years to the story in which the imprisoned handsome prince is released from a toad's body by a kiss from a beautiful princess. Consequently, they are certain that their managerial kiss will do wonders for the profitability of Company T(arget)... We've observed many kisses but very few miracles.[3]

The fact is, Buffett is right: The miracle-to-kiss ratio *is* low—far lower than those who pucker up might imagine.

Most studies put the percentage of mergers and acquisitions that fail to create shareholder value at over 60%. So whenever two companies come together in an embrace, the chances are high that the initiator of this act will destroy value in the capital with which it cements the relationship. Moreover, even if return on capital is not uppermost in the minds of management, it remains the case that the majority of acquisitions still fail to live up to their expectations, whether these be measured in cost savings, revenue enhancement, or profitability. Indeed, oftentimes they will seriously impair their entire business in the process.

In deploying the savings of his shareholders in this field, therefore, the odds are against Warren Buffett. Nevertheless, he is unabashed.

"What really makes us dance is the purchase of 100% of good businesses at reasonable prices," he says, and he has premised the growth in Berkshire Hathaway's economic value largely on the back of acquiring other companies.[4] This means finding the right businesses, buying them at the right price, and thereafter ensuring that they continue to perform in the fashion that he found attractive in the first place—the latter representing the rock on which so many acquisitions fail. So Buffett had better be sure of his case.

He is. When Warren Buffett commits to an acquisition, he chooses the businesses and managements with whom he wants to associate very carefully, sets out his stall to get these to come to him, stacks the odds in favor of consummating the marriage at a fair price, and thereafter elicits massive loyalty and complicity with his objectives.

Whether he is making acquisitions of controlling interests in other companies or investing in them, the same requirement is made of Warren Buffett: He has to make a judgment as to the appropriate valuation of the company in question. Nevertheless, it is with respect to his ventures into the stock market that his approach to this task has attracted most attention, and he is famous for at least three characteristics that he brings to bear in this arena. These are:

1 His ability to strip emotion from his analysis. "Success in investing," he says, "doesn't correlate with IQ once you're above the level of 25. Once you have ordinary intelligence, what you need is the temperament to control the urges that get other people into trouble investing."
2 His discipline with respect to price. "Rule No.1," he says, is "Never lose money." And "Rule No. 2: Never forget rule No.1."[5]

3 His preference for investing only in business franchises. "Look for the durability of the franchise," maintains Buffett when assessing an economic model. "The most important thing for me is figuring how big a moat there is around a business. What I love, of course, is a big castle and a big moat with piranhas and crocodiles."[6]

Yet, as recognizable as this identikit of Warren Buffett the investor remains when describing Warren Buffett the acquirer of entire corporations, it fails to capture the full likeness of a man who engages in an exercise in which the odds of failure are even higher than those of picking individual stocks that will outperform an index.

It cannot. The art of making successful acquisitions is more complex than investing in the stock market. It requires additional skills and it calls for a modification of those enumerated characteristics for which Buffett is most famous. This is "an extraordinarily difficult job," he confirms, "far more difficult than the purchase at attractive prices at fractional interest."[7]

Asked what he looks for when he acquires a controlling interest in another company, Buffett replied:

I would think very hard about getting into a business with fundamentally good economics. I would think of buying from people I can trust. And I'd think about the price I'd pay.[8]

This chapter will take each of these in order and delineate where the challenges exist in effecting successful corporate acquisitions, how Warren Buffett overcomes these, and where the modification of his best-known traits lies.

THE HIGH WALLS AND DEEP MOATS OF COSTS AND SERVICE

Economic terrain that is forever shifting violently is ground on which it is difficult to build a fortress-like business franchise. Such a franchise is usually the key to high business returns.

Warren Buffett[9]

Widen the moat: build enduring competitive advantage, delight your customers, and relentlessly fight costs.

Warren Buffett[10]

Having learnt his lesson the hard way in Berkshire Hathaway's textiles operations, the economics of the businesses that Buffett acquires are now of paramount importance to him.

Buffett was under no illusion as to the deficiencies of the textiles industry when he bought into it. He knew he would be selling a product that could not be differentiated from the offerings of his competitors, that those competitors were numerous, and that barriers to entry existed only to those without capital. He knew, therefore, that at best the returns on capital employed in this business would be low. Attempts to stay ahead of the curve, say by investing in state-of-the-art plant and machinery, would grant temporary reprieve but, in the long term, the benefits of these kinds of expenditures would fail to stick to Berkshire's ribs. Instead, because of competitive pressures, they would be passed on to consumers in the form of lower prices and higher quality.

The law of the economic jungle is that high returns on capital revert to the mean. Unless a business is characterized by sustainable competitive advantage, observes Buffett, it "earns exceptional profits only if it is the low-cost operator or if supply of its product or service is tight."[11] Recurrent capital expenditures in Berkshire's textiles business therefore would not become instruments of competitive advantage, but would be the price of staying in the game.

However, Buffett did believe that prescient management could stem the tide of these poor fundamentals and make a difference at the margin.

What he found was that these unattractive business economics are not susceptible to a cure by even the most skilled of managers. He says:

My conclusion from my own experiences and from much observation of other businesses is that a good managerial record (measured by economic returns) is far more a function of what business boat you get into than it is of how effectively you row.[12]

He also notes:

We could all go count restaurants for the next three miles and in five years, many of them will not be there with the same names. There are no prizes if you don't run them right. That's why I buy good businesses to begin with.[13]

Henceforth, therefore, Buffett would look to acquire businesses with economic characteristics that were the obverse of the textiles industry: in particular businesses possessed of sustainable competitive advantage, where the price of staying in the game, as measured by the level of capital expenditure required merely to maintain competitive position, is low.

Sustainable competitive positions produce the economic returns that Buffett is seeking. High levels of profitability on a low capital base, combined with low maintenance costs, produce the excess capital that can be recycled into growth opportunities within the industry (or elsewhere).

Given that he is renowned on the topic, however, it is commonly believed that ever since the Damascene revelation imparted by Charlie Munger, Warren Buffett has sought out durable competitive advantage in companies that occupy competitive positions of a certain type. Buffett's definition of the term "franchise" describes a company that offers a product or service that: "(1) is needed or desired; (2) is thought by its customers to have no close substitute; and (3) is not subject to price regulation."[14]

Since they are "virtually certain to possess enormous competitive strength ten or twenty years from now,"[15] companies that occupy such franchises are generally thought to be the ones that Buffett looks to own and invest in. And they possess the quality of last resort to which Buffett is attracted. "Franchises can tolerate mis-management. Inept managers may diminish a franchise's profitability, but they cannot inflict mortal damage."[16]

However, while Buffett's definition of a franchise might easily fit the more famous of the companies in which he has *fractional* stakes— such as Coca-Cola, Gillette, and American Express—it does not appear to cut the mustard with that long list of companies that Buffett owns outright.

Buffalo Evening News, Executive Jet, FlightSafety, and See's Candies all fit the bill. Each has an inimitable position in its industry. But where exactly are the castellations of H.H. Brown Shoe Co., Nebraska Furniture Mart, and Fechheimer Bros. Co.? How exactly do R.C. Willey Home Furnishings, GEICO, International Dairy Queen, and Borsheim's pull up the drawbridge against the competition?

This is an unlikely (and incomplete) list of companies for those seeking to identify businesses that possess strong franchises in the sense that most people would understand the phrase, and certainly not as it has come to be associated with Warren Buffett. As Buffett himself said in his year 2000 letter to the company's shareholders: "We have embraced the 21st century by entering such cutting-edge industries as brick, carpet, insulation and paint. Try to control your excitement."[17]

Nevertheless, all of these companies do occupy franchises of a sort.

Products and services "that have no close substitute" are not the sole preserve of companies that sell unique-tasting colas, state-of-the-art shaving systems, or fractional ownership of airplanes. Warren Buffett has found that sustainable competitive advantage can also be found in the combination of two factors: *permanently low-cost offerings and managerial excellence that is baked into a corporate service culture.*

BUSINESS ECONOMICS: THE NUMBERS GAME

GEICO's sustainable cost advantage is what attracted me to the company way back in 1951, when the entire business was valued at $7 million. It is also why I felt Berkshire should pay $2.3 billion last year [1996] for the 49% of the company that we didn't then own.

Warren Buffett[18]

Since GEICO is the Berkshire subsidiary that sells perhaps its most commodity-like product and therefore the company that we should least expect to occupy a franchise, it serves as a useful example of

Buffett's seemingly contradictory logic. It is distinguishable from other purveyors of auto policies purely by the fact that it is the low-cost operator in the industry.

This does not mean that the company is immune to the vagaries of that industry or, indeed, to mistakes of its own commission. In the 1970s, it ran into extremely severe operating difficulties. "They made all kinds of mistakes," says Buffett, they "didn't know their costs… and they got captivated by growth."[19]

However, the company *was* able to tolerate mismanagement. In Buffett's words, although "they did all kinds of things wrong… they still had the franchise. They still were a low cost operator."[20] This is what sustained them. And this is what will continue to sustain them. Buffett said in 1986, for instance:

> *The difference between GEICO's costs and those of its competitors is a kind of moat that protects a valuable and much-sought-after business castle. No one understands this moat-around-the-castle concept better than Bill Snyder, Chairman of GEICO. He continually widens the moat by driving down costs still more, thereby defending and strengthening the economic franchise.*[21]

In a difficult industry, characterized by intense competition, low barriers, or mixed results, because GEICO's cost structure relative to that of its competition can be forecast with near certainty, Buffett can assure himself that the advantage accruing from this is sustainable. GEICO will out-earn the industry.

So it is with Buffett's other subsidiary companies. He comments:

> *We don't care whether we're buying into a people-intensive business, a raw-material intensive business or a rent-intensive business. We want to understand the cost structure.*[22]

Nebraska Furniture Mart *et al.* share the same characteristic. They are low on the overhead, incidental, and running costs that other companies seem to accumulate by degree. Knowledge of this fact does not allow for its replication by a competitor. A company *might* be able to attain similar business economics at a given point in time. However, the ability to sustain and improve these economics comes from a managerial mindset that few possess. This advantage is passed on to the consumer in price and selection, setting up a virtuous circle whereby Buffett's companies tend to dominate the markets in which they operate. Thus, they garner economies of scale that, in reality, cannot be matched by the competition, and these are also passed on in price.

THE HUMAN PROPOSITION

I don't worry about the dumbest competitor in a business that's service-oriented.

Warren Buffett[23]

As well as being low cost, most of Berkshire's subsidiary companies are also essentially service providers, and quality of service at the point of execution is an essential element of the franchise in which Buffett is interested. Buffett is attracted to some industries in which players only have to be smart once. The Buffalo Evening News dominates its market, for instance. In order to emerge as number one, it had to do something clever in some point in its history. But thereafter, as *the* community bulletin board, it would have to do something dumb to lose its position. By comparison, retailers and their like have to be smart every day, and a major part of being smart is the provision of a customer experience that gets people to come back.

In 1996, for example, Buffett observed:

See's is different in many ways from what it was in 1972 when we bought it: It offers a different assortment of candy, employs different machinery and sells through different distribution channels. But the reasons why people today buy boxed chocolates, and why they buy them from us rather than from someone else, are virtually unchanged from what they were in the 1920s when the See family was building the business. Moreover, these motivations are not likely to change over the next 20 years, or even 50.[24]

Buffett's managers understand the service business. They know how to drive their passion for the business down to the point of execution, to people whom they may not be able to see but whom they know will share their ethos. It's a reflection of the same leadership skills that Buffett possesses and it all starts with the men and women who run the companies.

THE SAINTED SEVEN

The Blumkins, the Friedman family, Mike Goldberg, the Heldmans, Chuck Huggins, Stan Lipsey, Ralph Schey and Frank Rooney... are all masters of their operations and need no help from me. My job is merely to treat them right.

Warren Buffett[25]

I could no longer have fingertip control of all the details. That made my obsession with people even more intense.

Jack Welch[26]

In 1987 Buffett coined the collective term *The Sainted Seven* to describe Berkshire's subsidiary companies: Buffalo Evening News, Fechheimer, Kirby, Nebraska Furniture Mart, Scott Fetzer Manufacturing Group, See's, and World Book. By implication, he also applied the term to the managements of these companies. As his acquisition activity has continued apace, events have overtaken his prose and this epithet no longer quite captures its original meaning. Nevertheless, in respect of the kinds of people with whom he looks to associate, the phrase says it all.

Of the personnel in Berkshire Hathaway's insurance operations, for instance, Buffett tells his shareholders: "We have an advantage in attitude."[27] It doesn't stop there.

Buffett's managers are *doppelgängers* of himself and Munger. Those with whom he chooses to associate "work because they love what they do."[28] In short, like Buffett and Munger, *they are intrinsically motivated.* And this shines through in the economics of their businesses. Says Buffett:

We like to do business with someone who loves his business...
When this emotional attachment exists, it signals that important
qualities will likely be found within the business: honest account-
ing, pride of product, respect for customers, and a loyal group of
associates having a strong sense of direction.[29]

This is why The Sainted Seven run low-cost operations and enjoy
economies of scale in their local markets that cannot be matched. The
businesses are based on execution, attention to detail, and reputation.
For example, Buffett says of See's:

Cheerful, helpful personnel are as much a trademark of See's as is
the logo on the box. That's no small achievement in a business that
requires us to hire about 2000 seasonal workers. We know of no
comparably-sized organization that betters the quality of customer
service delivered by Chuck Huggins and his associates.[30]

Managements such as Chuck Huggins' at See's form an essential element
of the franchise that Buffett buys. They "unfailingly think like owners
(the highest compliment we can pay a manager),"[31] says Buffett and, as
such, they bring with them the business economics that he is looking for.

They are the business. They are the value. And for a man whose
capital allocation skills are too valuable to allow him to sweat the
details, they are the franchise.

Perhaps not surprisingly, Buffett has found that most managers who
fit the requirement of acting like owners are resident in enterprises
that are managed by their proprietors. This does not guarantee that an
individual will act like an owner in the management of a firm, however.
The institutional imperative is not choosy about whom it leads away
from the straight and narrow.

Therefore, in addition to running a check over the return and capital
intensity economics of every company he buys, Buffett runs a concomi-
tant check over managements' capital allocation policy—looking for
those who have "unfailingly" husbanded it wisely, rather than become
entrapped in dynamics from which they cannot escape, drawn to ventures long on psychic benefits but short on economic profitability.

To that end, Buffett will routinely retrieve a company's 20-year history, often going back as far as records will allow, and will always examine the realized capital allocation record of target companies over the period during which incumbent management has been in place. "We never look at projections, but we care very much about, and look very deeply at, track records," he says.[32]

Like a geologist analyzing a deep core sample of the earth's crust, from the fragmentary and layered information that this process makes available a vivid picture emerges to Buffett—of the inherent economics of a business model, including the amount of free cash flow that it generates, the element most easily usurped by the institutional imperative. Where managers have shown themselves immune to the imperative and skilled in their allocation of cash, checking these results against those attained by their direct competitors and the industry in general to gauge to what extent they have established a franchise, *then* Warren Buffett becomes interested. But only interested: There are other checks to be run.

Giving a lie to the economists' version of human nature, experimental work has shown what Warren Buffett has known all along— the rock on which he has built his leadership—that human beings care deeply about fairness and will reward it when present and punish it when absent.[33] Nevertheless, although Warren Buffett's managerial style may rely on the reciprocation of trust and fairness with effort, he is not so naïve as to believe that every competent manager uncovered by his research will possess the kinds of personal qualities that reflect this.

In those same experiments revealing that most people care about fairness, a significant minority—more than any manager would care to contemplate within his or her workforce—is also found to be selfish.[34] These are the natural-born cheats and free riders inside every organization, those who would bring down Buffett's hands-off approach to management if they stalked the corridors of Berkshire Hathaway.

Says Buffett of this type of individual:

You learn a great deal about a person when you purchase a business from him and he stays on to run it as an employee rather than as an owner. Before the purchase the seller knows the business intimately, whereas you start from scratch. The seller has dozens of opportunities to mislead the buyer—through omissions, ambiguities, and misdirection. After the check has changed hands, subtle (and not so subtle) changes of attitude can occur and implicit understandings can evaporate. *As in the courtship–marriage sequence, disappointments are not infrequent [emphasis added].*[35]

This was another lesson that Buffett had learned the hard way, at Dempster Mills. He corrected it at Berkshire Hathaway with Ken Chace. And he's been correcting it in every business association he has entered into since then. If he were to get the people side of the equation wrong, with *his* management style, acquisitions would fail in the integration process and the business economics he is attracted by would wilt on the vine.

"A new concept in business. It's called trust"[36]

Hence Buffett engages in the kind of "scuttlebutt" research that another of his heroes, Phil Fisher, recommended all investors to pursue. Buffett's network of acquaintances is huge. ("He has more tentacles out than anyone," says Welch.[37]) Largely these acquaintances exist inside the shareholder register of Berkshire Hathaway, and he sounds them out in order to establish the character of the management he is looking at. Do they have the integrity that he both requires and demands?

If they do, it will show up in their reputations. If not, it will very quickly be apparent. Of Jordan's furniture stores, acquired in 1999, Buffett had this to say, for instance:

Jordan's furniture is truly one of the most phenomenal and unique companies that I have ever seen. The reputation that Elliot and Barry [Tatelman] have earned from their employees, their customers, and the community is unparalleled. This company is a gem![38]

Once he is happy that he can trust managers, Buffett does so. It's as simple as that.

When he made the purchase of See's Candy he says, "We shook hands with Chuck [Huggins] on the compensation arrangement—conceived in about five minutes and never reduced to a written contract—that remains unchanged to this day."[39] And with regard to Borsheim's, as with Jordan's, although the company had no audited financial statements when be bought it, Buffett says that "nevertheless, we didn't take inventory, verify receivables or audit the operation in any way. Ike [Friedman] simply told us what was so—and on that basis we drew up a one-page contract and wrote a large check."[40]

However, you can only place such trust in the people that you deal with if you have done your homework beforehand.

Having established what he's looking for in the type of people with whom he wants to associate, and knowing how vital it is to the organization to get this right, Buffett is faced with a challenge, which makes finding these people and their businesses look easy by comparison. How does he get these paragons to sell their businesses to him—and at a fair price?

He cannot go out and buy them forcibly—hostile acquisitions would defeat the object of his hands-off managerial approach, which is to crowd in intrinsic motivation. The franchise, in other words, would be lost. Buffett is confronted with a very real dilemma, therefore. In the face of it, he has derived a cunning plan.

He does nothing; or close to it. He simply lets these people, rarities in the world of commerce and on whom Berkshire's future is premised, find him!

THE BUFFETTIAN VIRUS

How much better it is for the "painter" of a business Rembrandt to personally select its permanent home than to have a trust officer or uninterested heirs auction it off. Throughout the years we have had great experiences with those who recognize that truth and apply it to their business creations.

Warren Buffett[41]

When Buffett says that his acquisition strategy at Berkshire is to wait for the phone to ring, it does not do so by chance. The right type of managers, with the right type of businesses for sale, call Warren Buffett because, whether they know it or not, they have been infected by a virus that inclines them toward *him* at their point of sale.

As with their biological equivalent, successful viruses of the mind—such as the instrumental memes of Buffett's leadership—spread throughout a human population because they are bred for fitness. The most popular viruses tend to be those that play on our primary motivations to avoid loss and to reproduce: the danger and sex contained in any good soap opera.[42] But the microbe launched by the way in which Warren Buffett organizes and runs Berkshire Hathaway homes in on vendors where they are most susceptible—on the fears that they experience when they contemplate a transaction that will change their lives for ever.

Managements with businesses for sale approach Buffett, he says, "because a manager who sold to us earlier has recommended a friend that he think about following suit."[43] That's the virus in action. It says, "Berkshire Hathaway provides shelter from all your fears."

The DNA of the virus

We don't want managers... to ever lose any sleep wondering whether surprises might occur because of our... ownership.

Warren Buffett[44]

Buffett knows that the people with whom he wishes to associate feel the same way about the businesses they own and/or manage as he does about Berkshire Hathaway. Being careful not to squander their resources, they have crafted them over their lifetime (perhaps even generations); they love them and gaze on them as they would their children. They care deeply about what happens to them after they have been sold. Naturally, this makes them reluctant to let go, but let go they must, usually to diversify their wealth away from the single business they own. Nevertheless, this reluctance finds itself expressed in a desire to stay on as an interested manager—they want to monetize their interest ("sometimes for themselves," says Buffett, "but often for their families or inactive shareholders"[45]), not discard it.

Equally, Buffett knows that because of this, they are also dogged by uncertainty. Few, if any, will have sold a business before. Most will never have worked for a company that they did not also own. And they know that most corporate acquirers would not treat their businesses with the loving care that they have for years, or, in fact, treat themselves as they would want to be treated as employees.

Therefore, as much as the letters that Buffett takes care to draft in every annual report are put there for the benefit of his shareholders, they are also designed to reach a much larger audience, including potential vendors (or their acquaintances). Primarily this is where Buffett embeds his virus—a virus more potent since it can now be caught from reading the annual reports on the internet.

Revisiting a theme in his letter to the shareholders in 2000 that he has woven into his prose over many years, Buffett said:

> When a business masterpiece has been created by a lifetime—or several lifetimes—of unstinting care and exceptional talent, it should be important to the owner what corporation is entrusted to carry on its history. Charlie and I believe Berkshire provides an almost unique home. We take our obligations to the people who created a business very seriously, and Berkshire's ownership structure ensures that we can fulfill our promises. When we tell John Justin that his business will remain headquartered in Fort Worth, or assure the Bridge family that its operation will not be merged with another jeweler, these sellers can take those promises to the bank.[46]

Buffett is careful to ensure that individuals with businesses for sale are aware that Berkshire Hathaway presents them with a rare and unusual opportunity. He offers them the prospect of replacing uncertainty, fear, and suspicion with a known proposition. This is the DNA of Buffett's virus. People who care about their businesses and fret about their futures know *exactly* what to expect when they sell to Warren Buffett and stay on as managers.

Buffett's letters to his shareholders have established him as a leader among men, chairing a company with a clear and credible mission. A man of massive integrity, who upholds the highest standards of corporate governance, who will treat managers fairly, reward them appropriately, and grant them autonomy, trusting in their judgment as they fulfill this role. A man who will *change nothing* in the way the enterprise is run, except, perhaps, the compensation system, but only in a way that makes eminent sense: "We buy to keep, but we don't have, and don't expect to have, operating people in our parent organization."[47] And a man who presents sellers with a cast-iron guarantee that "this operational framework will endure for decades to come.[48]

The contrast with other buyers could not be more extreme—and Buffett is not loath to remind vendors of this fact. He told one prospective seller that practically all buyers except Berkshire Hathaway fall into one of two categories, each of which has "serious flaws" for the seller of a business that "represents the creative work of a lifetime and forms an integral part of their personality and sense of being."[49] These buyers will either be

> *a company located elsewhere but operating in your business or a business somewhat akin to yours. Such a buyer—no matter what promises are made—will usually have managers who feel they know how to run your business operations and, sooner or later, will want to apply some hands-on "help." If the acquiring company is much larger, it will often have squads of managers, recruited over the years in part by promises that they will get to run future acquisitions. They will have their own way of doing things and... human nature will at some point cause them to believe that their methods of operating are superior.[50]*

Or they will be "a financial maneuverer, invariably operating with large amounts of borrowed money, who plans to resell either to the public or to another corporation as soon as the time is favorable."[51]

In addition, Buffett laces his annual reports with other fragments of the virus addressing vendors' desire to diversify and preserve their wealth. Held out as an example, for instance, is Barnett Helzberg, Jr., the chairman of Helzberg's Diamond Shops, who, in Buffett's words, "owned a valuable asset that was subject to the vagaries of a single, very competitive industry, and he thought it prudent to diversify his family's holdings."[52]

As payment for assets Buffett offers sellers

a stock backed by an extraordinary collection of outstanding businesses. An individual or a family wishing to dispose of a single fine business, but also wishing to defer personal taxes indefinitely, is apt to find Berkshire stock a particularly comfortable holding.[53]

The virus multiplies

To ensure that only those vendors with the right kind of business approach him, however, Buffett places an ad in his annual reports so that people can check to see if their businesses fit his acquisition criteria. This first appeared in 1982 and he has repeated the exercise ever since, varying the prose only to alter the size requirements.

The original went as follows:

This annual report is read by a varied audience, and it is possible that some members of that audience may be helpful to us in our acquisition program. We prefer:

1 *Large purchases (at least $5 million of after-tax earnings).*
2 *Demonstrated consistent earnings power (future projections are of little interest to us, nor are "turn-around" situations).*
3 *Businesses earning good returns on equity while employing little or no debt.*
4 *Management in place (we can't supply it).*
5 *Simple businesses (if there's lots of technology, we won't understand it).*[54]

And Buffett urges potential vendors: "If you are running a large, profitable business that will thrive in… [the Berkshire] environment, check our acquisition criteria… and give me a call."[55]

Once the virus has gotten their attention, he knows that he will have elicited a psychological commitment at least to entertain the idea of selling their business to him. Indeed, as much as commitment that, to borrow a phrase from Cialdini, "grows its own legs" is something that Buffett avowedly avoids in his capital management, this is exactly the kind of process he is looking for as a leader in his prospective associations. "If you aren't interested now, file our proposition in the back of your mind," Buffett tells this constituency.[56]

Their immune systems are low. They are prone to infection.

Now, having committed to the idea that they will at least bear Buffett in mind when the moment comes to sell, each time a potential vendor subsequently reads one of Buffett's letters, it will *feed* the tendency within them to seek out support in favor of their prior conclusions. The virus will start to multiply, the legs of commitment to grow.

This process will be nurtured by each and every horror story of a business combination that foundered on a clash of cultures. It will luxuriate in tales of incumbent management ousted by new owners, of assets stripped, autonomy lost, companies broken up, and legacies destroyed:

> *You and your family have friends who have sold their businesses to larger companies, and I suspect that their experiences will confirm the tendency to take over the running of their subsidiaries, particularly when the parent knows the industry, or thinks it does.*[57]

And it will be fed annually by stories lifted straight out of Warren Buffett's letters to his shareholders.

Here potential vendors will find repeated testimony bearing witness to the fact that selling their companies need not feel like selling their children. He says:

> *You know some of our past purchases. I'm enclosing a list of everyone from whom we have ever bought a business, and I invite you to check with them as to our performance versus our promises.*[58]

Testimony of how folks, *just like them*, facing the same *uncertainty*, found everlasting contentment by selling their businesses to Berkshire Hathaway.

The social proof that Buffett puts on display and encourages them to check out works best in influencing other people's decision making when they are keying their behavior off relevant (similar) others, but even more so *in the presence of uncertainty*.[59] Past vendors to Berkshire Hathaway are similar to prospective vendors (Buffett has delineated their personal characteristics at length in his letters). And prospective vendors exist in a condition of uncertainty.

The virus overtakes their immune systems and they decide to sell to Buffett.

THE SAINTED SEVEN BECOME THE COMMITTED

Warren is an unusual guy because he's not only a good analyst, he's a good salesman, and he's a very good judge of people. That's an unusual combination. If I were to [acquire] somebody with a business, I'm sure he would quit the very next day. I would misjudge his character or something—or I wouldn't understand that he didn't really like the business and really wanted to sell it and get out. Warren's people knock themselves out after he buys the business, so that's an unusual trait.

Walter Schloss[60]

Here comes the twist. Now that these people are well and truly on the psychological hook—barbwired, so to speak—Buffett subjects them to a trial, an examination that they must pass if they are to enjoy the sanctuary that is on offer inside Berkshire Hathaway.

The trial is contained in this statement: "After some other mistakes, I learned to go into business only with people whom I like, trust, and admire."[61]

The purchase contract that Buffett draws up, such as it is, is one that every vendor knows is based purely on trust and the knowledge that Buffett only associates himself with managers whom he "would love to have as a sibling, in-law, or trustee of my will."[62]

Cialdini says that one way in which commitments influence our behavior is that people like and believe in what they have to struggle to get. Thus trials of initiation, common throughout human culture, help to ensure the lasting loyalty and dedication of those who make it through them. The more onerous the trial, the greater this effect.[63]

Move now to Berkshire Hathaway, the most exclusive of clubs. To get inside, vendors have to look deep within themselves. They have to reaffirm their intrinsic motivation to act like owners. They have to affirm their willingness to do so within another organization. They have to confirm their similarity with those on whom Buffett has already conveyed a blessing. To pass the test, they have to be made of the right stuff—and they know that Warren Buffett also knows, or will assuredly find out, whether they are or not. Says Buffett:

> *We do not wish to join with managers who lack admirable qualities, no matter how attractive the prospects of their business. We've never succeeded in making a good deal with a bad person.*[64]

Hence if he does decide to go with a manager, those characteristics for which he selects become massively reaffirmed by what amounts to a personal benediction from a demigod of finance.

"I have friends who wish that Warren Buffett would come talk with them, who wish that they were running their businesses so well that he would be interested in their companies," says Randy Watson of Justin Brands.[65]

"I love the association with him," says Bill Child of R.C. Willey. "Working for him is like getting a hole-in-one, or having a dream come true. It's a kind of climax to a wonderful business career. Warren is a great hero of mine."[66]

"I would like to recognize all those individuals who have helped to build our company over the past 61 years," wrote Seymour Lichtenstein, CEO of Garan, in the wake of its acquisition by Buffett in 2002. "It is indeed a credit to their efforts that Warren Buffett and Berkshire Hathaway have chosen to make this investment."[67]

Managers like these would not express such sentiments were Buffett the emotionless stock picker he is sometimes portrayed as. Only Buffett the warm, loyal, and fair-minded leader would attract them to his company. When they get there, managers such as these can no longer be called The Sainted Seven. They desperately want to sell their businesses to Warren Buffett. They are intensely keen to stay on as managers, reporting to him. They have been subject to a trial of personality. From then on, these people should be known as *The Committed*.

The bounty of The Committed

Chuck gets better every year. When he took charge of See's at age 46, the company's pre-tax profit, expressed in millions, was about 10% of his age. Today he's 74, and the ratio has increased to 100%. Having discovered this mathematical relationship—let's call it Huggins' Law—Charlie and I now become giddy at the mere thought of Chuck's birthday.

Warren Buffett[68]

Buffett's management task is made all the easier for their rites of passage.

The bounty of Buffett's selection process is that the excellence he identified within the managers he wants on board is both durable after he has acquired them and *increasing*. If their commitment was to act like owners prior to their blessing, they now act even more like owners. Thereafter, the definition of their personal and managerial qualities that granted them entry to Berkshire Hathaway (normally) as owners is the one to which they strive above all else to remain consistent when they get inside, as managers.

"The manager of a tightly-run operation usually continues to find additional methods to curtail costs, even when his costs are continually below those of his competitors," says Buffett, identifying the way personal commitments grow the legs for which he is looking.[69] His managers, already committed to running tight ships, continually cast around for reasons in support of their philosophy, constantly finding new ones, ignoring the temptations to add the costs that aggregate around others who do not share this mindset. This leaves Buffett's companies as the low-cost providers in their markets.

Similarly, referring to the institutional imperative, Buffett says, "Charlie and I have attempted to concentrate our investments in companies that appear alert to the problem."[70] Knowing this, Buffett can count on his managers' commitment to act like owners being sustained and bolstered.

One remarkable example of this will suffice. It summarizes the kinds of people with whom Buffett associates. At R.C. Willey, one of Berkshire's furniture store operators, CEO Bill Childs pursued a policy of closing his stores on Sundays for religious reasons and he wanted to continue this policy in a region in which the company had not previously operated. Buffett was skeptical that a new store could work against entrenched rivals that did open on Sundays, yet, as befits the freedom he gives his managers, he told Childs to follow his own judgment.

"Bill then insisted on a truly extraordinary proposition," says Buffett. He would buy the land himself and build the store (at a cost of around $9 million), sell it to Berkshire at cost if it proved to be successful, but exit the business, at his expense, if it was not.[71]

The store opened, was a huge success, and Berkshire wrote him a check for the cost. Adds Buffett:

And get this. Bill refused to take a dime of interest on the capital he had tied up over the two years... If a manager has behaved similarly at some other public corporation, I haven't heard about it.[72]

A by-product of the careful front-end-loaded selection process that brings people like Bill Childs on board "is the ability it gives us to easily expand Berkshire's activities," says Buffett:

We've read management treatises that specify exactly how many people should report to any one executive, but they make little sense to us. When you have able managers of high character running businesses about which they are passionate, you can have a dozen or more reporting to you and still have time for an afternoon nap. Conversely, if you have one person reporting to you who is deceitful, inept or uninterested, you will find yourself with more than you can handle. Charlie and I could work with double the number of managers we now have, so long as they had the rare qualities of the present ones.[73]

THE CLINCH

We do have filters… we really can say no in 10 seconds or so to 90%+ of all these things that come along simply because we have all these filters.

Warren Buffett[74]

There is still some unfinished business to attend to before these psychic benefits start to accrue to Berkshire, and that's the price at which the deal is finally struck. Buffett comments:

The sad fact is that most major acquisitions display an egregious imbalance: They are a bonanza for the shareholders of the acquiree; they increase the income and status of the acquirer's management; and they are a honey pot for the investment bankers and other professionals on both sides. But, alas, they usually reduce the wealth of the acquirer's shareholders, often to a substantial extent. That happens because the acquirer typically gives up more intrinsic value than it receives.[75]

This is the case because the institutional imperative, which informs managements that they must grow, can mean that they *need* to undertake acquisitions. This inclines them to overpay: It is a seller's market and the price they receive is, in effect, an unfair one.

To serve the interests of Berkshire's shareholders, Buffett cannot let this happen in his acquisitions. Therefore he restores the balance so that the price paid is fair to *both* parties. Consequently, he extracts the institutional dynamic from his side of the process, leaving the only dynamic in play on the vendor's side.

Earlier, I omitted two points that Buffett includes in his ad in the annual reports. These are that he prefers to see "an offering price (we don't want to waste our time or that of the seller by talking, even preliminarily, about a transaction when price is unknown)," and that he promises "a very fast answer to possible interest—customarily within five minutes."[76]

It is these two additions that restore the balance.

When Buffett does make a commitment to a transaction he ensures that it is rationally based. The specification in the ad that he wants to see an offering price immediately curtails any further dynamic to a commitment that might form in that instant. When that phone rings, he usually *knows* the economics of the business (he has already analyzed every company that fits his acquisition criteria). He knows that it is being run by people who act like owners (he's checked out their capital allocation record and their reputations). He knows that they have contracted the virus, that they are The Committed and will bring on board all that phrase implies. And he does not want to get involved in any "due diligence" other than that he has already performed.

Once a commitment is made, further due diligence invites the egregious imbalance that manifests itself in most acquisitions. Says Buffett:

> *The idea of due diligence at most companies is to send lawyers out, have a bunch of investment bankers come in and make presentations and things like that. And I regard that as terribly diversionary—because the board sits there entranced by all of that, by everybody reporting how wonderful this thing is and how they've checked out all the patents.*[77]

He continues:

> *If, however, the thirst for size and action is strong enough, the acquirer's manager will fill ample rationalizations for... a value-destroying issuance of stock.*[78]

The first-conclusion-stands, onward-ever-onward nature of this dynamic has been nicely illustrated by Stuart Oskamp, who carried out an experiment on a group of clinical psychologists using data from a real-life case. Historical background on the patient was summarized and organized into chronological sets of information that were presented to the judges in four successive stages. After stage one the judges made their initial clinical judgment. They were given the opportunity to review their diagnosis after each successive stage of due diligence. Oskamp discovered, however, that *as more information was presented, the number of changed answers decreased markedly and significantly*.

"This finding," he says, "suggests that judges may frequently have formed stereotype conclusions rather firmly from the first fragmentary information and then been reluctant to change their conclusions as they received new information."[79]

At the same time, Oskamp measured the confidence that each psychologist had in his judgment at each stage of the process. He found that as each new layer of information on the patient was revealed, these professionals became *convinced* of their own increasing understanding of the case. In fact, their confidence rose to such a degree that it dwarfed the increase in accuracy of their diagnoses: "The final stage of information seems to have served mainly to confirm the judges' previous impressions rather than causing them to revamp their whole personality picture [of the patient]."

Similarly, peeling back the onion on an acquisition target often serves only to reinforce a commitment already made. So much for the idea of due diligence at most companies. Frequently, as Buffett observes, people "go into it for their protection. Too often, they do it as a crutch—just to go through with a deal that they want to go through with anyway."[80]

And of course, as the supporting cast members in this dynamic catch a glimpse of the storyline, they edit their script accordingly and the entire troop polarizes further in the direction of executing the plot. Observes Buffett: "If the CEO is visibly panting over a prospective acquisition, subordinates and consultants will supply the requisite projections to rationalize any price."[81] That is, "both his internal staff and his outside advisers will come up with whatever projections are needed to justify his stance. Only in fairy tales are emperors told they are naked."[82] Thus it is that "while deals often fail in practice," according to Buffett "they never fail in projections."[83]

In contrast, when an acquisition opportunity presents itself to Buffett, he is not in the habit of seeking outside counsel on the wisdom of effecting acquisitions. "Don't ask the barber whether you need a haircut," he says.[84]

Thus Buffett is not exposed to any dynamic in the acquisition process. As the buyer he has no plan, *but the vendors do*. He has made no commitment; *they have*. The only institutional dynamics in play are on the other side of the fence. The balance is therefore on its way to being restored.

Now for one last push from the virus. Buffett's promise of normally a five-minute response to an offer is his version of "offer must end." It invokes the notion of scarcity, and our wiring has evolved to tell us that something that is difficult to possess is generally better than something that is easy to possess. Therefore we have a heuristic that allows us to judge an item's quality very quickly by its availability.[85]

If Buffett and Munger do not like the price, no matter how "attractive" the business, they will decline the deal. Door closed. The offer will not be entertained again. As Barnett Helzberg of the eponymous diamond store chain that Berkshire now owns says: "Basically the way to negotiate with Warren Buffett—you don't negotiate. He tells you the deal and that's the deal."[86] As the seller, therefore, you either pitch your business at the right price, or you can forget about selling to Berkshire Hathaway.

Now the price *is* approaching a fair one. Nevertheless, a delicate balance holds at this point—because the price has to be fair to both parties. Operating from a position of strength (because he has made it so), Buffett cannot afford to gouge on the price. He has designed his acquisition process to overcome the greatest downfall of most takeovers: the failure to elicit the complicity and loyalty of the human assets in the transaction. By redressing the second greatest failing of corporate acquisitions, the price paid, he does not want to ruin his good work by alienating the very people who are an integral part of the franchise he is buying. It just would not work that way. The people who join Berkshire Hathaway have to feel good about the whole process.

Therefore, he relaxes the strict discipline with respect to price for which he is renowned in his dealings in the stock market. "I used to be too price-conscious," says Buffett. "We used to have prayer meetings before we'd raise the bid an eighth and that was a mistake."[87]

He is helped in this departure by the advantage the tax code conveys on outright, versus fractional, ownership. He observes:

> *When a company we own all of earns $1 million after tax, the entire amount inures to our benefit. If the $1 million is upstreamed to Berkshire, we owe no tax on the dividend. And, if the earnings are retained and we were to sell the subsidiary—not likely at Berkshire!—for $1 million more than we paid for it, we would owe no capital gains tax. That's because our "tax-cost" upon sale would include both what we paid for the business and all earnings subsequently retained.*[88]

In contrast, if Berkshire were to own the same $1 million of earnings through an investment in a marketable security, on its distribution it would be subject to state and federal taxes of about $140,000.[89] Alternatively, if these earnings were retained by the investee company and subsequently captured by Berkshire as a capital gain, they would then be subject to "no less than $350,000" in tax, depending on Berkshire's capital gains tax rate (which varies between 35% and 40%).[90]

Thus, on an after-tax basis, identical cash flows are substantially more valuable to Berkshire if it owns the company (more than 80% of it, technically) than if it invests in its stock. This helps when deciding whether to quibble over an eighth.

Nevertheless, when Buffett listed those three qualities that he looks for in an acquisition—"getting into a business with fundamentally good economics... buying from people I can trust. And... the price I'd pay"—he added, "I wouldn't think about the price to the exclusion of the first two."[91] To attract the *right people* to Berkshire Hathaway, with the *right businesses*, he cannot afford to.

Thus the perfect acquisition candidate is allowed to move forward and assume his position in a perfect home.

The odds that the acquisition will continue to perform in the same fashion that first attracted Buffett are considerably raised. In the short term, he has removed the nagging uncertainty that wrecks most integration efforts. Where this is not addressed it saps motivation and the new entrant to the organization wilts under its weight.[92] In the long term, Buffett has elicited buy-in to his concept of acting like an owner from people who generally acted in this fashion before, but who will definitely act in this fashion going forward in order to remain loyal to the personal commitment they have made to do so.

To see this buy-in in action, let's move on to the conduct of Buffett's insurance operations. These will illustrate how he puts the managerial principles to which he aspires into practice and serve, by example, to show how Buffett influences the behavior of those whose activities he does not oversee on a day-to-day basis.

5

Insurance: Warren Buffett's Bank

Insurance can be a very good business. It tends to magnify, to an unusual degree, human managerial talent—or the lack of it.

Warren Buffett[1]

In an uncertain world, those who survived always had their emotional radar—call it instinct if you will—turned on. And Stone Age people, at the mercy of wild predators or impending natural disasters, came to trust their instincts above all else. So for human beings, no less than for any other animal, emotions are the first screen to all information received.

Nigel Nicholson[2]

Today, around 80% of Berkshire Hathaway's earnings are derived from the insurance industry. Clearly, Warren Buffett has made this business the centerpiece of his operations.

Yet one wonders why. Buffett says:

Insurance companies offer standardized policies that can be copied by anyone. Their only products are promises. It is not difficult to be licensed and rates are an open book. There are no important advantages from trade marks, patents, location, corporate longevity, raw material sources, etc., and very little consumer differentiation to produce insulation from competition.[3]

It is, therefore, "cursed with a set of dismal economic characteristics that make for a poor long-term outlook: hundreds of competitors, ease of entry, and a product that cannot be differentiated in any meaning-ful way."[4] In conclusion, the industry's economics "are almost certain to be unexciting," while "they may well be disastrous."[5]

This dismal description of the industry's fundamentals does not seem to square with Buffett's proclamation that "among all the fine businesses" that Berkshire owns, its insurance operations are those that have the "greatest potential."[6] Nevertheless, he can say this because his insurance companies are managed in a manner entirely distinct from most of the other companies that comprise the industry he so accurately portrays.

For Warren Buffett, there are three redeeming factors of insurance that allow him to thrive as others flounder. The first of these is the presence of the float, or the amount of money that an insurance com-pany gets to invest between the time premiums are taken in and when they are paid out as claims. Any returns earned over the cost of these flow straight to an insurance company's shareholders.

The second is the fact that, as Buffett says, "distribution channels are not proprietary and can easily be entered [so that] small volume this year does not prevent huge volume next year."[7] This means that when pricing is attractive in the industry, those with the capital to do so can write enormous amounts of business very quickly.

Neither of these is the sole preserve of Warren Buffet's insurance companies. They are available to all. But the existence of Buffett's third factor means that, overwhelmingly, they are Berkshire Hathaway's preserve: Insurance is a behavioral business, characterized like no other by behavioral shortcomings.

While logic would suggest that every effort should be made to gen-erate float at as low a cost as possible, since it is only in this form that it becomes a resource and only in this form that it can overcome the fundamental drawbacks of this industry, the fear of behaving in a man-ner consistent with this—stepping away from writing business when pricing is poor and doing nothing instead—is too much for most to confront. Which is why they don't. Which is why they chase prices down and produce the dismal characteristics of the industry that Buffett describes, destroying capital in the process.

It is as well that they do behave like this, however. For when capac-ity in this industry becomes scarce—when so much capital has been destroyed by the aberrant behavior of its participants that they can no longer write sufficient business to meet demand—that's when pricing improves. And this is when its unlimited distribution system becomes a most valuable asset to Warren Buffett, a man who has been able to adhere to logic, who is not prone to the fear that the industry contains, and who then strides into the marketplace to allocate as much capital to this sector as he can.

FUELING THE ROCKET

My gut told me that compared to the industrial operations I did know, this business [GE Capital] seemed an easy way to make money. You didn't have to invest heavily in R&D, build factories, and bend metal day after day. You didn't have to build scale to be competitive. The business was all about intellectual capital.

Jack Welch[8]

Warren Buffett's initial foray into the insurance industry was his purchase in 1967 of two local companies, National Indemnity Co. and National Fire and Marine, which both specialized in underwriting "unusual" risks. To this day, the writing of so-called super-catastrophe ("super-cat") policies remains Berkshire Hathaway's principal area of expertise.

On potentially large liabilities, such as insurance against earthquake damage, insurance companies generally like to lay off some of the risk to others in the industry, Berkshire Hathaway being one of them, which agree to pay claims above a specified amount. This is known as reinsurance. Sometimes the reinsurer also wants to do this, so it buys super-catastrophe insurance. That's where Warren Buffett comes in.

National Indemnity is now the US's most prominent writer of super-cat policies and forms an integral part of Berkshire's interest in this business. But Buffett never forgot his introduction to the insurance industry, one Saturday morning in 1951, at the feet of GEICO's investment officer Lorimar Davidson. GEICO was a writer of auto policies and its chairman was Buffett's hero, Ben Graham; hence his visit. GEICO became a major holding in Buffett's personal portfolio, subsequently an investment of Berkshire Hathaway, and eventually, in 1996, a wholly owned subsidiary of that company. It is now the seventh-largest insurer in the US and the eighteenth-largest insurer overall.

Then in 1998, Buffett doubled the size of Berkshire's float with the acquisition of General Re, whose operations are concentrated in reinsurance.

There is a sense in which Buffett is ideally suited to the insurance industry. His calculator brain and the fact that "he automatically thinks in terms of decision trees and the elementary math of permutations and combinations" make him a natural underwriter of risk.[9] Nevertheless, the actuarial calculation of the price of risk is not where Warren Buffett's competitive advantage lies. Sat in a darkened room and asked to assay the appropriate price for a particular risk, Buffett would not fare materially better than any other competent underwriter in the industry (although he might be the quickest to produce the answer). Aside from Ajit Jain, a special case whom we'll talk about in Chapter 9, nor would any underwriter he employs.

However, the fact is that underwriters do not ply their trade in darkened rooms. Prices are not set in isolation; they are set in the distracting hubbub of the marketplace. They are subject to the frailties of our cognitive apparatus. And *this* is where Buffett's competitive advantage comes from: the intellectual capital that sets him apart.

Capacity at the speed of thought

When Warren Buffett measures the profitability of an insurance company, he compares its underwriting loss to the size of its float.[10] Taken over a number of years, this ratio provides an indication of the cost of funds generated by insurance operations. "A low cost of funds signifies a good business: a high cost translates into a poor business."[11]

If an insurance company can maintain high standards in its underwriting practices, it can consistently generate low-cost capital, which it can then deploy elsewhere. In effect, it is provided with permanent access to a very low-cost loan if it does this. That is exactly the strategy Buffett pursues: borrowing cheaply (for nothing, if possible) and growing the size of the borrowed funds (in his case) at a compound growth rate of 25.4%.

This is Warren Buffett's bank, the fortress wherein resides his capital, the position of strength from which he allocates it, not only in the insurance industry itself but also elsewhere, and the alchemist's lab wherein he transforms it from low cost to high return.

It is not a bank that is available to all, however. The characteristics of the industry see to that.

In commodity industries such as insurance, one factor above all others destroys profitability: excess capacity. And capacity in the insurance industry is of a particular nature, with a behavioral component setting it apart from almost any other business.

"In most industries, capacity is described in physical terms," says Buffett.[12]

> *In the insurance world, however, capacity is customarily described in financial terms; that is, it's considered appropriate for a company to write no more than X dollars of business if it has Y dollars of net worth. In practice, however, constraints of this sort have proved ineffective. Regulators, insurance brokers, are all slow to discipline companies that strain their resources. They also acquiesce when companies overstate their true capital. Hence, a company can write a great deal of business with very little capital if it is so inclined. At bottom, therefore, the amount of industry capacity at any particular moment depends on the mental state of insurance managers [emphasis added].[13]*

"Capacity," says Buffett, "is an attitudinal concept, not a physical fact."[14] In the insurance industry, *capacity is created at the speed of thought.*

So saying, the industry is condemned to mediocrity. The attitudinal concept to which Buffett refers is conditioned within humans by emotions and cognitive biases ensuring that, in the insurance industry as in no other, capacity is created on the basis of fear, not economic logic.

LONELY LOGIC

We believe it is true that virtually no major property-casualty insurer—despite protests from the entire industry that rates are inadequate and great selectivity should be exercised—has been willing to turn down business to the point where cash flow has turned significantly negative.

Warren Buffett[15]

At Berkshire we will never knowingly write policies containing promises we can't keep.

Warren Buffett[16]

Buffett says that there are

three basic rules in running an insurance company:

1 *Only accept risks you are able to properly evaluate... and confine your underwriting to business that, after an evaluation of all relevant factors, including remote loss scenarios, carries the expectancy of profit;...*
2 *Limit the business accepted in a manner that guarantees you will suffer no aggregation of losses from a single event or from related events that will threaten your solvency; and*
3 *Avoid business involving moral risk: No matter what the rate, you can't write good contracts with bad people. While most policyholders and clients are honorable and ethical, doing business with the few exceptions is usually expensive.*[17]

Guided by these principles, Buffett told his shareholders in 1989 that Berkshire's insurance businesses would be "perfectly willing to write five times as much business as we write in 1988—or only one-fifth as much."[18] Nothing has changed since then. "We cannot control market prices," says Buffett. "If they are unsatisfactory, we will simply do very little business. No other major insurer acts with equal restraint."[19]

In the commodity industry that is insurance, Warren Buffett distinguishes himself by his "total indifference to volume."[20] This is logical. If this business is to act as his bank, the first thing he must do is preserve his capital *and* source it at low cost. This cannot be achieved by accepting business at any price: You have to possess the mental resolve to turn it away when it is poorly priced.

Would that this were easy, but ceding (even unprofitable) business to the competition is something that does not come naturally. Even Buffett has to gird his loins against the part of human nature that prizes more highly something that is under threat of being taken from us. Says Buffett:

> As markets loosen and rates become inadequate, we again will face the challenge of philosophically accepting reduced volume. Unusual managerial discipline will be required, as it runs counter to the normal institutional behavior to let the other fellow take away business—even at a foolish price [emphasis added].[21]

The institutional dynamic at play here is mediated by psychological reactance, or what Charlie Munger calls "deprival super-reaction syndrome." This is the feeling that you get, in Charlie's words, "(A) when something you like is taken away from you and (B) when you almost have something you like and 'lose' it." Either way, says Charlie, the result is a "powerful, subconscious, automatic" emotion that "distorts your cognition."[22]

It does so by making you want it more. It is a feeling that is extremely difficult to tolerate. The same instinct that tells a two-year-old to go after a toy snatched from it compels companies to hang on to, or fight for, the business within its grasp. And most do.

Typically (in adults) this feeling is mediated by justifications that make the item appear more valuable than it was previously.[23] One of these is created by the notion of scarcity. Most insurance companies are afraid to pass up business to another, says Buffett, for fear that they will never get it back. They envisage their slice of market share as a scarce resource, and humans always value items that are difficult to get more highly than those that are abundant. In addition, it has been found in experiments on this subject that we value scarce items *most* highly when we have to compete for them—exactly the emotion that Buffett has recognized as being in play when one insurance company contemplates watching "another fellow taking away its business."[24]

Since few are willing to let business go, overcapacity is normally the result—pricing deteriorates and profitability follows suit (with a lag that depends on the nature of the policies written). The downside of this is that, as profitability deteriorates, the weakest players in the industry are tempted to patch up the growing hole in their businesses by writing *more* policies at inadequate rates just to get the cash *today*. It's only human nature that they should do this. Writing insurance policies is an exercise in temporal discipline. In theory, insurance companies should be happy to forgo the small early reward of the premium, however set, in preference to the large late reward that takes the form of profit accruing on a well-priced risk. That's how low-cost float is generated.

In practice, in the same way as many of us decide before dinner to skip dessert (a small early reward) in order to lose weight (a large late one), only to succumb to temptation when the waiter brings the dessert menu, at times it appears that any business will do, as long as it brings in cash flow today. (Tomorrow, when the claim is made, will look after itself.)[25]

Buffett bemoans the existence of "cash flow" underwriting, as it is known, since he recognizes that "in a business selling a commodity-type product, it's impossible to be a lot smarter than your dumbest competitor."[26] This is when the red ink in the industry really starts to flow and, says Buffett, "some unattractive aspects of human nature have manifested themselves in the past when this has happened."[27]

Sensing trouble, some insurance companies succumb to Shefrin's "get-evenitis" and up the ante. In other words they take on even more risk in the hope that they can break even—"scrambling for business when underwriting losses hit record levels—it is likely to cause them at such a time to redouble their efforts," observes Buffett.[28] "These companies," he continues, "hope that somehow they can get lucky on the next batch of business and thereby cover up earlier shortfalls," and this further exacerbates the problems of the industry.[29]

However, in a self-correcting process, the aberrant behavior described above eventually erodes the capital of the industry to the point where it can no longer provide sufficient cover to meet demand. As the industry becomes capacity constrained, so pricing improves— holding out the possibility of returning to levels consistent with making profits.

The flowers that bloom in this desert can nevertheless be short-lived. Says Buffett:

> *When over-capacity finally corrects itself, the rebound to prosperity frequently produces a pervasive enthusiasm for expansion that, within a few years, again creates over-capacity and a new profitless environment.*[30]

This is a cycle of behavior that, if not as predictable as the migration of wild animals, is certainly as periodic. Just like migratory animals, insurance companies move in herds; it's safer that way.

It is the anonymity of the crowd that allows insurance companies to coalesce in the downside of the industry's cycle (even those that recognize that they are fooling themselves in ascribing higher value to business under threat of being taken away than it actually warrants). This instinctive behavior—instinctive because it is evolutionarily sound, if not economically logical—is more powerful when:

○ Peer perceptions of ability are important (about which, handily, Buffett does not care: "I keep an internal score card. If I do something that others don't like but I feel good about, I'm happy. If others praise something I've done, but I'm not satisfied, I feel unhappy"[31]).

○ The willingness to admit errors in judgment to peers is a factor (which, it just so happens, is the inverse of Buffett's attitude to oversights: "Of course, it is necessary to dig deep into our history to find illustrations of... mistakes—sometimes as deep as two or three months back"[32]).

○ One's willingness to take a risk is modified by the prospect of looking stupid if the decision goes against you (which Warren Buffett, not unsurprisingly, is content to risk: "[Charlie and I] are willing to look foolish as long we don't feel we have acted foolishly"[33]).

Thus herding is not a form of conduct in which Warren Buffett seeks shelter. He doesn't feel the need. He doesn't key his behavior off the behavior of others. Standing alone holds no fear for him; it never has. This is why he has the resolve to step away when prices deteriorate, why he glories in the loneliness of being logical.

This element of his wiring is a genetic gift and there are numerous examples of this trait in his personal life, which would be trivial if they did not signify more consequential behavior. He eats hamburgers or steak in *any* restaurant he visits, for instance.[34] He quaffs Coca-Cola instead of wine at dinner in fancy restaurants with fine company, and this septuagenarian chairman of a major public corporation snacks continuously on See's candies and Dairy Queen ice creams on the dais at his annual general meetings.[35]

In high school he wore sneakers all year round even when it was snowing—"most of us were trying to be like everyone else," said a friend at the time, "I think he liked being different"—while in later years he bought suits, five at a time, all in the same "style," which was no style at all.[36]

However, the most extraordinary example of Buffett's refusal to bow to social influence on behavior can be found in his living arrangements. Here he flouts one of the most fundamental of human conventions: He is married to one woman, lives with another, *and conducts public relationships with both.*[37]

If Warren Buffett is not troubled by standing out from the crowd, this is also a quality that he looks for in the behavior of the insurance companies he acquires. "We hear a great many insurance managers talk about being willing to reduce volume in order to underwrite profitably, but we find that very few actually do so," he says.[38] In Phil Liesche at National Indemnity, for example, Buffett found an exception:

> *If business makes sense, he writes it: if it doesn't, he rejects it...*
> *Jack Ringwalt, the founder of the National Indemnity Company,*
> *instilled this underwriting discipline at the inception of the com-*

pany, and Phil Liesche has never wavered in maintaining it. We believe such strong-mindedness is as rare as it is sound—and absolutely essential to the running of a first-class casualty insurance operation.[39]

Nor is Buffett given to myopia. He calculates the value of a dollar spent today against the opportunity cost of not investing it personally.[40] When you can compound the value of your savings at a rate of 20%+ per annum, the jam today vs. jam tomorrow decision is made for you.

Equally, Buffett is aware of the human tendency to discount the value of late rewards so heavily that they pale in comparison to rewards in the present. Classically, in his own diet he too is confronted with the dessert–willpower challenge. And just as Pinker notes that we will place the alarm clock across the room so we will not turn it off and go back to sleep, or put tempting snacks out of sight and mind,[41] Buffett goes to similar lengths. When he strives to lose weight, he incentivizes himself with money—not to receive a sum if he maintains his diet, but to lose it if he does not (playing on his own loss aversion; this guy is really wired), and customarily he will write a substantial check to his daughter, payable on a specified date in the future *unless* his weight has dropped by that time.[42]

Buffett puts a mental cudgel in place at his insurance companies in order to ensure that they keep their eyes firmly fixed on the long term. A major part of Berkshire's insurance managers' remuneration package is premised on the ultimate cost of their float. So even as they tuck into their main course, one eye on the dessert trolley in the corner, they know that their bonus will not be proportionate to the volume of food they consume but inversely proportionate to their weight when they get on the scales. They, too, stand to lose if they over-eat.

Knee deep in the big muddy

Of course, an insurance company's dogged resolution to stick with writing policies, even when prices are depressed, describes nothing other than the institutional imperative at work; it's entrapment. But there is *another* form of entrapment that can lie in wait in these situations, illustrated by Martin Shubik.[43] In his game "How Much Would You Pay for a Dollar?" Shubik auctions a dollar bill to the highest bidder, drawn from a class of students. No communication is allowed between bidders and the two highest bidders have to pay what they bid, even though only the highest wins.

Consider, therefore, the predicament of someone who has just bid 95 cents, only to have the only other player left in the game bid $1. If that person quits at this point, he or she is sure to lose 95 cents—but this loss can be reduced to only 5 cents by raising the bid to $1.05 (if this wins the auction). The problem is that the other person faces the same calculation. Caught "knee deep in the big muddy,"[44] in order to minimize their losses opponents in situations such as these usually continue clobbering each other until one of them gives up, and the bidding often reaches a few dollars.

This situation is analogous to that in the insurance industry. Companies are selling a commodity product, differentiated chiefly by price. Thus when they set their prices, they are, in effect, bidding for customers. An insurance company's loss, if it does not win the contest, is similar to that of the loser in Shubik's game, except that in this case, its loss is measured by the market share, scale, and psychic and material benefits that go hand in hand with corporate size, and that accrue to their chief executives. So they, too, can get caught knee deep in the big muddy, clobbering each other into submission.

Not Warren Buffett. Importantly, Buffett makes no such psychic and material commitment to the industry, so he is able to walk away when the fighting starts, and he derives no psychic or material benefit from Berkshire's size. The calculation he performs is not insurance centric, it's global. He measures his use of capital against all other possible uses and thus if the pricing environment in the insurance industry is unfavorable, the numbers won't add up for him in the way that they might for others who do not share his perspective. And if the price is not right, he is happy to do nothing.

BUSY DOING NOTHING

One English statesman attributed his country's greatness in the nineteenth century to a policy of "masterly inactivity." This is a strategy that is far easier for historians to commend than for participants to follow.

Warren Buffett[45]

Peter Ustinov, the actor, raconteur, and wit, tells a story of the time he went to watch the performance of a screen actor in a stage play. This particular individual had been schooled in the art of "method acting," a form of performance suggesting that he should fret about the stage giving physical expression to every emotion he was attempting to portray. Ustinov found this a great distraction. After some time, he could stomach no more and cried from the balcony: "Don't just do something. Stand there!"

Recall that the attribution error suggests that for those on the outside looking in (Mr. Ustinov, your peers, board, and shareholders, for instance), the characteristics of your performance will be ascribed not to the *situation* in which you find yourself (to which *you* will attribute your performance), but to *your personal qualities*.

On the inside, all of us who are monitored in our work instinctively know this, which is why we feel uncomfortable when it looks as though we are doing nothing.

Thus, with the best will in the world, even if, like Buffett, an underwriter possesses the discipline not to herd and/or the capacity not to succumb to myopia, writing business—*any business*—is far, far easier than writing none at all. Insurance companies are frightened of standing still. It's deeply unconventional to do so. And it also invites a volatility in corporate results that shareholders loathe.

However, as Ben Franklin once said: "Never confuse motion for action." Warren Buffett doesn't. "The trick is," he says, "when there is nothing to do, do nothing."[46]

Never was a man so content to *appear* to be doing nothing as is Warren Buffett. Never has a man been so content to do the unconventional. And never was an insurance executive so willing to

embrace what others are afraid of: "Berkshire happily accepts volatility," says Buffett, "just as long as it carries with it the expectation of
increased profits over time."[47]

Concomitantly, never has a manager been so content for those
working for him also to do nothing. Buffett attributes that act properly
to the situation, and not improperly to the individual. When volume
shrinks in Berkshire's insurance operations, its managers "will hear no
complaints from corporate headquarters," says Buffett, "nor will
employment or salaries suffer."[48]

In fact, Buffett has made this a rule, a specification carefully
designed to elicit the behavior he is looking for—this one recognizing
that humans tend to make the best of what is available to them (we are
"resourceful, evaluative maximizers," as Michael Jensen would have
it[49]). Comments Buffett:

> We don't engage in layoffs when we experience a cyclical slow-
> down at one of our generally profitable insurance operations. This
> no-layoff policy is in our own self-interest. Employees who fear
> that large layoffs will accompany sizeable reductions in premium
> volume will understandably produce scads of business through
> thick and thin (mostly thin).[50]

RATIONAL PRICING

> Though certain long-tail lines may prove profitable at combined
> ratios of 110 or 115, insurers will invariably find it unprofitable to
> price using those ratios as targets. Instead, prices must provide a
> healthy margin of safety against the social trends that are forever
> springing expensive surprises on the insurance industry.
>
> Warren Buffett[51]

In theory, pricing in the insurance industry should be relatively
straightforward. Gauging risk in this arena is akin to a scientific
process in which statistical measures that have been tried and tested
for over 200 years can be brought to bear.

In practice, while all insurance companies possess the skills necessary to rate risks properly, the correct price for policies written in the future has to be judged not merely in relation to an actuarial calculation, but also in relation to an estimate of the *actual* profitability of policies currently in force. To do this, an insurance company has to estimate the size of the reserves it should set aside to cover the expected liability stemming from claims that are in process, but not yet settled. Whereas actuarial assessments of probability frequencies are objective, the estimation of reserves is far more subjective.

Proper reserving is an essential element in the economics of an insurance business because claims account for the vast majority of its overall operating costs. An insurance company therefore needs to make an accurate calculation of required reserves if it is to have an idea of its costs—*which it then uses as a basis to judge the expected profitability of the new business it is writing.* If it gets this calculation wrong, it will get its pricing wrong.

Given the subjectivity involved in this process, however, estimates of reserves are always wrong—but normally in the direction of setting them too low. Typically, insurance companies delude themselves that reserves are adequate when in fact they are not, which means that they routinely underestimate the costs of their business and on this basis set their prices too low, as Buffett witnessed at GEICO. He says:

> *When insurance executives belatedly establish proper reserves, they often speak of "reserve strengthening," a term that has a rather noble ring to it. They almost make it sound as if they are adding extra layers of strength to an already-solid balance sheet. That's not the case: instead the term is a euphemism for what should more properly be called "correction of previous untruths" (albeit non-intentional ones).*[52]

And such "self-delusion in company reserving almost always leads to inadequate industry rate levels," says Buffett. "If major factors in the market don't know their true costs, the competitive "fall-out" hits all—even those with adequate cost knowledge."[53]

Overconfidence

Smart, hard-working people aren't exempt from professional disasters from overconfidence. Often they just go around in the more difficult voyages they choose, relying on their self-appraisals that they have superior talents and methods.

Charlie Munger[54]

There are several cognitive reasons for insurance companies getting this calculation wrong, generally in the direction of under- rather than over-reserving. I will deal with one of these here—overconfidence—and leave the others until later in the book, since they affect the quality of all decisions made under general conditions of uncertainty, not just those in the insurance industry.

Charlie Munger observes that most people consider themselves to be above-average drivers, even though, in the aggregate, this cannot be the case.[55] Such overconfidence has been found in tasks of far greater moment than a person's assessment of his or her driving skills, however. It is a condition found in any situation in which humans have to make a judgment as to their abilities relative to others.

Typically when they design experiments to test for overconfidence, psychologists set a series of questions—often trivia—and ask respondents to choose a range for each answer such that they are 90% confident that the correct answer will lie within it. The common finding on these tests is that way in excess of 10% of the answers lie outside the stipulated range.

In similar fashion, when they come to estimate the reserves that should be set aside against claims, most insurance companies are aware of the prudence of being conservative and (implicitly) will choose a range of estimates designed to capture the actual outcome. But even as they strive for this and set their confidence limits accordingly, more than likely they will exhibit the same overconfidence that most of us do in all walks of life (which explains why books, including this one, never get finished on time). What they believe is conservatism turns out not to be. They aim too low and subsequently price too low.

Buffett faces the same challenge of estimating reserves correctly—and he fails it on a regular basis too, normally missing on the low side. However, in understanding his own cognitive apparatus, Buffett may be alone in the industry in comprehending the nature of overconfidence and incorporating this truth into the conduct of the managers of his insurance subsidiaries. Business that looks profitable to most is business that Berkshire Hathaway will turn away.

SEPTEMBER 11, 2001

At Berkshire we have estimated our September 11 insurance loss was $2.2 billion… huge. Nevertheless, it's one Berkshire can easily bear. We have long been in the super-cat business and we have been prepared, both financially and psychologically, to handle them when they occur. This won't be our last hit.

Warren Buffett[56]

Buffett also carries another psychological principle with him when he goes into bat in the insurance industry. He uses one of those cognitive biases that ruins pricing in this business to his own ends, once it has been ruined. That bias is scarcity.

True scarcity—rather than its imagined variety, the fear that business ceded will never be regained—is what Warren Buffett waits for (in more normal times).

It occurs when the claims experience of insurance companies debilitates them so badly that they lack the financial resources to supply the capacity the market needs; on a regulatory and/or fiduciary basis, they simply cannot absorb sufficient risk. This can happen because pricing has been too low for several years and the chickens have come home to roost, or because a major catastrophe or series of catastrophes has overwhelmed the industry, taking those who mispriced these risks with them.

On September 11, 2001, with the felling of New York's twin towers, that scarcity was delivered in the most awful way, one that Warren Buffett could neither have imagined nor welcomed.

Unpalatable to contemplate, disasters of this nature nevertheless call forth the premise on which Buffett writes all of his insurance policies. Because he and his managers refuse to write business that does not hold out the promise of being profitable, Berkshire's financial strength remains intact during those periods when others are threatened with going to the wall. When capacity has been drained from the industry, Warren Buffett stands ready to provide cover.

Naturally, given the circumstances, he will be able to do so at prices that now offer the prospect of profitability. Capacity shortages in commodity industries push up pricing. The more than $40 billion hit that the insurance industry took in the wake of the terrorist attack on the US will have no less an effect.

Buffett said in the wake of September 11:

Near-term prospects—very near-term—for this business are good. We are the Fort Knox of the insurance business at a time when financial strength is a top priority for buyers of reinsurance.[57]

When capacity is short in the catastrophe market, Berkshire Hathaway provides an oasis of protection. Buffett's customers who still need to lay off some of their risks are drawn to him as never before. What they once had in abundance has suddenly dried up. And if humans are wired to value items more highly when they are made scarce by the process of social competition, we have been conditioned to value them even more highly when what was once in abundance disappears.[58] As this emotion overwhelms those in need of cover, they become even more willing to pay for it. In the wake of September 11, therefore, pricing in reinsurance markets rose by between 35% and 50%.

Similar scarcity manifested itself in a much more normal and far more acceptable fashion in the mid-1980s. Back then, Buffett was in his element. In 1984 he told his shareholders:

For some years I have told you that there could be a day coming when our premier financial strength would make a real difference in the competitive position of our insurance operation. That day may have arrived. We are almost without question the strongest property/casualty insurance operation in the country, with a capital position far superior to that of companies of much greater size.[59]

In the following year, Berkshire was still in the catbird seat and volumes were going through the roof:

In past reports, I have told you that Berkshire's strong capital position—the best in the industry—should one day allow us to claim a distinct competitive advantage in the insurance market. With the tightening of the market, that day has arrived. Our premium volume more than tripled last year... Berkshire's financial strength (and our record of maintaining unusual strength through thick and thin) is now a major asset for us in securing good business.[60]

Customers were beating a path to its door:

We correctly foresaw a flight to quality by many large buyers of insurance and reinsurance who belatedly recognized that a policy is only an IOU—and who, in 1985, could not collect on many of their IOUs. These buyers today are attracted to Berkshire because of its strong capital position. But, in a development we did not foresee, we are also finding buyers drawn to us because our ability to insure substantial risks sets us apart from the crowd.[61]

Buffett's understanding of human behavior was such that he manipulated the situation somewhat. In 1985 he told his shareholders that "our largest insurance company, National Indemnity Company, broadcast its willingness to underwrite large risks by running an advertisement in three issues of an insurance weekly. It solicited policies of only large size: those with a minimum premium of $1m and, remarkably, produced 600 replies and yielded premiums totalling about $50m."[62] What Buffett did not tell his shareholders, however, was that the advertisement stipulated that respondents had to name their price. If Buffett did not like the price, the understanding was that they would not get a second chance.[63] Therefore he created an even greater illusion of scarcity. (There was no such manipulation post-September 2001.)

Buffett also knows that Berkshire's financial strength pays off not just under conditions of scarcity but also under conditions of *anticipated* scarcity. He told his shareholders in 1996:

> *After a mega-catastrophe, insurers might well find it difficult to obtain reinsurance even though their need for coverage would then be particularly great. At such a time, Berkshire would without question have very substantial capacity available—but it will naturally be our long-standing clients who have first call on it. That business reality has made major insurers and reinsurers throughout the world realize the desirability of doing business with us. Indeed, we are currently getting sizeable "stand-by" fees from reinsurers that are simply nailing down their ability to get coverage from us should the market tighten.*[64]

And again:

> *Periodically... buyers remember Ben Franklin's observation that it is hard for an empty sack to stand upright and recognize their need to buy promises only from insurers that have enduring financial strength. It is then that we have a major competitive advantage. When a buyer really focuses on whether a $10 million claim can easily be paid by his insurer five or ten years down the road, and when he takes into account the possibility that poor underwriting conditions may then coincide with depressed financial markets and defaults by reinsurers, he will find only a few companies he can trust.*[65]

Indeed, it was to capitalize on this competitive advantage that Buffett made the acquisition of General Re. It is curious, however, that in doing so he should end up diluting, rather than fortifying, Berkshire Hathaway's competitive advantage (at least in the medium term).

In order to explore why this is so, we should move on to Part II of this book, which will discuss the General Re acquisition in more detail, extract some of the lessons associated with this debacle, and pave the way for presenting in detail Warren Buffett's model for the management of capital.

Part II
Capital Manager

6

The Man for All Seasons

I don't want you to think we have any way of learning or behaving so you won't make a lot of mistakes. I'm just saying that you can learn to make fewer mistakes than other people—and how to fix your mistakes faster when you do make them. But there's no way that you can live an adequate life without many mistakes.

Charlie Munger[1]

A man has as many social selves as there are individuals who recognize an image of him in their mind... it may be a perfectly harmonious division of labor, as where one tender to his children is stern to the soldiers or prisoners under his command.

W. James[2]

Such is the aura surrounding Buffett that many people feel everything he touches should turn to gold. If it does not, then they are ready to leap to the offensive. Held up as an oracular demigod, they want to see him bleed like a mortal. And plenty are willing to take the shot that might draw blood.

In the latter part of the 1990s, the bullets were flying from the new-economy camp. As the price of technology stocks soared, Buffett was accused of missing out in spectacular fashion. He was not in step. Berkshire Hathaway was underperforming the S&P and, for a time, the wounds looked deep. However, they healed as quickly as the tech bubble burst, and Buffett's stock roared back against a declining market.

The events of September 11, 2001 provided the skeptics with more deadly ammunition—handed to them, this time, by Buffett himself. In the aftermath, General Re laid him wide open. Buffett told his shareholders that September 11 had exposed severe shortcomings in that company's underwriting standards. In total, Berkshire reported a $2.3 billion charge for the quarter against a "guess" of its liability in relation to the claims originating from the terrorist attack on the World Trade Center. Of this, $1.7 billion was attributable to General Re.[3]

Buffett owned up and accepted the blame, explaining that each of his golden rules of conduct in running an insurance company had been broken at General Re. *He was bleeding.*

General Re should have epitomized Warren Buffett's trinity of strengths. Now what some consider to be an amazing admission had blown a hole in the very substance of his organizational frame, in:

1 His ability to underwrite risk.
2 His decentralized management style.
3 His skill in effecting acquisitions.

A close examination of this debacle will uncover where Buffett's error lay. In the process, it will reveal Warren Buffett as a mortal, not a god, as a man who does make mistakes. It will also describe him as a man who manages change in the realm of capital allocation, not by antici- pating it but by reacting to it. This immediately characterizes his mis- takes as less damaging to Berkshire's wellbeing. And in delineating Buffett as a man who is not afraid to effect change at the human level when he has to, it will also reveal Buffett as a proactive leader.

Warren Buffett defies stereotyping. He is several in one: He is the man for *all* seasons.

WHEN TIME RAN OUT

A mega-catastrophe is no surprise: One will occur from time to time, and this will not be our last. We did not, however, price for manmade mega-cats, and we were foolish in not doing so. In effect, we, and the rest of the industry, included coverage for ter- rorist acts in policies covering other risks—and received no addi- tional premium for doing so. That was a huge mistake and one that I myself allowed.

Warren Buffett[4]

One year after acquiring General Re, and after several elaborations of the rationale behind the acquisition, Warren Buffett finally told his shareholders the real reason for buying that company—but only obliquely. Writing in Berkshire's annual report of 1999, with its stock nearly 50% below the high it had reached in the previous year, Buffett addressed the subject of share repurchases.

"We will not repurchase shares unless we believe Berkshire stock is selling well below intrinsic value, conservatively calculated," he said, revisiting a point on the allocation of capital he had made many times before. Then he continued:

Recently, when the A shares fell below $45,000, we considered making repurchases. We decided, however, to delay buying, if indeed we elect to do any, until shareholders have had the chance to review this report.[5]

The shareholders—and the stock market—got the message. For the first time in Buffett's stewardship of Berkshire Hathaway, its stock price was trading at a sufficient discount to his informed estimate of the company's intrinsic value for him to consider buying some of it back. Naturally, once the intended audience got wind of Warren Buffett's personal assay of Berkshire's value, the price rose rapidly and the issue became redundant once more.

Now do the math. If $45,000 was a discount to intrinsic value, this means that, at the $81,000 price at which Buffett effected the all-stock purchase of General Re, Berkshire Hathaway shares must have been trading at a handsome premium to intrinsic value. It was this that persuaded Buffett to do the transaction.

General Re was founded in 1921 and, at the time of its acquisition by Berkshire Hathaway, was one of the three largest reinsurers in the world, operating in 31 countries and providing reinsurance coverage in over 150. Chaired and managed by Ron Ferguson, a man with whom Buffett was professionally well acquainted, Buffett knew its business well and it was described by many as a perfect fit for Berkshire. (Ferguson's formula for value creation was, for instance, based on the size and cost of the company's float and the return on float.[6])

Prior to this acquisition, however, Warren Buffett had shown an aversion to using his own stock as a medium of exchange in a transaction. He had done so only very sparingly, and only then as a small fraction of the deals that otherwise had been paid for out of Berkshire's cash. He tells his shareholders:

> *Other things being equal, the highest stock market prices relative to intrinsic value are given to companies whose managers have demonstrated their unwillingness to issue shares at any time on terms unfavorable to the owners of the business. When the buyer makes a partial sale of itself—and that is what the issuance of shares to make an acquisition amounts to—it can customarily get no higher value set on its shares than the market chooses to grant it [whereas the target company can normally negotiate a very full price].[7]*

He adds:

> *The acquirer who barges ahead... must give up $2 of value to receive $1 of value. Under such circumstances, a marvelous business purchased at a fair sales price becomes a terrible buy. For gold valued as gold cannot be purchased intelligently through the utilization of gold... valued at lead.[8]*

According to Buffett, however, one opportunity does present itself in avoiding the "destruction of value for old owners" if shares are issued for acquisitions, and this is when "the acquirer's stock sells at or above its intrinsic business value. In that situation, the use of the stock as currency may enhance the wealth of the acquiring company's owners."[9]

Such was the case in the summer of 1998.

Buffett first considered a merger with General Re as early as September 1996 when Berkshire's shares were changing hands for around $32,000. In July of the following year he met with Ron Ferguson to discuss the matter. However, according to the legal documents supplied for the deal, "during this period, the relationship between the market prices of Berkshire's Common Stock and General Re's Common

Stock was such that Mr. Buffett was not willing to consider a transaction that would provide any premium to the General Re stockholders."[10]

That was to change by May 6, 1998. "Since the prior meetings, the value of Berkshire's stock had increased in relationship to the value of General Re's Common Stock," says the documentation.[11] In fact, having appreciated by around 140% since Buffett first took a look at General Re, Berkshire's stock had caught fire. The cult surrounding Buffett was in full force. Large capitalization stocks, particularly those of global branded goods companies, were leading the market up and Buffett's genius was being highlighted by the enormous returns he was making on his investments in the likes of Gillette and American Express and, particularly, his large holding in Coca-Cola, purchased in 1988 and 1989. In anticipation of Buffett's next act of "brilliance," investors were happy to pay a premium to the underlying value of Berkshire Hathaway.

In the meantime, Ron Ferguson continued to buy back General Re stock in the belief, which he had held for several years, that it was trading below intrinsic value.[12] Consequently, Buffett met with Ferguson again—this time to discuss the combination of the two companies *and* financial terms. Buffett proposed an exchange ratio of shares and, as a result of that meeting, the merger between the two companies was announced on June 19.

The stated rationale

The transaction will allow General Re to better serve its clients by accepting attractive reinsurance opportunities that it has declined or been unable to write in the past, due to constraints on its earnings volatility. Removing the constraints will enhance long-term profitability. The combination will allow General Re to retain, rather than to cede to other reinsurers, more of the business it writes, which will increase funds available for investment. Berkshire will allow General Re to grow its international business as quickly as it desires and will provide General Re with abundant capital.

Joint Proxy Statement/Prospectus[13]

In explaining why he had traded 22% of Berkshire Hathaway's equity in the $22 billion acquisition of General Re, at a 21.8% premium to the price the stock market considered correct, Buffett spoke a word from the lexicon of rationales for corporate takeovers that he had uttered on only one previous occasion, *in the ill-fated purchase of Waumbec Mills*, which exemplified his entrapment in textiles. That word was "synergy," "a term widely used in business to explain an acquisition that otherwise makes no sense" according to Buffett in 1985.[14]

The synergies on offer were real, are still available, and have indeed been partially exploited.

This acquisition was a major departure from the methodology that Buffett had previously pursued in expanding Berkshire's domain. General Re was not an owner-managed enterprise. Nor did it have managers who acted like owners. Ron Ferguson and his team had, as Buffett pointed out, eschewed volatility, accepting lower profits in exchange for smoother returns. This might maximize the stock price in the short to medium term, but not the long. However, management at General Re were not incentivized to maximize long-term intrinsic value. They had stock options. The higher the interim price of General Re the better, and if the stock market wanted growth and/or linear results, it was in their best interests to deliver these.

Hitherto, Buffett's approach to acquisitions had been premised on reinforcing behavior that was already in place. To get General Re's managers to act like owners required that he *change* their behavior. In its first two years under Berkshire's ownership, the new acquisition misfired badly. In 1999 Buffett reported that Berkshire had incurred a $1.4 billion underwriting loss that had raised his precious cost of float to 5.8%.[15] The warning signs were there.

Nevertheless, accepting that it's okay to cede business to the competition, growing comfortable with the concept of detaching from the herd, learning to put off early rewards, being content in doing *nothing*, and shaking off a resolute commitment to be in the business of insurance rather than the business of allocating capital all take time to learn.

In order to engineer the reorientation of General Re's management toward a new owner with a completely different imperative, Buffett put in place the minimum specifications that he uses elsewhere at Berkshire. Most importantly, he redesigned managements' remuneration packages and replaced their option schemes with "incentive compensation plans… directly tied to the variables of float growth and cost of float, the same variables that determine value for owners."[16]

By 2000, the short-term evidence was encouraging of a longer-term improvement. Buffett reported:

> *The news has turned considerably better. Ron Ferguson, along with Joe Brandon, Tad Montross, and a talented supporting cast, took many actions during 2000 to bring the company's profitability back to past standards. Though our pricing is not fully corrected, we have significantly repriced business that was severely unprofitable or dropped it altogether.*[17]

Then time ran out.

THE MISTAKE

> *Your company is run on the principle of centralization of financial decisions at the top… and rather extreme delegation of operating authority to a number of key managers at the individual company or business unit level… This approach produces an occasional major mistake that might have been eliminated or minimized through closer operating controls. But… it enables us to attract and retain some extraordinarily talented individuals—people who simply can't be hired in the normal course of events—who find working for Berkshire to be almost identical to running their own show.*
> *Warren Buffett*[18]

Buffett spoke the above words in 1977—and they prophesied the failure at General Re.

Buffett's oversight in acquiring General Re was not so much that he had underestimated the chance that the previously unthinkable would happen. September 11 merely revealed something he had missed in his assessment of the company. He is not a details man. He doesn't kick the tires on his acquisitions as most do. His due diligence is based on a personal assessment of the man in charge of the company. If he trusts him, he trusts that the company he is buying bears all the characteristics that a full due diligence check would uncover.

Indeed, the comparative advantage of his acquisition strategy is premised on running the kind of company that others are willing to join. Taking people on trust and liberating them from close operational control thereafter are the cornerstones to this approach. At General Re, he was let down.

Berkshire's other reinsurance operations also took a hit on September 11. Nevertheless, Buffett was able to tell his shareholders that results from these "continue to be very satisfactory."[19] The difference? "That unit has consistently adhered to the three underwriting rules I stated, and we've been paid appropriately for the risks we have underwritten," he added.[20]

Buffett's surprise and disappointment were that General Re's underwriting was revealed by this tragedy to have been woefully inadequate, not only previously accepting mispriced risks (as one of the costs of smoothing operating earnings Buffett was aware of this and was in the process of fixing it), but also aggregating exposure to losses from a single event or related events and, by Buffett's inference, writing business with customers who could not be expected to conduct themselves with probity when the claims were filed.

General Re was not Ron Ferguson. Having participated with General Re in many of its reinsurance contracts, Buffett would have had a keen sense of the company's underwriting standards. What he ignored was the capacity in this business for human error to magnify the consequences of error.

In 1999 Buffett told his shareholders:

> *General Re has the distribution, the underwriting skills, the culture, and—with Berkshire's backing—the financial clout to become the world's most profitable reinsurance company. Getting there will take time, energy and discipline, but we have no doubt that Ron Ferguson and his crew can make it happen.*[21]

The weakness of this opinion lay in the company's culture. It appears that it was a mile deep in Ron Ferguson but an inch wide in the company he managed. However, Buffett could only have known the full extent of the shortfall in standards at General Re if he had gone through its book of business with a fine-tooth comb. Indeed, it's unlikely that even Ferguson knew of this shortfall.

Buffett made a similar mistake with his investment in Salomon Inc. Buffett and Munger liked, admired, and trusted John Gutfreund, the company's CEO. Buffett told his shareholders in 1987:

> We first got to know him in 1976 when he played a key role in GEICO's escape from near-bankruptcy. Several times since, we have seen John steer clients away from transactions that would have been unwise, but that the client clearly wanted to make— even though his advice provided no fee to Salomon and acquiescence would have delivered a large fee.[22]

But operations within Salomon were not an accurate reflection of the integrity of its chairman and the company was almost brought to its knees by the actions of one its employees, Paul Mozer, who was caught placing false bids for bonds at US Treasury auctions.[23]

When the wrong behavioral rules are in place, their gaming can be difficult to detect. Even Jack Welch, the king of operational controls, found this out. Subsequent to GE's purchase of Kidder Peabody it was discovered that Joseph Jett (Kidder's $9 million cash bonus "Man of the Year" in 1993) had fraudulently exploited a remuneration system that encouraged him to feather his own nest rather than the company for which he worked.[24]

Nevertheless, there is no getting away from the fact that, at General Re, Buffett had made a mistake. It was not his first. It will not be his last.

A CAREER OF MISTAKES

A particularly encouraging point about our record is that it was achieved despite some colossal mistakes made by your Chairman

prior to Mike Goldberg's arrival. Insurance offers a host of opportunities for error, and when opportunity knocked, too often I answered.
Warren Buffett[25]

Back in the days before Buffett finally admitted to himself that he should foreclose on one of his biggest mistakes, buying Berkshire Hathaway in the first place, he was preoccupied with the prospect of a return to the rates of inflation that had characterized the US economy in the 1970s.

Buffett had not yet benefited to the full from the explosion of cognition that would transform his view of the world and at this time—unheard of now—he premised his stock selection on the outlook for the macro economy. He wrote in his letter to shareholders in 1984:

We believe substantial inflation lies ahead although we have no idea what the average rate will turn out to be. Furthermore, we think there is a small, but not insignificant, chance of runaway inflation. Such a possibility may seem absurd, considering the rate to which inflation has dropped. But we believe that present fiscal policy—featuring a huge deficit—is both extremely dangerous and difficult to reverse.[26]

With that kind of forecast of rampant inflation in mind, Buffett had long since positioned Berkshire's equity portfolio in commodity stocks that would prove a hedge against rising prices. In 1980 he commented:

We have a much larger interest in the aluminum business than in practically any of the operating businesses we control and on which we report in more detail. If we maintain our holdings, our long-term performance will be more affected by the future economics of the aluminum industry, than it will be by direct operating decisions we make concerning most companies over which we exercise management control.[27]

The supposition *was* absurd; his forecast was wrong. The inflation never did materialize and, instead, has been declining on a secular basis ever since. Back then, if Buffett had factored this fact into his valuation of equities, the discount rate he employed to value the future cash flows of businesses would have been much lower. Consequently, he would not have been so bearish about valuations for most of the bull market that ensued for the next 20 years.

It is difficult to conceive, but Berkshire's returns could have been materially higher. Yet Buffett's career has been pockmarked with error.

His first brush with extending his investment approach beyond the confines of the US stock market, in the acquisition of Guinness, ended in disappointment and a sale of stock.

Or referring to a period in the 1990s when noises made by President Clinton with regard to pharmaceutical pricing sent that industry into a stock market tailspin, Buffett says, "We should've had enough sense to recognize that the pharmaceutical industry as a group was undervalued."[28] It would have proven to be a valuable investment.

Buffett tells his shareholders:

Some of my worst mistakes were not publicly visible. These were stock and business purchases whose virtues I understood and yet I didn't make. It's no sin to miss a great opportunity outside one's area of competence. But I have passed on a couple of really big purchases that were served up to me on a platter and that I was fully capable of understanding. For Berkshire's shareholders, myself included, the cost of this thumb-sucking has been huge.[29]

Why have Buffett's mistakes failed to reduce Berkshire Hathaway's performance to the mediocre? Why, indeed, haven't some of them, such as the General Re acquisition, reduced his track record to rubble? A fuller explanation will have to wait until the next chapter. Suffice to say in this chapter that Buffett's mistakes do not come from anticipating change, strangling that beast, and imposing his supremacy over it—which would compound the error should he be wrong. They come only after he has reacted to change and the opportunities this creates.

MANAGING CHANGE

Also, combining General Re with Berkshire's other income-generating businesses will increase General Re's flexibility in managing its insurance investments.

Joint Proxy Statement/Prospectus[30]

One of Buffett's unspoken rationales behind the acquisition of General Re was to effect a tax-free switch out of equities, which he considered to be generally overvalued.

In 1997 Buffett made net sales of about 5% of his equity holdings.[31] The following year, he "trimmed or substantially cut" many of his smaller positions.[32] This was not unprecedented. He has sold stocks in the past, but normally only when higher returns are on offer elsewhere and he faces capital constraints in exploiting these opportunities. Yet at the same time as raising cash from these sales, he was also sitting on more than $15 billion in cash equivalents. If he did have his eye on higher returns, he hardly needed to realize assets to go after them.

More likely, his decision to sell reflected his jaundiced view of valuations. Selling his larger holdings would, however, have led to a substantial capital gains tax liability, a tax that Buffett is highly averse to paying, particularly with respect to his strongest franchise holdings.

The opportunity presenting itself with the acquisition of General Re was that it offered Buffett the next best thing. He could use the very valuation of the stocks he held, expressed as they were in the valuation of Berkshire Hathaway, to buy a company that owned an investment portfolio far more heavily weighted toward fixed-income securities than equities.

Approximately 80% of Berkshire's $50 billion of investment assets was held in the stock market prior to the merger. By contrast, at year-end 1997, General Re held only around 20% of its $24 billion of investment assets in equities.[33] Thus Buffett reduced his exposure to expensive stocks from 80% to roughly 61% without paying a cent in taxes.

As of writing, and since the acquisition of General Re, the S&P 500 has fallen by 24% and bonds have yielded a total return of around 26%.

Not bad timing. But Buffett's preoccupation is not with the timing of his investments, it's with their pricing. He had his eye on supercharging the returns from the enormous float he had acquired with General Re, which, perforce, had been invested on such a conservative basis under its previous ownership, and on beefing up Berkshire's "other income-generating businesses" in order to allow his now much larger insurance operations to become aggressive when the time is right.

In spite of the fact that the stock market was generally overvalued, around the turn of the twentieth century it had become distinctly two-tiered. New-economy stocks were enjoying an enormous bull market. Meanwhile, old-economy stocks—particularly of the small- and mid-capitalization variety—were in the midst of a full-blown bear market.

When prices fall in a bear market, companies find one avenue for raising capital—the stock market—closed to them. In addition, other forms of finance, such as corporate debt, can also become expensive. Compounding this problem, as Buffett told his shareholders in 2000, "was that the market for junk bonds [also] dried up as the year progressed."[34] He continued:

> In the two preceding years, junk bond purchasers had relaxed their standards, buying the obligations of ever-weaker issuers at inappropriate prices. The effects of this laxity were felt last year in a ballooning of defaults. In this environment, "financial" buyers of businesses—those who wish to buy using only a sliver of equity—became unable to borrow all they thought they needed... Because we analyze purchases on an all-equity basis, our evaluations did not change, which means we became considerably more competitive.[35]

Warren Buffett is happy to reinvest in his existing businesses for as long as they possess high-return investable opportunities. But he loves bear markets because they allow him to accelerate the process of change at Berkshire Hathaway.

In the normal course of events change is relatively glacial: at the margin harvesting Berkshire's excess cash and allocating it to new ventures when they are priced attractively, at the fringe of variation in the likes of Flight Safety and Executive Jet where change begets opportunity, or at the trailing edge of variation in shoe manufacturing where inertia provides a different type of opportunity.

With the acquisition of General Re, however, Buffett went more liquid than ever before. Value was available in abundance and he took the opportunity to reorient the company by buying (take a deep breath now) Jordan's Furniture, 76% of MidAmerican Energy; CORT Business Services, the national leader in "rent-to-rent" furniture; U.S. Liability and its two sister companies that, combined, comprise a medium-sized writer of unusual risks; Ben Bridge Jeweler, a 65-store West Coast retailer; Justin Industries, the leading maker of Western boots and the premier producer of brick in Texas and five neighboring states; Shaw Industries, the world's largest carpet manufacturer with annual sales of about $4 billion (making it Berkshire's largest business outside of the insurance industry); Benjamin Moore Paint; Johns Manville Corp., the nation's leading producer of commercial and industrial insulation, which also has major positions in roofing systems and a variety of engineered products; 90% of MiTek Inc., a producer of steel connector products and design engineering software; XTRA Corporation, a leading operating lessor of transportation equipment; nearly all of Fruit of the Loom's apparel business, a company in bankruptcy; and finally Garan, another leading manufacturer of apparel.

All told, Buffett has laid out cash in excess of $10 billion to effect these 13 transactions. The compounding machine has gone to work and Buffett has transformed Berkshire Hathaway from what was (mistakenly) perceived by many as a holding company for stock market investments into (unmistakably) an operating company.

Notwithstanding the fact that if the stock market once again offers general value Buffett will increase his holdings of fractional ownerships, speculation that this reorientation of Berkshire Hathaway is part of his grand plan for succession may not be far off the mark. Although Lou Simpson at GEICO has an enviable track record as an investment manager and will probably take over in this capacity when Buffett leaves the scene, the cult surrounding Buffett's skill in stock picking will die with him. The legacy that will live on beyond him, however, is that tied up in the corporate culture he has established within Berkshire's operating companies.

And after he has gone, it is this that will sustain the growth in Berkshire's intrinsic value; that's what Buffett has been doing with General Re's float since 1998. It is a float that was available when Buffett first contemplated the acquisition of General Re in 1996. The opportunity, in terms of the relative pricing of both companies and the bear market in old-economy stocks, was not.

As a manager of capital, therefore, rather than anticipate change, Buffett reacted to it.

We will find out below that as a leader of those who manage capital on his behalf, he is often found to be more proactive.

EFFECTING CHANGE

If earnings have been unwisely retained, it is likely that managers, too, have been unwisely retained.

Warren Buffett[36]

Warren Buffett only works with people whom he likes, trusts, and admires, *and* who act like owners.

If a manager ceases to do the latter, so important is this mindset in looking after other people's money that, no matter the personal relationship he has with Buffett, he had better watch out.

If a Berkshire manager loses focus, Buffett has found it almost impossible to right his behavior via persuasion. "I'd say that the history that Charlie and I have had of persuading decent, intelligent people who we thought were doing unintelligent things to change their course of action has been *poor*," he says.[37] The laws of human nature are such that Buffett cannot change them. (Nor does he want to: He wants to work with them.) That leaves a change of management as Buffett's only option. It's not an option that he likes to use: "Management changes, like marital changes, are painful, time-consuming and chancy."[38] This helps to explain why he places so much emphasis on the front-end of his role in this regard, in the selection of the managers with whom he wants to associate. But almost from day one of his transformation into a manager who also invests, Buffett has been effecting change and doing the necessary dirty work that comes with that job.

When the management of Dempster Mills, the first company of which he took control, showed themselves reluctant to stop investing in projects with low return and send the excess cash to him instead, Buffett had them removed. Harry Bottle, who came via a recommendation from Charlie Munger, was put in charge and he took a knife to costs, closed plants, sold down inventory, and laid off employees.[39]

Echoing Jack Welch's "We could be humane and generous to the people we let go... By moving early, more jobs were available for them,"[40] Buffett was to comment on the human cost of this necessity: "If we'd kept them the company would have gone bankrupt... I've kept close tabs and most of them are better off."[41]

When Buffalo Evening News ran into trouble in its competition with the Courier Express, Buffett removed its management too, replacing them in 1980 with the trusted Stan Lipsey.[42] Like Harry Bottle, Lipsey brought to bear the operational controls that Buffett thought necessary. Buffett wasn't prepared to do this himself, but he was prepared to have an agent do it on his behalf.

In 1986, after K & W Products, a small Berkshire subsidiary that produced automotive products, had "stumbled badly," Buffett allowed Charlie Munger, who oversaw K & W, to bring Harry Bottle in once more. He was made CEO and in the following year K & W's profits set a record.[43]

In 1999, Buffett took the unusual step of moving a CEO from one subsidiary, Cypress Insurance Company's Brad Kinstler, and installing him as CEO of Fechheimer Brothers, a manufacturer of uniforms that Berkshire had bought in 1986 and had struggled at the top since the two brothers who had founded the company had departed the scene some years earlier.[44]

When insurance subsidiary Home and Auto experienced a shortfall in underwriting standards in the early 1970s, Buffett made John Seward a "battlefield promotion."[45] In 1978, Frank DeNardo was brought in to straighten out National Indemnity's California Worker's

Compensation business, which had been a disaster.[46] And when GEICO ran into similar operating difficulties in the early 1990s, a time when Buffett owned more than half of the company, he was evidently displeased with the way in which Bill Snyder, the successor to Jack Byrne as CEO, had expanded the company into noncore areas and made a number of acquisitions. Subsequently, in 1993, Snyder decided to "retire early," which is when Tony Nicely and Lou Simpson became co-CEOs.[47]

Ron Ferguson has also retired. The *new* management team at General Re is Joe Brandon and Tad Montross.

The surprisingly interventionist aspect of Buffett's management style is not confined to those companies of which he is either sole or majority owner. It seems apparent that he has also worked behind the scenes at those companies in which he has major investments.

"At board meetings, criticism of the CEO's performance is often viewed as the social equivalent of belching," says Buffett.[48] While he sits on a company's board, Warren Buffett is not afraid to belch (although he does weigh this against the danger of not being invited back[49]).

When Coca-Cola's chairman, Douglas Daft, announced his intention to acquire Quaker Oats in 2000, the stock market gave its public verdict by marking the company's share price down sharply to reflect the impending destruction of value from the deal. The board duly took notice and forced Daft into an embarrassing climb-down. According to James Williams, a board member and chairman of the executive committee of Sun Trust Banks Inc., Buffett was the most vocal dissenter in the meeting at which the deal was discussed, claiming that the proposed price was too high.[50]

The boards on which Buffett sits can be active. Daft's predecessor, Doug Ivester, was removed from his post by Coca-Cola's board. It is conceivable that Buffett was instrumental in this decision. Daft had the company chasing centrally set targets that, it turned out, bore no relation to what was achievable in the wake of a crisis enveloping its emerging markets and a deflationary grip closing around its developed ones. In this sense, earnings were retained unwisely and Ivester had ceased to act like an owner.

Similarly, Gillette also endured a period in which its stewardship fell from the straight and narrow (which will be expanded on in Chapter 9). In turn, it lost the services of Alfred Zeien and then, soon afterwards, of his replacement as chairman, Michael Hawley.

And in July 2002 Coca-Cola announced that it would start to treat stock option costs as expenses, using a method recommended by Buffett. Washington Post, on whose board Buffett also sits, followed suit. (It may only be a matter of time at Gillette as well.) Donald Graham, Washington Post's chairman and chief executive, attested to what we already know: "I and everyone on the board and in management have been listening to Warren Buffett and think his arguments are pretty persuasive."[51]

❖❖❖

Warren Buffett makes mistakes. He manages change and effects change. He is a confident man—"I've never had any self doubt. I've never been discouraged," he says. "I always knew I was going to be rich."[52]

He is not, however, an overconfident chief executive.

Buffett learns from his mistakes. He has calibrated his confidence. He accepts reality and changes managers of capital when he has to. He has also developed a model for his own management of capital, which allows him to manage change by responding to it, rather than attempting to master it as an overconfident individual might.

Says Buffett:

> *The modern manager refers to his "portfolio" of businesses—meaning that all of them are candidates for "restructuring" whenever such a move is dictated by Wall Street preferences, operating conditions or a new corporate "concept."*[53]

In contrast, the man for all seasons has a model for all seasons. Consequently, the compounding continues. In order to appreciate more fully why this is the case, let's proceed to the next chapter in which Buffett's model for the management of capital will be delineated in detail.

7

The Circle of Competence

In complex environments, the successful expert is creating a "simulation" of the system in their head that is populated with information from many different sources. Somehow the diversity of information in their brain creates an emergent solution to the problem.

Norman Johnson[1]

We try to think about things that are important and knowable. There are important things that are not knowable... and there are things that are knowable but not important—and we don't want to clutter up our minds with those.

Warren Buffett[2]

In choosing not to equip Berkshire Hathaway with a strategic plan, Warren Buffett has robbed himself of one of the essential instruments of leadership: a road map. Paradoxically, however, he remains firmly in charge of Berkshire Hathaway's destiny, confident of meeting the target he has set for the company. That is because he has established a Circle of Competence within which he conducts his capital management.

Inside his Circle of Competence, Buffett understands the laws that apply in the allocation of capital. He is capable of qualifying opportunity. He is also able to pinpoint the origin of his mistakes so that he can amend his decision rules if need be. And it is Buffett's Circle of Competence that gives him the sense of control that all humans crave in the face of uncertainty, and that most CEOs have "found" in the adoption of their more conventional strategic plans. Buffett reiterates:

We don't have a master plan. Charlie and I don't sit around and strategize or talk about the future of various industries or anything of that sort. It just doesn't happen... We simply try to survey the whole financial field and look for things that we understand, where we think they have a durable competitive advantage, where we like the management and where the price is sensible.[3]

Buffett is renowned for the objectivity he brings to bear in the judgments with respect to comprehension, competitive advantage, management, and price to which he alludes above. He appears to conduct his analysis and proceed to action, or inaction, without emotion. However, while it is true that Buffett's competitive edge in the management of capital does come from his objectivity, this is not achieved by being, in some hitherto unexplained way, emotionless. Emotions cannot, should not, be extracted from decision making. They are a necessary input to the process—especially important in the forward-looking, risky decisions at which Warren Buffett excels. It is only when they become too strong that they interfere with the capacity to make effective judgments.

As an allocator of capital—as a human—you have to have balance. Warren Buffett has that balance. Every decision he takes in the allocation of capital is taken from a position of utmost psychological security. His Circle of Competence is indispensable in this regard. But he has also put the groundwork in ahead of time to ensure that he is comfortable with the behavior suggested by managing capital within this circle and according to its dictates. It is Buffett's *emotional balance* that, ultimately, gives him the objectivity that elevates and sustains his unusual approach to capital management above the average.

THE CIRCLE OF COMPETENCE

Thomas J. Watson Sr. of IBM followed the same rule: "I'm no genius," he said. "I'm smart in spots—but I stay around those spots."

Warren Buffett[4]

I've learned the perimeter of my circle of competence. If you name almost any big company in the US, I can tell you in five seconds whether or not it is within my circle of competence, and if it is I've probably got some sort of fix on it.

Warren Buffett[5]

Unique among allocators of capital, Warren Buffett and Charlie Munger do not peer into the socioeconomic future when they make decisions on behalf of their shareholders. "We will continue to ignore political and economic forecasts, which are an expensive distraction for many investors and businessmen," Buffett claims.[6]

Buffett and Munger do not believe that the economy lends itself to forecasting in the sense in which forecasting has come to be practiced. Just like the stock market in which he also allocates capital, the economy is a "complex adaptive system" that is poised in a critical state. One small change within the economy can either lead to a proportional outcome or ignite an avalanche of related effects that generate an outsized result. In the short and medium term, the direction and scale of events are therefore dictated by contingencies that cannot be determined.

In order to produce meaningful forecasts in such systems, says Per Bak, "one would have to measure everything everywhere with absolute accuracy, which is impossible. Then one would have to perform an accurate computation based on this information, which is equally impossible."[7]

Warren Buffett concurs. He observes:

Years ago no one could have foreseen the huge expansion of the Vietnam War, wage and price controls, two oil shocks, the resignation of a president, the dissolution of the Soviet Union, a one-day drop in the Dow of 508 points, or treasury bill yields fluctuating between 2.8% and 17.4%.[8]

Nevertheless, the admission of his own inability to predict these kinds of events has not prevented Buffett from rationally managing the capital at his disposal.[9]

In defining the boundaries of Berkshire Hathaway's deployment of capital, Buffett refers to a representation of the universe that he carries in his head. This is a meta-model, a synthesis of the array of mental models that he brings to bear in his analysis of the world.

It is a model that does not go for completeness. It is a model that recognizes that some things that are knowable are not important. It also accepts that other things that are important are unknowable. It is a model that, to the exclusion of all else, focuses on the important *and* knowable.

Buffett prefers to make his capital allocation decisions within the realm of the important and knowable. This is his strike zone, if you will, where he is happy to swing his bat at the pitches thrown his way. It encapsulates a universe in which he can make an objective assessment of the opportunities presenting themselves to him, a universe in which the variables he considers in his decision making are so manifest that he can almost touch them, and where he is so sure of them that he can essentially eradicate uncertainty.

In order to administer this state of cognition, Buffett proscribes for himself the Circle of Competence shown in Figure 2. He draws this according to the following instructions:

1 He *establishes* what he knows by identifying *truths*, the dynamics that sit behind them, and their relationships to each other.
2 He *ensures* that he knows by a process of *inversion* whereby he seeks to disprove his prior conclusions.
3 He *checks* that he knows by seeking out *feedback* from the consequences of his decisions.

TRUTHS

Our job really is to focus on things that we can know that make a difference. If something can't make a difference or if we can't know it, then we write it off.

Warren Buffett[10]

I look for what's permanent, and what is not.

Warren Buffett[11]

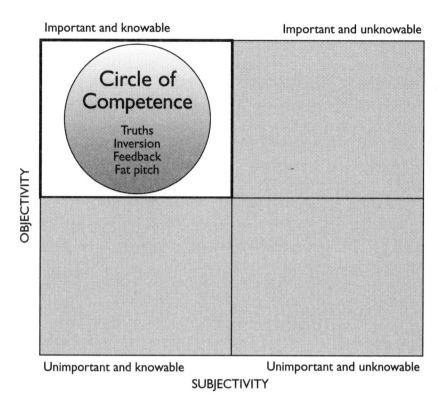

Figure 2 The Circle of Competence

Warren Buffett says that he and Charlie Munger view themselves "as business analysts—not as market analysts, not as macroeconomic analysts, and not even as security analysts."[12]

As such, when Buffett embarked on his investment career, he analyzed every company in the United States that had publicly traded securities. In effect, he started at A and worked his way through the alphabet. He says:

As you're acquiring knowledge about industries in general and companies specifically, there isn't anything like first doing some reading about them and then getting out and talking to competitors and customers and suppliers and past employees and current employees and whatever it may be. Virtually everything we've done has been by reading public reports and then maybe asking questions around and ascertaining trade positions and product strengths or something of that sort.[13]

Increasingly, as he conducted this research, Buffett developed the mental models that would allow him to create order out of what he was learning.

Thus, while he readily acknowledges that all businesses are subject to change over time, he has established that, in the realm of the business analyst, there exist incontrovertible truths that *do* apply and *can* be expected to hold in the long term, even in complex systems.[14]

Buffett found these truths in the laws of business economics: in the numbers game of capital intensity, in the capital requirements needed to maintain the status quo and those needed to grow the business, in the inevitability of the forces of mean reversion, and in the protection against these afforded by franchises, however these are defined.

He found them in the human proposition: in the hardwiring that governs the behavior of managers and determines the effectiveness of his and their leadership, and in the same hardwiring that governs the interaction between the firm and its customers, and managements and their shareholders.

He found them in the fundamental premise of value creation: that it is dependent on a manager's ability to generate incremental earnings on capital "equal to, or above, those generally available to investors."[15]

He found them in the equation for value: in which he incorporates a combination of *business economics* and the *human proposition* into a calculus that allows him to judge price.

And he found them in the essential characteristic of complex adaptive systems, which is that they will *deliver opportunities to him*: "The fact that people will be full of greed, fear, or folly is predictable. The sequence is not predictable," says Buffett.[16] Therefore, even though he doesn't know when, where, or how opportunities will present themselves, he does know that "it's almost certain there will be opportunities from time to time for Berkshire to do well within the circle we've staked out."[17]

Buffett's Circle of Competence surrounds those industries and companies in which he feels confident of being able to identify, comprehend and forecast the dynamics contained in his truths. Perhaps not surprisingly, he restricts this universe of the important and knowable to the simple. "The finding may seem unfair," he says, "but in both business and investments it is usually far more profitable to simply stick with the easy and the obvious than it is to resolve the difficult."[18]

Although Buffett will attest that his mental models have improved over time, the size of his Circle of Competence with regard to the businesses he feels capable of valuing has not changed since those early forays. That's how immutable the laws of business economics are.

However, as befits the explosion of cognition that came later, Buffett has increasingly secured the perimeter of his Circle with regard to his understanding of the way in which human behavior shapes these fundamentals. These were the lessons that Buffett learnt when he transitioned from cigar butt investor to capital manager and, perforce, to leader. He confirms:

Charlie and I have learned a lot about a lot of businesses over 40 or 50 years. However, in terms of the new things that would come to us, we were probably about as good judges of 'em at the end of the second year as we would be today. But I think there's a little plus to having [been around at it]—more in terms of human behavior and that sort of thing than knowing the specifics of a given business model.[19]

INVERSION

It is, of course, irritating that extra care in thinking is not all good but also introduces extra error... The best defense is that of the best physicists, who systematically criticize themselves to an extreme degree... as follows: The first principle is that you must not fool yourself and you're the easiest person to fool.

Charlie Munger[20]

There is a school of thought that humans accept all information they encounter as initially correct, and subsequently recode the information that is found to be false. Warren Buffett's behavior suggests that he ascribes to this view.[21]

Buffett believes that transforming an area of knowledge into a Circle of Competence, and keeping it that way, can only be achieved if he constantly stress tests what he believes to be true. Charlie Munger, for instance, says that both he and Buffett "are very good at changing our prior conclusions."[22] The reason is that they are both in the habit of inverting their arguments. Says Charlie:

> *The mental habit of thinking backward forces objectivity. One of the ways you think a thing through backward is you take your initial assumption and say, Let's try and disprove it.*[23]

He continues:

> *For example, if you were hired by the World Bank to help India, it would be very helpful to determine the three best ways to increase man-years of misery in India—and, then, turn around and avoid those ways. So think it backward as well as forward. It's a trick that works in algebra and it's a trick that works in life. If you don't, you'll never be a really good thinker.*[24]

Thus Buffett and Munger, two like-minded individuals who are inclined to agree on most things, overcome the potential that this has to damage their cognition by constantly trying to knock down their arguments, calling on the use of all of their mental models to do so. If the arguments still stand after they have been run through these—Buffett calls Munger "the abominable no-man"[25]—then they might, indeed, have some merit.

FEEDBACK

> *Part of what you must learn is how to handle mistakes and new facts that change the odds.*
>
> Charlie Munger[26]

The only way that Buffett can validate the decision rules originating within the Circle of Competence is to seek out, *and take*, feedback from them.

"Agonizing over errors is a mistake," says Buffett. "But," he adds "acknowledging them and analyzing them can be useful."[27] In keeping with this philosophy, Buffett conducts his post-decisional analysis, not on the ones he gets right (false positives will not provide him with the information he is looking for), but rather on the ones he gets wrong.

This is why Buffett is so ready to own up to his own mortality. He told his shareholders in 1986 in one of his regular confessionals:

> *As you can see, what I told you last year about our loss liabilities was far from true—and that makes three years in a row of error. If the physiological rules that applied to Pinocchio were to apply to me, my nose would now draw crowds.*[28]

Buffett keeps a starkly honest internal scorecard of his own performance, in which he leaves his psyche nowhere to hide. Crucially, he counts against him the mistakes that most of us allow ourselves to get away with—his mistakes of omission:

> *What's an error is when it's something we understand and we stand there and stare at it and we don't do anything. Conventional accounting, of course, does not pick those up at all. But they're in our scorebook.*[29]

And he considers the way in which his score is put together—flukes do not count.

In settings in which feedback on decisions is unambiguous and timely, such as in meteorology and games of bridge, practitioners have been found to develop a very good sense of their ability to judge relative to those who make decisions in settings in which feedback does not possess these characteristics.[30] Buffett—who, not without coincidence, is an excellent bridge player—wants to calibrate his judgmental accuracy in the same way.

He wants to reduce the number of errors he makes. But, more importantly, *he wants to be able to produce a forecast range in which he can be relatively certain that the outcome will lie.* This is the essence of properly calibrated confidence. It illuminates why Buffett tells his shareholders:

> *I want to be able to explain my mistakes... If we are going to lose your money, we want to be able to get up there next year and explain how we did it.*[31]

It also explains why Buffett reduces the ambiguity that can be contained in post-decisional feedback by being so honest with himself.

Having established the truths of his Circle of Competence, acquired the habit of inverting his arguments, and sought out feedback on the quality of the decision rules he is using, Buffett's task in using this model in his management of Berkshire's capital is to find value. The necessary tool that allows him to do this is, naturally, another incontrovertible truth: the equation for value.

THE EQUATION FOR VALUE

> *The value of any stock, bond or business today is determined by the cash inflows and outflows—discounted at an appropriate interest rate—that can be estimated to occur during the remaining life of the asset.*
>
> *Warren Buffett*[32]

> *We just read the newspapers, think about a few of the big propositions, and go by our own sense of probabilities.*
>
> *Warren Buffett*[33]

Buffett tells us that the equation for value—described in the first quotation above—was set down nearly 70 years ago by John Burr Williams.[34] With some manipulation of the terms used, Buffett deploys this equation in every sphere of his capital allocation at Berkshire:

It applies to outlays for farms, oil royalties, bonds, stocks, lottery tickets, and manufacturing plants. And neither the advent of the steam engine, the harnessing of electricity nor the creation of the automobile [will change] the formula one iota—nor will the Internet. Just insert the correct numbers, and you can rank the attractiveness of all possible uses of capital throughout the universe.[35]

There are two elements to this catch-all equation: (1) the forecast of future cash flows, and (2) the certainty attached to the production of that forecast cash flow, with the latter determining the rate at which the cash flows are discounted to present value. The greater the risk in an enterprise (for instance), the higher the discount rate that should be used in the equation, and the lower the value of the business for any given production of cash. You do not know a business if you cannot make judgments with respect to (1) and (2). Those that Buffett feels capable of judging define his Circle of Competence.

The risk facing any investor, says Buffett, is that the return on an investment does not protect his or her purchasing power against inflation, plus an opportunity cost that can be measured by the return the investor could have earned elsewhere. The same risk faces any allocator of capital and although, according to Buffett, this cannot be calculated "with engineering precision, it can in some cases be judged with a degree of accuracy that is useful."[36]

Stable frequencies and the accuracy of cognition

With one very important exception, which I will delineate in Chapter 9, in pursuing this degree of accuracy Buffett is inexorably drawn to quantifiable, knowable *ranges* of odds, of the type that manifest themselves in the property casualty insurance industry in which he feels so comfortable setting prices. The universe of the important and the knowable cannot be that unless Buffett can specify the probabilities contained within it. What he looks for are stable frequencies.

A useful analogy in this regard is a game of poker.[37] This is a complex process containing a range of possible outcomes, just like the operation of any business. In any particular hand, the probability of a particular combination of cards being a winning hand can only be imprecisely *estimated*. Yet at the same time, if thousands of hands are dealt, these "hidden" odds—the game's stable frequencies—reveal themselves. They are knowable quantities.[38]

The way Buffett sees it, the same is true for companies that are impervious to material change. In those that make essentially the same pitch over and over again, stable frequencies will manifest themselves out of the complexity of the economy within which they operate. Not fixed odds, but a knowable range. Not an immutable range either, but a range in which change can be forecast.

From Buffett's quoted investments, for instance, Coca-Cola and Gillette offer among the world's best-known, market-dominant brands to people who wake up thirsty every morning and/or who need a shave. They place their affordable, easy-to-distribute products within arm's reach of desire, and back this up with constant psychological reinforcement and conditioning through their advertising. Effectively, they play games where draws are always made from the same pack, where the rules remain unchanged, and where the chain of events is kept to a minimum. This allows Buffett to prune the decision tree of his forecast and attach odds that can be calculated with a meaningful degree of certainty.

Businesses such as these could more properly be described as a continuum rather than a branching tree. Buffett himself describes them as *The Inevitables*.[39] He says:

> *Forecasters may differ a bit in their predictions of exactly how much soft drink or shaving-equipment business these companies will be doing in ten or twenty years. Nor is our talk of inevitability meant to play down the vital work that these companies must continue to carry out, in such areas as manufacturing, distribution, packaging and product innovation. In the end, however, no sensible observer... questions that Coke and Gillette will dominate their fields worldwide for an investment lifetime.*[40]

Buffett's other, wholly owned franchises present essentially the same fundamentals, albeit in weaker form. There are only a few companies in the world that Buffett feels comfortable describing as Inevitables.

"To the Inevitables in our portfolio, therefore," he says, "we add a few *Highly Probables*," by implication adjusting for the reduced certainty he has in forecasting the timing and quantity of their cash flows and judging the risk attached to these.

"Experience... indicates," he adds, "that the best business returns are usually achieved by companies that are doing something quite similar today to what they were doing five or ten years ago."[41] In their own way, the Highly Probables—NFM, GEICO, Borsheim's, Executive Jet, *et al.*—occupy the continuum that Buffett is looking for. "With the businesses *we* think about, I think that the moats that I see now seem as sustainable to me as the moats that I saw 30 years ago," he says.[42] Shielded from major change, drawing from the same deck sequentially through time, they throw off the knowable statistics that allow for the proper estimation of the important in the value equation. Their *business economics* do not present such a robust defense against reversion to the mean, but their *human proposition* does.

This is the objectivity that Buffett is seeking: business processes that generate statistical backgrounds allowing him to bring calibrated confidence to bear, to produce forecasts that *can* be made; a *range* of these that *can* be specified, containing risks that *can* be assessed. Thereafter, incorporating the yield on 10-year bonds (normalized for the business cycle), he discounts the weighted average of these forecasts back to a net present value. Then he waits.

THE FAT PITCH

We try to exert a Ted Williams kind of discipline. In his book The Science of Hitting, *Ted explains that he carved the strike zone into 77 cells, each the size of a baseball. Swinging only at balls in his "best" cell, he knew, would allow him to bat .400; reaching for balls in his "worst" spot, the low outside corner of the strike zone, would reduce him to .230. In other words, waiting for the fat pitch would mean a trip to the Hall of Fame; swinging indiscriminately would mean a ticket to the minors.*

Warren Buffett[43]

Be aware that Buffett runs the equation for value in his head. Charlie Munger says that he's never actually seen Buffett perform a discounted valuation calculation. *In essence, that's how intelligible it should be.*

Buffett has an Excel spreadsheet in his brain, which helps, but there should be so few variables in his equation and so little ambiguity that the math is simple.[44] He is not looking for absolute precision. "It is better to be approximately right than precisely wrong," he maintains.[45] He has not reduced this to a numerical science. "Read Ben Graham and Phil Fisher, read annual reports and trade reports, but don't do equations with Greek letters in them," he says.[46] It's more a question of *knowing* the range of possible outcomes. When this is the case, the rest follows.

To Buffett, allocating capital to positive-net-present-value ventures in the strike zone is routine. Says Munger:

> I've heard Warren say since very early in his life that the difference between a good business and a bad one is that a good business throws up one easy decision after another, whereas a bad one gives you horrible choices—decisions that are extremely hard to make. For example, it's not hard for us to decide whether or not we want to open a See's store in a new shopping center in California. It's going to succeed.[47]

Indeed, Buffett says that economic goodwill at See's "has grown, in an irregular but very substantial manner, for 78 years. And, if we run the business right, growth of that kind will probably continue for at least another 78 years."[48]

Similarly, at GEICO, Buffett is content to let CEO Tony Nicely expand as he wishes, professing "there is no limit to what Berkshire is willing to invest in GEICO's new-business activity."[49] The economics of this business are such the cost/value relationship of investing in it sits comfortably in the realm of Figure 2 where Buffett wants to allocate capital. Opportunities to do so are pitches at which Buffett is happy to let his operating managers swing.

However, as important as reinvesting in existing businesses is, the capital management decisions that have really counted at Berkshire

Hathaway—the big ideas—have been far less routine. Buffett and Munger recognize that in those capital allocations of sufficient moment to shape the fortunes of an entire corporation, it is much too difficult to gain an edge by making hundreds of smarter-than-the-next-guy decisions. There just aren't that many large-scale opportunities of value for which Buffett believes it is also possible to make a reliable judgment *in respect of value*. Comments Munger:

> *It's not given to human beings to have such talent that they can just know everything about everything all the time. But it is given to human beings who work hard at it—who look and sift the world for a mispriced bet—that they can* occasionally *find one.*[50]

"Therefore," Buffett tells his shareholders, "we adopted a strategy that required our being smart—and not too smart at that—only a very few times."[51]

Buffett and Munger differ on how many occasions they have been smart in their joint career—Buffett estimates around 25; Munger closer to 15—but, without being so, Berkshire's performance would have been merely ordinary.[52] Big ideas, such as the initial purchase of See's and GEICO, are the fat pitches of Figure 2 that Buffett waits for. They should be so obviously in the strike zone that they are "no-brainers."

"You know when you've got a big idea," says Buffett. Fifty years ago, for instance, when he scanned Moody's looking for cigar butts, the no-brainers would jump off the pages at him. When value was defined in relation to tangible assets, the tangibility that Buffett looks for was a given. "I've got half a dozen xeroxes from those reports... that I keep just because it was so *obvious* that they were *incredible*," he says.[53] Although Buffett has displaced the cigar butt equation with the more complex equation for value, his Circle of Competence still allows him to identify the pitch that he can hit to the bleachers.

Buffett knows that these pitches will be thrown every now and then. When they are, he enjoys a considerable advantage over base-ball players like Ted Williams. "Unlike Ted," observes Buffett, "we can't be called out if we resist three pitches that are barely in the strike zone."[54]

Buffett has no compulsion to act. "But," he adds, "if we let all of today's balls go by, there can be no assurance that the next ones we see will be more to our liking."[55] Equally, although Buffett is confident that, if he and Charlie were to deal with the evaluation of numerous fat pitches in a short space of time, their judgment would prove to be reasonably satisfactory, he also observes:

> *We do not get the chance to make 50 or even 5 such decisions in a single year. Even though our long-term results may turn out fine, in any given year we run a risk that we will look extraordinarily foolish.*[56]

Herein lies the rub. The philosophy underpinning Buffett's capital management, he says, "frequently leads us to unconventional behavior both in investments and general business management."[57]

Buffett's willingness to reject any opportunity when the equation for value does not add up can lead to long periods of torpor. His countervailing eagerness to bet when he knows the odds are with him, quite possibly in enormous size, also induces volatility in Berkshire's results. In the short term, whether he's passing up obvious home runs in, say, technology stocks or striking out in General Re, Buffett can quite easily *look* misguided.

At the same time, he is under no illusions as to the consequences of failing to spot, and connect with, the fat pitch: "If Charlie and I were to draw blanks for a few years in our capital-allocation endeavors, Berkshire's rate of growth would slow significantly," he notes.[58] The pressure for more normal capital management (don't just stand there, do something) means that Buffett can be called out by his shareholders if he simply shoulders his bat.

In the face of this intense pressure, he shrewdly observes:

> *Failing conventionally is the route to go. As a group, lemmings may have a rotten image, but no individual lemming has ever received a bad press.*[59]

The condemnation that Buffett's unconventional behavior invites, should it fail to produce the results expected to go with it, is suggestive of adverse imaginable outcomes. And this engenders a problem in terms of the accuracy of Buffett's cognition and his objectivity.

When imaginable outcomes evoke strong emotions, human judgment normally becomes extremely *insensitive* to differences in probabilities.[60] Buffett professes: "Charlie and I... like any proposition that makes compelling mathematical sense," and he has premised his capital management on an ability to embrace *any* such proposition.[61] If he were unable to cope with the emotional consequences of this approach and lose sight of the probabilities on which his analysis is based, the consequences would be disastrous.

MAINTAINING EMOTIONAL BALANCE IN THE STRIKE ZONE

[The] capacity to be made uncomfortable by the mere prospect of traumatic experiences, in advance of their actual occurrence, and to be motivated thereby to take realistic precautions against them, is unquestionably a tremendously important and useful psychological mechanism, and... probably accounts for many of man's unique accomplishments. But it also accounts for some of his most conspicuous failures.

Joseph LeDoux[62]

I do only the things I understand.

Warren Buffett[63]

Experiments revealing the effect of strong emotions on decision making feature subjects who are given painful electric shocks of varying intensity, but with known probability.[64] In the countdown period up to its delivery, their physiological responses to the impending shock (the chemistry of their emotions) is measured, and it is found that their emotional responses are correlated with their expectations about the *intensity* of the shock, not the *probability* of receiving it.

The reason for this is that we cannot weigh decisions without emotions. For much of the twentieth century the field of psychology denied this. It was dominated by the notion that "cold" cognition and emotion existed in isolation from each other and it was held that where the two did meet, emotions represented "an interruption to an otherwise logical (and preferred) mode of being."[65]

Hitherto, it has been maintained that the objectivity that Warren Buffett brings to bear in his decision making can be explained by his ability to extract the emotion from the exercise. This cannot be true. In and of itself, pure cognition is incapable of triggering action. After analysis, we only proceed to action in the light of the affective, or emotional, responses that analysis elicits. We make decisions because their likely outcomes are perceived as good, bad, safe, risky-but-worth-it, smart, dumb-but-what-the-hell, because they *feel* right or wrong, and so on.[66]

These are the emotional markers that accompany every decision, the mobilization of a motivational state that precedes action. The capacities to plan cognitively, evaluate the merits and consequences of a decision, and construct imaginable outcomes are inseparable. People in whom the ability to generate anticipatory emotions has become impaired tend to be very poor at making forward-looking decisions. Frontal lobotomy patients, for example, who are unable to evoke emotional responses to unseen but imagined events, become confined to the present, are highly impulsive, and take unjustified risks. In games where they are faced with a choice of drawing cards from a high-risk deck that pays out handsomely but only sparingly, or a low-risk deck that pays out less but more frequently, they normally lose all their money very quickly. In spite of a strong desire to win and a thorough understanding of the game, they are incapable of experiencing the anxiety that should normally accompany risk taking. Thus, they consider the risky draws to be less risky than they are.[67]

If accurate judgments are to be made in the face of uncertainty, therefore, emotions cannot be removed from the process. However, in order to remain sensitive to the probability distributions contained in uncertainty and assess them reasonably, emotions do have to be kept in balance. Says Buffett:

Plenty of people have higher IQs, and plenty of people work more hours, but I am rational about things. But you have to be able to control yourself; you can't let your emotions get in the way of your mind.[68]

Buffett's Circle of Competence delivers a large part of his emotional balance. Within it he *knows* the knowable. In here, he is in control of the capital allocation process. More importantly in his Circle of Competence, he *feels* in control and, emotionally, this is very valuable. "Imagine the cost to us..." he tells his shareholders, "if we had let a fear of unknowns cause us to defer or alter the deployment of capital."

In order to be doubly sure that he retains this feeling of security, Buffett has also prepared the ground ahead of time. He perceives all of the imaginable outcomes of his unconventional behavior as benign: He has shareholders who are also his partners; he incorporates a margin of safety into every decision he takes; and, although Berkshire Hathaway does employ some debt on its balance sheet, from the point of view of this affecting Buffett's willingness to be aggressive in his capital management, Berkshire is essentially debt free. It's time to move on to Figure 3.

SHAREHOLDER-PARTNERS

Eysenck proposed that highly anxious people attend preferentially to threat-related stimuli and interpret ambiguous stimuli and situations as threatening.

George F. Lowenstein[69]

I really like my life. I arranged my life and so that I can do what I want... I tap dance to work, and when I get there, I think I'm supposed to lie on my back and paint the ceiling.

Warren Buffett[70]

When Buffett set up his Partnership in 1956 he told those who backed him: "All I want to do is hand in a scorecard when I come off the golf course. I don't want you following me around and watching me shank a three-iron on this hole and leave a putt short on the next."[71] That's

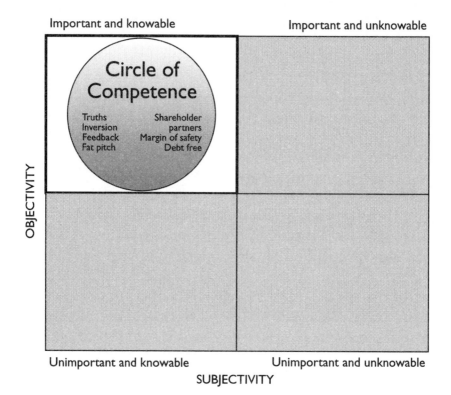

Figure 3 Maintaining emotional balance in the strike zone

essentially the way in which he runs Berkshire Hathaway. *Buffett wants to be the one who analyzes and puts right his mistakes, not his shareholders. For when people make decisions looking over their shoulders they become anxious and, in that state, are prone to concentrate more on the possible than the probable. In doing this, they tend to make decisions that can be most easily defended after the fact rather than those that are the most appropriate.*[72] This means that they gravitate toward the conventional. But the conventional is average and Warren Buffett does not want to be average.

In managing Berkshire, Buffett treats even the smallest of its shareholders as equal owners in the enterprise. Therefore, if he is to feel comfortable in being unconventional, he has to have their mandate to do the unconventional. Crucially, and not without a design that will be delineated in the next chapter, Buffett is able to attest that "Berkshire probably ranks number one among large American corporations in the percentage of its shares held by owners with a long-term view."[73] These people understand Berkshire's operations, approve of the policies of its chairman, share his expectations, and allow him to focus on the logical rather than the defensible.

"We are under no pressure to do anything dumb," says Buffett. "If we do dumb things, it's because we do dumb things. But it's not because anybody's making us do it."[74]

MARGIN OF SAFETY

Confronted with a challenge to distill the secret of sound investment into three words, we venture the motto Margin of Safety.
                                                            Benjamin Graham[75]

I still think those are the right three words.
                                                            Warren Buffett[76]

In the wake of the General Re acquisition, his biggest mistake to date comprising the largest and most unexpected loss in the history of the insurance industry, Buffett was still able to state: "We are as strong as any insurer in the world and our losses from the attack, though punishing to current earnings, are not significant in relation to Berkshire's intrinsic business value."[77]

By waiting for the premium over the intrinsic value of Berkshire's stock price to expand in relation to the discount on General Re's price, Buffett built a cushion into its purchase. He also maintained a cushion against adversity by adhering to underwriting standards in Berkshire Hathaway's insurance businesses that guarantee its financial security in the face of occasional, exceptionally large losses.

"We had a margin of safety and it turned out we needed it," Buffett told his shareholders in the wake of September 11. And he employs a margin of safety in every decision he makes, not just in the underwriting of risk or the subdivision of capital management that is investing, Graham's preoccupation. Nor is Buffett's current margin of safety principle the same as the one he used when he traded in cigar butts. The protection Buffett looks for between the price he can pay for a stock and its value *used* to reside in the discount it sold at in relation to the value of the assets on its balance sheet. Now that he buys and invests only in going concerns, this principle has morphed into an *objective assessment of intrinsic value.* That is, Buffett's margin of safety is *built into* his equation for value—into his forecasts and their range—not brought into it after the fact. This explains why he is able to use the risk-free rate on long bonds as his discount rate.[78] He doesn't have to beef this up to incorporate risk, and this is an essential element of identifying the fat pitch.

Crucially, Buffett would not be able to calibrate his margin of safety if he allocated capital to enterprises that are subject to major variance. The introduction of change into the calculation would be analogous to the addition of new cards to the pack in a game of poker. If this were to happen, the previously identifiable probability distribution of possible outcomes on which Buffett relies would vanish—only to become apparent once more if we started the iteration process all over again. *However, if sufficient new cards were added to the pack on a regular enough basis, the system would never settle down into one that would lend itself to forecasting in the way Buffett understands the term.*

DEBT FREE

We will reject interesting opportunities rather than over-leverage our balance sheet. This conservatism has penalized our results but it is the only behavior that leaves us comfortable, considering our fiduciary obligations to policyholders, depositors, lenders and the many equity holders who have committed unusually large portions of their net worth to our care.

Warren Buffett[79]

Stress makes people suggestible.

Charlie Munger[80]

In conjunction with his margin of safety principle, Buffett also protects himself from anxiety by employing very little debt in his company. "You ought to conduct your affairs so that if the most extraordinary events happen, you're still around to play the next day," he says,[81] and the concentration of his capital management into 15 to 25 big ideas precludes taking on the type of interest payments that most companies would consider appropriate. Many companies that take on debt that does not fit with their risk profile fail to show up for the next day's game, not because their fundamental proposition is flawed, but because temporary cash flow problems cause them to default.

Accordingly, Buffett says:

We do not wish it to be only likely that we can meet our obligations; we wish that to be certain. Thus we adhere to policies—both in regard to debt and all other matters—that will allow us to achieve acceptable long-term results under extraordinarily adverse conditions, rather than optimal results under a normal range of conditions.[82]

This "restriction" has impeded Berkshire's returns. Buffett told his shareholders in 1989:

In retrospect, it is clear that significantly higher, though still conventional, leverage ratios at Berkshire would have produced considerably better returns on equity than the 23.8% we have actually averaged. Even in 1965, perhaps we could have judged there to be a 99% probability that higher leverage would lead to nothing but good. Correspondingly, we might have seen only a 1% chance that some shock factor, external or internal, would cause a conventional debt ratio to produce a result falling somewhere between temporary anguish and default.[83]

However, in Buffett's view he has made no mistake: "We wouldn't have liked those 99:1 odds—and never will."[84]

By chasing the additional return that extra leverage would afford, Buffett would also have had to take on what he describes as "a small chance of distress or disgrace."[85] *By ensuring that he is free of this particular imaginable outcome, he grants himself the emotional security to consider swinging at fat pitches without fearing the consequence that he might mis-specify one or two of them as such.*

ENLIGHTENED CAPITAL MANAGEMENT

If options aren't a form of compensation, what are they? If compensation isn't an expense, what is it? And, if expenses shouldn't go into the calculation of earnings, where in the world should they go?

Warren Buffett[86]

References to EBITDA make us shudder—does management think the tooth fairy pays for capital expenditures?

Warren Buffett[87]

During the Enlightenment in the eighteenth century, a representation of the universe manifested itself that made sense of cause and effect for the first time in human history. It was a short step from there to the derivation of the forecasting techniques that would allow the calibration of risk and return and facilitate the advent of modern capitalism.[88] The "light" in Enlightenment was switched on when intellectuals were able to utilize newly discovered laws of nature to create a simulation of the system in their heads, which was capable of explaining the mechanism that underpinned observable outcomes.

Warren Buffett's Circle of Competence is such a system. The accuracy of his cognition has been similarly enhanced and his capital management enlightened.

Stan Lipsey, Buffett's lieutenant at Buffalo Evening News, says that Buffett "can take a complex system and make it simple. I have sent a number of people who have business problems to Warren. They've traveled to Omaha; they've come back, and said, *He just made it so simple.*"[89]

Buffett's Circle of Competence explains why. He has turned down the noise. He concentrates on the important and knowable. *He knows these*. Cause and effect are lit bright for him, infused with insights into human behavior that were not available to Renaissance man.

It is this state of enlightenment that grants Buffett—"the sage"—his unerring ability to puncture reality and dispel accepted wisdom on options and EBITDA, for example. It is this enlightenment that has allowed him to translate his Circle of Competence into the decision rules enabling him to act like an owner. In Part III of this book, we will delineate these and make them available to any CEO who would seek to emulate Buffett.

Part III

To Act Like an Owner

8

The User's Manual

Understanding intrinsic value is as important for managers as it is for investors. When managers are making capital allocation decisions... it's vital that they act in ways that increase per-share intrinsic value and avoid moves that decrease it. This principle may seem obvious but we constantly see it violated. And, when misallocations occur, shareholders are hurt.

Warren Buffett[1]

I have been asked by a number of people just what secrets the Blumkins bring to their business. These are not very esoteric. All members of the family: (1) apply themselves with an enthusiasm and energy that would make Ben Franklin and Horatio Alger look like dropouts; (2) define with extraordinary realism their area of special competence and act decisively on all matters within it; (3) ignore even the most enticing propositions failing outside of that area of special competence; and, (4) unfailingly behave in a high-grade manner with everyone they deal with.

Warren Buffett[2]

As a manager, the twin dividend that Warren Buffett receives from staying within his Circle of Competence is derived from the wisdom of his capital allocation and the bond of trust that this has cultured between himself and his shareholders. In turn, this bestows discretion on Buffett in his management of their capital.

It is important that this is so. A company becomes the embodiment of its capital allocation decisions. In both psychological and economic terms, once these decisions have been made they can be difficult and costly to undo—and they can have an untoward bearing on the nature of future capital management. In a world in which he does not know when, where, or how opportunity will present itself, except that it *will*, Warren Buffett allocates capital where *he* sees fit, when *he* sees fit, and at the pace *he* sees fit.

He does this in a pragmatic style dictated by the precepts of price versus value, rather than according to a grand plan. Buffett has yielded to the marketplace when he has had to, withdrawn from the game when necessary, and ceded ground where conditions have dictated. Constrained only by the circumference of his circle, he has also leapt on opportunity and risk when these two have been offered in the right combination.

Tomorrow, he will do the same. In proportion to the scale and nature of the opportunities presenting themselves, Berkshire Hathaway will change shape once more, possibly to something resembling a prior manifestation or, since its future is not bound by legacy businesses, most likely into a novel form.

Berkshire Hathaway is thus a product of the irregular environment in which it operates, not an imposition of Warren Buffett's will upon it. In this way, Berkshire Hathaway's behavior, while highly unusual, is nevertheless evolutionarily sound. Crucially, as Buffett picks his way through this environment, *sans* strategy, he carries his shareholders with him—otherwise he would not be able to do so. He thinks like an owner. He acts like an owner. So do they.

"When proper temperament joins with proper intellectual framework," says Buffett, "then you get rational behavior."[3]

THE PROPER INTELLECTUAL FRAMEWORK

We've been deploying capital since I was 11. That's our business.
                                                            Warren Buffett[4]

We didn't give up on the beaches of Dunkirk, and we are not going to give up now.
                          Anonymous, non-executive director of Marconi[5]

Warren Buffett tells his shareholders that one of management's favorite rationalizations for issuing stock in a takeover is "We have to grow."[6] But, he asks:

Who... is the "we"? For present shareholders, the reality is that all existing businesses shrink when shares are issued. Were Berkshire to issue shares tomorrow for an acquisition, Berkshire would own everything that it owns now plus the new business, but your interest in such hard-to-match businesses as See's Candy Shops, National Indemnity, etc. would be automatically reduced.[7]

The only thing that grows assuredly in this context is managerial domain. In order to emulate Warren Buffett, therefore, the first thing a CEO must do is adopt the right mindset. They may have come up through the ranks as an operational manager, but if their predisposition as a chief executive is to *manage*, the institutional imperative will color any "rational" debate about the conduct of the firm.

For example, one aspect of the institutional imperative not covered thus far is the common finding in studies of group decision making that—"as if governed by Newton's First Law of Motion," Buffett reminds us—the process of deliberation serves only to polarize the opinions of the group further in the direction of their pre-deliberation bias.

In one such study, Schkade *et al.* first asked individuals to reach a judgment on a number of legal cases. Subsequently, they aggregated the same individuals into juries so that they might further deliberate the cases and discovered that, after deliberation, the dollar verdict of the jury was typically higher, often far higher, than the median judgment of the same jury as individual members.[8] The manifestation of this "severity shift," as Schkade and his colleagues call it, stems, they believe, from the existence of a systematic rhetorical advantage held by members of the group. In this case, it was the rhetorical advantage enjoyed by those members of society who argue for higher dollar awards.

Accordingly, all CEOs need to establish where the rhetorical advantage lies within the companies that they manage. At the UK telecommunications company Marconi, the rhetorical advantage lay in becoming a leading player in that industry, and it clung doggedly to a growth strategy that, like so many others in this industry, eventually brought the company to its knees. "Managers frequently have trouble putting themselves in the shoes of their shareholder-owners," observes Buffett.[9]

It is clear at Berkshire Hathaway that Buffett's predisposition is not to pursue a pre-ordained strategy, but to allocate capital. *In order to act like an owner, first you must think like an owner.* And Buffett explicitly embeds this rhetorical advantage into the deliberation process that precedes his capital management. The intellectual framework to which he adheres in this respect considers the following points in turn:

1 "Does it make more sense to pay [the capital] out to the share-holders than to keep it within the company?"
2 "If we pay it out, is it better off to do it via repurchases or dividend?"
3 "If you have the capital and you think that you can create more than a dollar, how do you create value with the least risk?"
4 "The cost of every deal that we do is measured by the second best deal that's around at a given time—including doing more of some of the things we're already in."[10]

Buffett's task in corporate governance is to calculate the current intrinsic value of the enterprise, which naturally includes the intrinsic value of current investable opportunities and an option value on opportunities not yet in view. The results of this calculation, which he compares to the value at which Berkshire trades in the marketplace, informs Buffett of the relative merit of capital retention versus payout.

If capital is retained, he thinks through the risk attached to the cash flows that it might produce. And he defines his cost of capital as an opportunity cost.

In other words, in managing the enterprise, Buffett defers to mental models contained in his Circle of Competence. The lesson for any who would seek to emulate Buffett's capital management is to do the same.

Establish a Circle of Competence. This is exactly what Buffett looks for in *his* managers, such as the Blumkins whom he refers to at the head of this chapter. It's exactly what any CEO should do.

Your Circle of Competence should contain some of the essential elements of Buffett's: truths, the equation for value, the patience to wait for value, and an intimate knowledge of how your cognitive apparatus functions. It should be infused with and surrounded by an array of mental models. And it should play its part in delivering emotional balance.

Assuredly, each CEO's Circle of Competence will be materially different from Buffett's in terms of what is considered important and knowable. "I'm sure Bill Gates would apply the same principles," says Buffett. "He understands technology the way I understand Coca-Cola or Gillette."[11]

All capital management should take place within the circle. Practitioners should have a sense of when they are operating comfortably within it. And CEOs have to know enough about its construction to realize when they are approaching its perimeter.

Only in this way can CEOs put themselves in a position to decide the best use of their shareholders' capital. Once they think like an owner, they will be ready to act like an owner. In order to do this, Buffett's "proper intellectual framework" needs to be combined with his "proper temperament" or attitude.[12]

THE PROPER TEMPERAMENT

We do not want to maximize the price at which Berkshire shares trade. We wish instead for them to trade in a narrow range centered at intrinsic business value.

Warren Buffett[13]

For reasons that will become apparent later in this chapter, and even more so in the next, Buffett's overriding objective in his communications with his shareholders is to facilitate market efficiency in the pricing of Berkshire Hathaway's stock price—that is, to ensure, as far as he is able, that it bears a close relationship to its intrinsic value.

Buffett knows that "management cannot determine market prices." However, he recognizes that "it can, by its disclosures and policies, encourage rational behavior by market participants."[14] Therefore,

Buffett reports fully and fairly on Berkshire Hathaway's operating results and outlook. He says:

> When Charlie and I read [annual] reports, we have no interest in pictures of personnel, plants or products... We're very suspicious of accounting methodology that is vague or unclear, since too often that means management wishes to hide something. And we don't want to read messages that a public relations department or consultant has turned out. Instead, we expect a company's CEO to explain in his or her own words what's happening.[15]

He continues:

> What needs to be reported is data... that helps financially-literate readers answer three key questions: (1) Approximately how much is this company worth? (2) What is the likelihood that it can meet its future obligations? And (3) How good a job are its managers doing, given the hand they have been dealt?[16]

And he maintains:

> What Charlie and I would want under that circumstance would be all the important facts about current operations as well as the CEO's frank view of the long-term economic characteristics of the business. We would expect both a lot of financial details and a discussion of any significant data we would need to interpret what was presented.[17]

Consequently, Warren Buffett reduces the noise/signal ratio that Berkshire Hathaway emanates to the marketplace in which its stock price is set. Buffett presents the investment community with data that it requires to make an informed judgment with respect to value. *And he tells it like it is.*

"The primary test of managerial economic performance is the achievement of a high earnings rate on equity capital employed (without undue leverage, accounting gimmickry, etc.) and not the achievement of consistent gains in earnings per share," maintains Buffett.[18] Therefore, he provides Berkshire's shareholders with the information required for them to make a judgment in respect of whether he has passed this test and, more importantly, whether he is likely to pass it in the future. He observes:

> *In our view, many businesses would be better understood by their shareholder owners, as well as the general public, if managements and financial analysts modified the primary emphasis they place upon earnings per share, and upon yearly changes in that figure.*[119]

Buffett does not seek to dress up Berkshire's results for public consumption. "Many managements view GAAP not as a standard to be met, but as an obstacle to overcome," he says,[20] and he professes that "accounting consequences do not influence our operating or capital-allocation decisions."[21]

As a corollary, Buffett also tells his managers that "they should not let any of their decisions be affected even slightly by accounting considerations. We want our managers to think about what counts, not how it will be counted."[22]

Buffett conditions his shareholders not to extrapolate current results when these are unsustainably positive. Instead, he encourages them to expect a reversion to what he considers to be Berkshire's mean. "We may have years when we exceed 15%," he tells them, "but we will most certainly have other years when we fall far short of that— including years showing negative returns—and those will bring our average down."[23]

He also facilitates their ability to imagine the *challenges* contained in compound growth. He told them in 1998:

> *Charlie and I will do our best to increase intrinsic value in the future at an average rate of 15%, a result we consider to be at the very peak of possible outcomes. In the meantime, you should understand just what an average gain of 15% over the next five years implies: It means we will need to increase net worth by $58 billion.*[24]

Conversely, Buffett is also at pains to ensure that Berkshire's share-holders are capable of imagining the *benefits* of compound growth. In Chapter 1 I attempted to overcome the difficulty that many of us have in conceptualizing the power of compound growth—we become anchored in the early part of the calculation where the numbers are small—by conjuring up an image of my son as being taller than the Empire State Building.

Warren Buffett simply refuses to split his stock. And, since the pub-lication of the 2000 annual report, he has backed this up with a sum-mary measure of the growth in Berkshire's book value since 1964 versus the rise in the market value of the S&P 500, with dividends reinvested, over the same period. "As the table on the facing page shows," Buffett tells his shareholders, "a small annual advantage in our favor can, if sustained, produce an anything-but-small long-term advantage."[25] The latest reading from that table in Buffett's 2001 letter is 194,936% versus 4,742%, respectively.[26]

Buffett shares his latest thinking on what can be achieved at Berkshire with the cards that are dealt him, including revisions to long-held targets:

> *I think the probability of us achieving 15% growth in earnings over an extended period of years is so close to zero that it's not worth considering. The businesses we have are good businesses in the aggregate. They will do well. But they won't do anything like 15% growth per annum. So we will take a good rate of progress from those businesses and we'll superimpose acquisitions upon that which will add to that. But we can't do 15% over time.*[27]

Last, in telling it like it is, Buffett rarely talks about Berkshire Hathaway's stock price. In fact, he restricts his comments in this regard to the few occasions when price and intrinsic value per share have parted company by a degree exceeding his margin of safety. Buffett wants his shareholders to think about the fundamentals of intrinsic value, not to become fixated by the machinations of a stock price, the short-term prediction of which Buffett believes is impossi-ble, distracting, and dangerous. He says:

*Charlie and I hope that you do not think of yourself as merely own-
ing a piece of paper whose price wiggles around daily and is a candidate for sale when some economic or political event makes you
nervous. We hope that you instead visualize yourself as part owner
of a business that you expect to stay with indefinitely, much as you
might if you owned a farm or apartment house in partnership with
members of your family.*[28]

Buffett's communication with the investment community is not conducted through an investor relations department. Except for once a
year, he does not meet with investors. He does not talk with analysts.
He does not hold conference calls with either party. The few sell-side
analysts that do research his stock receive no help or guidance from
him, his quarterly reports to shareholders are brief and, apart from
the occasional letter in the interim, he rarely makes a public comment on Berkshire's operations. However, purely by dint of honesty,
transparency, and consistency, Buffett achieves his objective. "Over
the long term," he says, "there has been a more consistent relationship between Berkshire's market value and business value than has
existed for any other publicly-traded equity with which I am
familiar."[29]

Achieving this objective is not the obsession of an unusual man. He
comments:

*If the holders of a company's stock and/or the prospective buyers
attracted to it are prone to make irrational or emotion-based decisions, some pretty silly stock prices are going to appear periodically.
Manic-depressive personalities produce manic-depressive valuations. Such aberrations may help us in buying and selling the
stocks of other companies.* But we think it is in both your interest
and ours to minimize their occurrence in the market for
Berkshire *[emphasis added].*[30]

The interest that it serves to have Berkshire Hathaway's stock efficiently priced stems from the following:

○ "We receive our rewards as owners, not managers," Buffett tells his shareholders.[31]

○ It creates a fair market for Berkshire's stock, which is vital for the relationship he wishes to conduct with his shareholders.

○ It obviates the effect that mispricing a company's stock can have on the conduct of its managers.

We will expand on the first two of these points below, leaving a more lengthy discussion of the final point to the following chapter.

REWARD THE RIGHT BEHAVIOR

Charlie and I don't consider ourselves to be richer or poorer based on what the stock does. We do feel richer or poorer based on what the business does. We look at the business as to how much we're worth, not the stock price—because the stock price doesn't mean a thing to us.

Warren Buffett[32]

What could be more exhilarating than to participate in a bull market in which the rewards to owners of businesses become gloriously uncoupled from the plodding performances of the businesses themselves.

Warren Buffett[33]

When Warren Buffett says that he and Charlie Munger receive their rewards as owners, rather than as managers, he does not mean that a greater part of their wealth is realized through the ownership of Berkshire Hathaway's stock.[34] *He means that they receive their rewards from the growth in Berkshire's intrinsic value*, which, by arrangement, is closely mirrored by the performance of its stock.

Given the presence of the institutional imperative, Buffett recognizes that the alignment of the interests of managers and shareholders is a must. For him, the source of this alignment comes from within. Acting like an owner sits at the core of Buffett's being and his financial reward for doing so, based overwhelmingly on his ownership of Berkshire stock, serves only as a bonus. However, being a keen student of human nature, Buffett's prescriptive advice to others would be that, if the remuneration package is wrong, the behavior it induces is also likely to be wrong.

For example, Buffett says:

> *It's been a huge advantage at GEICO to have a plan that's far more rational than the one that preceded it. And that advantage will do nothing but grow stronger over time. That's because compensation is our way of speaking to employees generally... It tells them what we think the rational measurement of productivity and performance in the business is. And over time, that gets absorbed by thousands and thousands of people. It's the best way of getting them to buy into our goals.*[35]

However, in assuming that the alignment of the interests of managers and shareholders can be achieved by tying managerial compensation to the company's stock price performance, we have forgotten to answer the question implicit in Warren Buffett's reward structure: Is a balance held between intrinsic and stock market value?

The Efficient Market Hypothesis says that there is, so the question has never been asked. Therefore, many managers "start with the assumption, all too common," says Buffett, "that their job at all times is to encourage the highest stock price possible."[36]

If the stock market is not *always* efficient, this assumption could not be further from the truth. Consequently, until and unless a company is efficiently valued on the stock market, the use of stock as reward in a compensation package must be put on hold. In the interim, companies should seek, as Buffett does, to reward the behavior that counts. This means basing compensation on intrinsic value and changes in that value.

A CEO's focus—put there by pay if it has to be that way—should be firmly on the business *and not its stock price*. "Charlie and I let our marketable equities tell us by their operating results—not by their daily, or even yearly, price quotations—whether our investments are successful," says Buffett.[37] The same rule should apply to a CEO's remuneration. Buffett notes:

> As Ben Graham said, "In the long run, the market is a weighing machine—in the short run, a voting machine." I have always found it easier to evaluate weights dictated by fundamentals than votes by psychology.[38]

For his part, Buffett finds it relatively easy to evaluate the weights dictated by fundamentals with regard to Berkshire Hathaway's intrinsic value, particularly the present value of its existing operations. The more challenging element in his equation is to work out what rate of return he will make with the capital as it comes in.[39] Since the average company is not as insulated against change as Berkshire Hathaway's, Buffett infers that these tasks are likely to be more difficult for the average remuneration committee, so the calculation of intrinsic value will not be easy and will lack the apparent precision that exists in a stock market value. "A business that constantly encounters major change also encounters many chances for major error," says Buffett.[40]

At each link in the chain of compound events that determine such a company's fortunes, there resides a probability of failure. The more links, the higher the probability of eventual disappointment. This need not cause any problems to the art of valuing or planning the business concerned, although it will surely reduce its intrinsic value, as long as the number of compound events and probabilities attached to each is knowable with some degree of certainty, or if a range can be specified with a degree of accuracy in the Buffett mold.

The greater the range of possible values for each variable, the wider the dispersion in the estimate of intrinsic value. *This is no problem; it is simply a reflection of reality.* The problems start when we deny this reality.

Buffett himself admits that "intrinsic value is necessarily an estimate." And he notes that he and Charlie might differ by 10% in their appraisals of Berkshire Hathaway's intrinsic value.[41] By implication, the task of the CEO and the board of directors in this regard is to calibrate their confidence, establish the range of intrinsic value, and remunerate based on changes to that (measured over a period of time that makes sense).

This is challenging. And it is not as convenient as using a price taken from the stock market. Nevertheless, "if you aren't certain that you understand and can value your business far better than Mr. Market, you don't belong in the game," says Buffett.[42]

Naturally, to do this you have to think like an investor—as long as that investor is Warren Buffett. The parenthetic payoff is one that Buffett already enjoys. He says:

> *Charlie and I see CEOs all the time who, in a sense, don't know how to think about the value of the business they're acquiring. Therefore, they go out and hire investment bankers.*[43]

Learning how to think about the equation for value will solve this problem and much more:

> *If you learn to think intelligently about how to invest successfully in businesses, you'll become a much better business manager than you will if you aren't good at understanding what's required for successful investment.*[44]

When and if intrinsic and stock market values are held in rough balance, remuneration committees might consider incentivizing managements with that other favorite alignment instrument, the stock option. Currently, where options are employed, Buffett advises that they should be structured carefully—"absent special factors they should have built into them a retained-earnings or carrying-cost factor"[45]— and priced realistically. He notes:

> *When managers are faced with offers for their companies, they unfailingly point out how unrealistic market prices can be as an index of real value. But why, then, should these same depressed prices be the valuations at which managers sell portions of their businesses to themselves?*[46]

While Buffett is not averse to his subsidiary managers owning Berkshire stock, he does not use options in his remuneration packages. When options are fed down the organization to people who do not have responsibility for overall corporate performance, they violate his incentivization principle of only rewarding results that are within a manager's bailiwick.

"It's silly to imagine someone here working very hard at some small job with our aggregate market value around $90bn thinking that their effort will move the stock," says Buffett. (It's also dangerous if that person decides to take a free ride on the back of everyone else's efforts.) But, he continues:

> *Their effort may well move the number of policyholders we gain— or the satisfaction of those policyholders. Therefore, if we can find ways to pay them based on that, we're far more in synch with what they can actually do. And they know it makes more sense.*[47]

More importantly, to Buffett's mind, options also fail the alignment test on a more serious basis. He explains:

> *Ironically, the rhetoric about options frequently describes them as desirable because they put managers and owners in the same financial boat. In reality, the boats are far different. No owner has ever escaped the burden of capital costs, whereas a holder of a fixed-price option bears no capital costs at all. An owner must weigh upside potential against downside risk; an option holder has no downside.*[48]

This characteristic of options can be particularly dangerous in the management of capital, further discussion of which is more appropriate to the following chapter.

SET ACHIEVABLE TARGETS

For a major corporation to predict that its per-share earnings will grow over the long term at, say, 15% annually is to court trouble.

That's true because a growth rate of that magnitude can only be maintained by a very small percentage of large businesses.

Warren Buffett[49]

While investors and managers must place their feet in the future, their memories and nervous systems often remain plugged into the past.

Warren Buffett[50]

Warren Buffett has allowed his Circle of Competence to determine the composure of Berkshire Hathaway's business mix. His cornerstone insurance businesses grant him access to low-cost float and, "in a way that industries such as printing or steel cannot," he can if he wishes operate these "at quarter-speed much of the time and still enjoy long-term prosperity."[51] By incorporating this fundamental into his management of Berkshire's capital, Buffett has been able to compound its intrinsic value at a rate approximating 26% per annum.

Yet until very recently, for the duration of this achievement, Buffett's long-term target rate of return for Berkshire has been "just" 15% per annum. And as Berkshire has grown in size, Buffett has become increasingly vocal about the appropriate expectation of what he can deliver.

Buffett set himself this target in light of the fact that the long-term average return on equity in the US is around 12%. This is the stable frequency, the truth. It is what is produced in a dynamic, free-market economy in which below-average returns get "fixed"—either by incumbents who fear for their jobs, in the market for corporate control, or via bankruptcy—and in which above-average returns face remorseless attack.

It follows that the long-term return from equities is around the same. Over a long enough period of time, the return an investor can earn from an equity should equate to the return that a manager can earn on it—another truth. "If the business earns 6% on capital over 40 years and you hold it for 40 years, you're not going to make much different return than a 6% return—even if you originally buy it at a huge discount," says Munger, echoing Buffett's point in Chapter 1.[52] So Buffett's 15% goal was not one that was picked out of thin air.

Buffett acknowledges that, in order to provide a service to those who save with him, he has to beat the average return that they can earn from investing in a basket of other companies:

Meeting with my seven founding limited partners [on May 5, 1956], I gave them a short paper titled "The Ground Rules" that included this sentence: "Whether we do a good job or a poor job is to be measured against the general experience in securities."[53]

Nothing has changed since and, with Berkshire's fundamentals and his Circle of Competence, Buffett figures that he should be able to allocate capital more efficiently than the average CEO. Hence the long-held 15% and the current revisions to that number. This is what Buffett considers to be realistically achievable over the long term and he is at pains to remind his shareholders that, in spite of his track record to date, a growth rate in excess of 15% per annum over the long term is unattainable and should not be aimed for. Anyone who believes otherwise "should pursue a career in sales, but avoid one in mathematics," advises Buffett.[54] For example, he says:

Examine the record of, say, the 200 highest earning companies from 1970 or 1980 and tabulate how many have increased per-share earnings by 15% annually since those dates. You will find that only a handful have. I would wager you a very significant sum that fewer than 10 of the 200 most profitable companies in 2000 will attain 15% annual growth in earnings-per-share over the next 20 years.[55]

EMBRACE VOLATILITY

Charlie and I have always preferred a lumpy 15% return to a smooth 12% return.

Warren Buffett[56]

Buffett suggests that a manager's capital allocation record should be judged over a period of five years, at a minimum. Equally, he would never entertain the idea of committing to an *annual* value creation target. He recognizes that the fermentation process that is a business cannot be controlled to the nth degree. The stream of cash that it produces is naturally irregular. It has to be because it is reacting with, and to, a world that is naturally complex and inherently unpredictable. Buffett has amassed his results by waiting for opportunities to pop up into his strike zone.

Rather than settling for those opportunities that happen to exist in the present, at the edge of his strike zone, which must be taken if corporate results are to be smoothed, Buffett has selected for the best of what an irregular world has to offer. And he embraces the volatility that comes with this logic. It is an advantage in attitude.

Nowhere is this more evident than in Berkshire Hathaway's insurance operations, where Buffett is both candid about its nonconventionality and convincing of its business sense:

> *Note that we are not spreading risk as insurers typically do, we are concentrating it. Most insurers are financially unable to tolerate such swings. And if they have the ability to do so, they often lack the desire.*[57]

He notes:

> *Wide swings in earnings hurt both credit ratings and p/e ratios, even when the business that produces such swings has an expectancy of satisfactory profits over time. This market reality sometimes causes a reinsurer to make costly moves, among them laying off a significant portion of the business it writes… or rejecting good business simply because it threatens to bring on too much volatility.*[58]

This is not to say that Buffett ignores current results. "In most cases, they are of great importance," he says. Analyzing current results is part of the process of continually securing the perimeter of his Circle of Competence. "But," he adds, "we *never* want them to be achieved at the expense of our building ever-greater competitive strengths."[59]

"We simply measure whether we are creating more than a dollar of value per dollar spent—and if that calculation is favorable, the more dollars we spend the happier I am," says Buffett.[60] If this calculation is not favorable, he sits on his hands:

> You do things when the opportunities come along. I've had periods in my life when I've had a bundle of ideas come along, and I've had long dry spells. If I get an idea next week, I'll do something. If not, I won't do a damn thing.[61]

This means being in a state of preparedness. "Our basic principle is that if you want to shoot rare, fast-moving elephants, you should always carry a loaded gun," says Buffett.[62] In other words, capital *has* to be husbanded and, if need be, raised in an opportunistic fashion:

> Unlike many in the business world, we prefer to finance in antic-ipation of need rather than in reaction to it. A business obtains the best financial results possible by managing both sides of its balance sheet well. This means obtaining the highest-possible return on assets and the lowest-possible cost on liabilities... We have no abil-ity to forecast interest rates and—maintaining our usual open-minded spirit—believe that no one else can. Therefore, we simply borrow when conditions seem non-oppressive and hope that we will later find intelligent expansion or acquisition opportunities.[63]

Such an opportunity presented itself in May 2002 when Buffett took out the world's first ever negative interest loan, or what he calls a SQUARZ.[64] The SQUARZ, via which Buffett raised $400 million, pays its holders 3% interest per annum. In addition, those who bought the security receive a warrant to buy Berkshire Hathaway stock in five years' time at a 15% premium to its price on issue of the SQUARZ. In return for this privilege, SQUARZ holders will pay Berkshire a 3.75% installment payment per annum on the warrants.

"Despite the precedent," says Buffett, "a negative coupon security seemed possible in the present interest rate environment."[65] He was able to persuade investors to lend Berkshire money because the com-pany was back in vogue. Essentially, Buffett took advantage of a win-dow of opportunity in order to raise capital in the present by issuing shares in the future at low cost. In the meantime, he granted himself the opportunity of creating value on the capital raised over and above its cost to him. The SQUARZ works in the same way as low-cost float, but it only exists because the time was right for Buffett.

Except for the SQUARZ, Buffett's "fund-first, buy-or-expand-later policy almost always penalizes near-term earnings," he notes.[66] So too does his willingness to build competitive advantage at the expense of current results. This is of no concern. By staying within his Circle of Competence and avoiding the institutional imperative, "idle" capital in Buffett's hands retains an intrinsic value far in excess of that suggested by its short- or medium-term returns. "If we find the right sort of business elephant within the next five years or so, the wait will have been worthwhile," says Buffett.[67]

Berkshire Hathaway's shareholders are confident of Buffett's ability to find the right elephant and to keep his powder dry until it looms into view. Consequently they, and the buyers of the SQUARZ, are willing to "pay" for the option value that Buffett creates by standing ready and to credit this to Berkshire's stock market value. Likewise, they also credit Berkshire's value with the anticipation of the *future* exploitation of a competitive advantage that is built into the present. The CEO whose compensation is tied to intrinsic value has nothing to lose by mimicking Warren Buffett.

Buffett concludes:

We obviously expose Berkshire to lumpy financial results. That's totally acceptable to us. Too often insurers (as well as other businesses) follow sub-optimum strategies in order to "smooth" their reported earnings. By accepting the prospect of volatility, we expect to earn higher long-term returns than we would by pursuing predictability.[68]

GET SHAREHOLDER-PARTNERS

If [companies] focus their thinking and communications on short-term results or short-term stock market consequences they will, in large part, attract shareholders who focus on the same factors. And if they are cynical in their treatment of investors, eventually that cynicism is highly likely to be returned by the investment community.

Warren Buffett[69]

We are almost certainly the leader in the degree to which our shareholders think and act like owners.

Warren Buffett[70]

Buffett says that he does not understand the CEO who wants lots of stock activity. "That can be achieved only if many of his owners are constantly exiting," he observes. "At what other organization—school, club, church, etc.—do leaders cheer when members leave?"[71]

If this were the case, then Buffett would not be able to fulfill his function as corporate saver—the proper function of the stock market. If the turnover in Berkshire Hathaway shares approximated that of the average company listed in the S&P 500 index, around one year, his shareholders would not be saving *with* him; they would speculating *via* him.

Nevertheless, Buffett also realizes two things:

1 "To obtain quality shareholders is no cinch... Entering members of a shareholder 'club' cannot be screened for intellectual capacity, moral sensitivity or acceptable dress. Shareholder eugenics, therefore, might seem a hopeless undertaking."[72]
2 Liquidity is an important factor to many shareholders: "Of course, some Berkshire owners will need or want to sell from time to time."[73]

By telling it like it is, Buffett kills both these birds with one stone.

If we ran a private business with a few passive partners, we would be disappointed if those partners, and their replacements, frequently wanted to leave the partnership. Running a public company, we feel the same way.[74]

But if investors do wish to take their leave, Buffett says that he tries "through our policies, performance, and communications, to attract new shareholders who understand our operations, share our time horizons, and measure us as we measure ourselves."[75]

He calls these "policies and communications" his "advertisements."[76] Just as he tells the advertising agencies working on behalf of Berkshire's subsidiary companies that a person has to be exposed to each advertisement seven times before the message begins to sink in, Buffett wants to be able to condition his shareholders in the same way. If he can continue to attract the sort of shareholder who aligns his or her philosophy with his, this will enable him to elicit a commitment from them in the same fashion that he elicits a durable and growing commitment from those managers who sell their businesses to him.

"Just as important," adds Buffett, if he "can continue to be uninteresting to those with short-term or unrealistic expectations," Berkshire shares should "consistently sell at prices reasonably related to business value."[77]

Thus, new investors will be encouraged by the fact that what they are buying is what they will get—any increase in intrinsic value from their point of entry will be mirrored in the market value of the stock—which encourages a long-term perspective. And short-term investors will not be presented with a valuation anomaly that they perceive they can exploit.

Accordingly, Buffett can attest that "the annual percentage turnover in Berkshire's shares is a small fraction of that occurring in the stocks of other major American corporations." That small fraction is around 3%. Given that, for most of the period over which Buffett has measured that turnover, he and Munger have owned almost half of Berkshire's stock, this means that *on average* each shareholder maintains his or her position in the stock for over 16 years.

Serendipitously, this keeps Berkshire shareholders on the register long enough for Buffett's conditioning of them to take effect. And "if properly informed," says Buffett, Berkshire's shareholders "can handle unusual volatility in profits so long as the swings carry with them the prospect of superior long-term results."[78]

"We can therefore ask our CEOs to manage for maximum long-term value," he continues, "rather than for next quarter's earnings."[79] In contrast, he observes that "very few CEOs of public companies operate under a similar mandate, mainly because they have owners who focus on short-term prospects and reported earnings."[80]

HARVEST THE TRUST

Capital Cities possesses both extraordinary properties and extraordinary management. And these management skills extend equally to operations and employment of corporate capital... While control would give us the opportunity—and the responsibility—to manage operations and corporate resources, we would not be able to provide management in either of those respects equal to that now in place. In effect, we can obtain a better management result through non-control than control.

Warren Buffett[81]

Naturally, Warren Buffett's Circle of Competence and his track record have engendered a great deal of trust between him and Berkshire's shareholders. The CEO to whom this is new should recognize that trust such as this can only be established over the long term. "No matter how great the talent or effort, some things just take time," says Buffett. "You can't produce a baby in one month by getting nine women pregnant."[82] CEOs should also recognize that trust can be destroyed in an instant: "Once management shows itself insensitive to the interests of owners shareholders will suffer a long time from the price/value ratio afforded their stock."[83]

Equally, Buffett observes:

A manager who consistently turns his back on repurchases, when these clearly are in the interests of owners, reveals more than he knows of his motivations. No matter how often or how eloquently he mouths some public relations-inspired phrase such as "maximizing shareholder wealth"... the market correctly discounts assets lodged with him. His heart is not listening to his mouth—and, after a while, neither will the market.[84]

Buffett's attitude as a shareholder when the right management is in place is that he does not need to assert control of their behavior; a CEO is given the freedom to act when he is trusted. "The first-class managers with whom we have aligned ourselves [in our quoted investments]," attests Buffett, "can focus their efforts entirely upon running the businesses and maximizing long-term values for owners."[85]

By arrangement, Berkshire Hathaway's shareholders treat Buffett in the same way. Thus, even though Buffett has been hit by two bolts from the blue in the recent past that would have tested the metal of any chief executive, his resolve to manage capital in the way he thinks fit has not weakened.

Between June 1998 and March 2000, Berkshire Hathaway's stock price halved in value.[86] In the process, it unwound *all* of its outperformance versus the S&P 500 since 1984 and did much to dim the aura that had come to surround Buffett. He was forced to make a confession to his shareholders:

> *We had the worst absolute performance of my tenure and, compared to the S&P, the worst relative performance as well... My "one subject" is capital allocation, and my grade for 1999 most assuredly is a D.*[87]

Then in 2001, after taking an enormous hit in the reinsurance division, through which Berkshire has more exposure than any other player in the industry to catastrophic events, Buffett was forced to issue another apology.

In both periods, Warren Buffett was failing unconventionally. As he knew he might, he did *look* extraordinarily foolish. The test was on.

The *Financial Times* opined in the wake of 1999's dismal performance:

> *Oh, Warren. The man sometimes known as the world's greatest investor... has started to affect a small-boy-in-trouble tone to his keenly read annual letters.*

It zeroed in on what it considered the greatest risk to Berkshire Hathaway:

> *More worrying for Buffett would be if the contrite-schoolboy act*
> *began to grate on loyal Berkshire Hathaway investors, for whom*
> *the gap between the chairman's investment wisdom and his short-*
> *term investment performance has never been so wide.*[88]

The implication of the article was clear. As much as Buffett professes that "gyrations in Berkshire's earnings don't bother us in the least," he also adds, "we are most *comfortable*, however, when we have share-holder/partners who can also accept volatility" [emphasis added].[89] And the last time Buffett felt a high degree of discomfort, he folded the Buffett Partnership.

Over 30 years on from 1969, Buffett is standing firm. As Berkshire Hathaway's manager, he can act like its owner because he has share-holders who think like owners. And he continues to make decisions based on the force of logic *because he has a mandate to do so.*

Warren Buffett's Circle of Competence delivers the emotional balance required in his management of Berkshire's capital. "I have no stress whatsoever—zero," says Buffett.[90] He is in control. He has reduced his capital management down to near certainties. He has managers who are intrinsically motivated to act like owners. He has devised rules of behavior that tap into and enhance this motivation. And he stays inside a Circle of Competence in which he *feels* in control.

Berkshire's shareholders bless this arrangement. They are happy to keep their savings with Buffett, content that he is acting in their best interests and that no change is required.

❖❖❖

Buffett's Circle of Competence is an emergent solution to the problems contained in capital management, not least the alignment that must exist between managers and owners. That solution cannot necessarily be guessed at by analysis of its parts, only by comprehension of the interactive workings of the whole.

The circle is infused with mental models. They gave birth to it and, indeed, they support the dynamic process that maintains and occasionally alters its circumference. Their diversity is vital in this regard.

And it is in this diversity that Buffett has borne witness to the alternative to his Circle of Competence.

Invoking the spirit of the algebraist Carl Jacobi—whose injunction it was, notes Munger, to "Invert. Always invert"[91]—Buffett has considered how he would have to behave in order to mismanage Berkshire's capital and break the bond of trust between its manager and its owners. The conclusion he has come to is that he would have to inhabit a Circle of Illusory Competence.

Rather than sticking to the important and knowable, he would have to fail to question what is knowable. Rather than *establishing* what he knows by searching for truths, he would have to *persuade* himself of what he "knew." Instead of *ensuring* that he knows by inverting his arguments, he would have to *convince* himself of what he purported to know. In place of *checking* the veracity of his model by seeking feedback, he would have to live in *denial* of the consequences.

It may seem like a tall order to behave so perversely; it is not. The construction of the Circle of Illusory Competence comes so naturally to humans that Buffett has *enshrined* his capital management in its prescriptive alternative.

Crucially, Buffett would not have been able to identify the behavioral rules applying in his Circle of Competence, and keeping it that, without knowing how the mind works in order to construct its inverse—without seeking the lessons of failure.

With Buffett acting as illustrator, therefore, in Chapter 9 we will explore that other essential in his user's manual, an exposition of the governing principles of the Circle of Illusory Competence. This will allow us to analyze the mechanism and consequences of *blinkered*, as opposed to *enlightened*, capital management.

9

The Circle of Illusory Competence

The elementary part of psychology—the psychology of misjudgment, as I call it—is a terribly important thing to learn. There are about 20 little principles. And they interact, so it gets slightly complicated. But the guts of it is unbelievably important. Terribly smart people make totally bonkers mistakes by failing to pay heed to it.

Charlie Munger[1]

I've often felt there might be more to be gained by studying business failures than business successes... my partner, Charles Munger, says all he wants to know is where he's going to die—so he won't ever go there.

Warren Buffett[2]

In the dying years of Berkshire's textiles business, Ken Chace would come to Buffett with carefully constructed plans to upgrade and expand operations. Buffett rejected them all. He commented:

The promised benefits from these textiles investments were illusory. Many of our competitors, both domestic and foreign, were stepping up to the same kind of expenditures and, once enough companies did so, their reduced costs became the baseline for reduced prices industrywide.[3]

Buffett's Circle of Competence gave him a perspective that Chace lacked: the outside view of one removed from the fray versus the inside view of one in the thick of it. Buffett notes:

> *The CEO of a multi-divisional company will instruct Subsidiary A, whose earnings on incremental capital may be expected to average 5%, to distribute all available earnings in order that they may be invested in Subsidiary B, whose earnings on incremental capital are expected to be 15%.*[4]

This is the CEO's outside view. It presents a clear, detached picture of where capital should be allocated. But he continues:

> *If his own long-term record with incremental capital is 5%—and market rates are 10%—he is likely to impose a dividend policy on shareholders of the parent company that merely follows some historical or industry-wide payout pattern.*[5]

This is his inside view, which lacks perspective.

Buffett terms this tendency to modulate between the inside and outside view "schizoid behavior."[6] His task in leading those who manage capital within Berkshire is to get them to tap into the outside view that exists in all of them when putting money to work in their governance of the company's subsidiaries. If Buffett can prevent schizoid behavior within Berkshire, as he eventually did with Chace, then the institutional imperative telling managers to reinvest where there is no likelihood of value creation will be diminished and more excess capital will be sent to Omaha.

Buffett does this by bringing his detached perspective to bear on the conduct of his managers, in "Ken, you won't beat the historical average"[7] mode. More importantly, he brings it to bear on his own conduct.

Buffett owns and operates franchises because of mean reversion; he associates with the right personality types because human nature is resistant to change; he swings only at fat pitches because the market is generally efficient; he buys only good businesses because "when a management with a reputation for brilliance tackles a business with a reputation for bad economics, it is the reputation of the business that remains intact,"[8] and he structures his acquisitions in a particular fashion because successful mergers are difficult to effect. By imposing these operating restrictions on himself, Buffett is admitting to the significant base rate probability of failure should he behave any differently. And, unlike Ken Chace before Buffett was able to change him, as well as countless other managers who remain close to the fray, Warren Buffett always takes base rate probabilities into account before he takes his wallet out on behalf of Berkshire's shareholders.

Buffett's outside view—his detached and global perspective on the task at hand—defines him as a capital manager and a leader. His Circle of Competence delivers this. It allows him to let go and trust in the natural laws governing outcomes.

Other CEOs are not so trusting. As far as we have come since the Renaissance, something is rotten in the state of capital management. Says Buffett:

> Adam Smith felt that all noncollusive acts in a free market were guided by an invisible hand that led an economy to maximize progress. Our view is that casino-type markets and hair-trigger investment management act as an invisible foot that trips up and slows down a forward-moving economy.[9]

At this juncture in the evolution of capitalism, we have torn down the walls of intellect but not yet conquered the impediments of psychology and emotion, merely put up make-do ladders against them. We would do well to share Buffett's insights as to why this is the case.

THE CIRCLE OF ILLUSORY COMPETENCE

> Pascal said in essence, "The mind of man at one and the same time is both the glory and the shame of the universe."… It has this enormous power. However, it also has these standard misfunctions that often cause it to reach wrong conclusions.
>
> Charlie Munger[10]

> If we have a strength, it is in recognizing when we are operating well within our circle of competence and when we are approaching the perimeter.
>
> Warren Buffett[11]

In his analysis of the flaw in Ken Chace's arguments in favor of upgrading Berkshire's textile operations, Buffett provides a clue as to why many managers are content to reinvest in industries in which the base rate probability of creating value is low:

Viewed individually, each company's capital investment decision appeared cost effective and rational; viewed collectively, the decisions neutralized each other and were irrational (just as happens when each person watching a parade decides he can see a little better if he stands on tiptoes). After each round of investment, all the players had more money in the game and the returns remained anemic.[12]

Adopting the inside view and considering a problem individually, rather than in its global context, is instinctive. Buffett knows this because he has identified two problems in the management of capital.

The first lies in the nature of the environment in which he must make his forecasts; the second in the brain that he uses to make them. These two problems threaten to meet in the remarkable ability of that organ to eradicate the uncertainty that complex systems naturally contain.

It eradicates uncertainty because it can: Complex systems may be inherently unpredictable, but they are also eminently comprehensible. It eradicates uncertainty because it needs to: In order to step forward into the otherwise unknown, humans feel compelled to be in the driving seat. And it eradicates uncertainty because it has limited processing power.

When faced with an avalanche of information, Buffett's brain is no different than any other. It is only able to process and react to a small proportion of the data that confronts it; it is "boundedly rational."

Recalling his investment career before he set up his partnership, for instance, Buffett says:

I used to feel when I worked back in New York that there were more stimuli hitting me all the time, and if you've got the normal amount of adrenaline, you start responding to them. It may lead to crazy behavior after a while.[13]

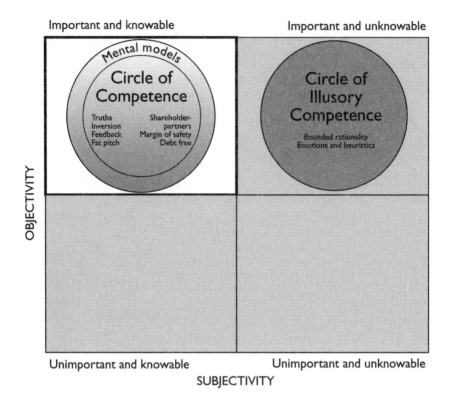

Figure 4 The Circle of Competence and its inverse

That "crazy behavior" threatened to occur because, by evolutionary legacy, his brain has learned to overcome its capacity constraint by deferring to emotions (hence Buffett's adrenaline) and heuristics, depicted in Figure 4.

Emotions compensate for the fact that we lack "a comprehensively rational mechanism for sorting the relevant from the irrelevant and weighing the relevant aspects accordingly."[14] In other words, emotions evolved *because* we are boundedly rational. Amid the clutter of information vying for our attention, they tell us what information we *should* be taking note of.

This is evolutionarily sound, but the driver of selection in evolution is survival. On the savannah plains, it turned on our ability to respond to danger and opportunity, the aims being to safeguard our wellbeing and to mate. Today, self-preservation and procreation are more reasonably assured and the preoccupations of most humans are qualitatively different. However, our brains have not forgotten that the primary aim of their body hosts is to replicate genes and for this reason emotions can be maladaptive in the post-industrial arena where capital needs to be allocated.

Heuristics share a similar problem. Rather than crunching through the analysis of problems longhand, which makes a significant call on the brain's processing power, we have learned to default to short cuts. These were tried and tested in a different environment and they equip us with cognitive biases that affect the way we process information. Says Charlie Munger:

> *The basic neural network of the brain is there through broad genetic and cultural evolution. It uses a crude, shortcut-type of approximation. However, it's not good.*[15]

The awareness of these emotions and heuristics in himself and his observation of their existence in others explains why Buffett filters the information to which he has to respond as a manager of capital to fit the bounds of his rationality. "Our filters are filters against consequences from our own lack of talent," confirms Munger[16] and, fittingly, Buffett's Circle of Competence is now represented in Figure 4 as being surrounded by the mental models responsible for its construction and maintenance.

Buffett's "filtered rationality" is a response to bounded rationality. It acts as an antidote to what Charlie Munger has termed a "lollapalooza effect."[17] Cognitive biases and emotions seldom exist in isolation. They like to act in concert. When they do—in a lollapalooza—they can, for example, persuade people to a Circle of Illusory Competence in which they come to "know" the unknowable. The consequences of this for the quality of decisions made in capital management can be easily guessed.

This starts with the hindsight and hubris of Figure 5.

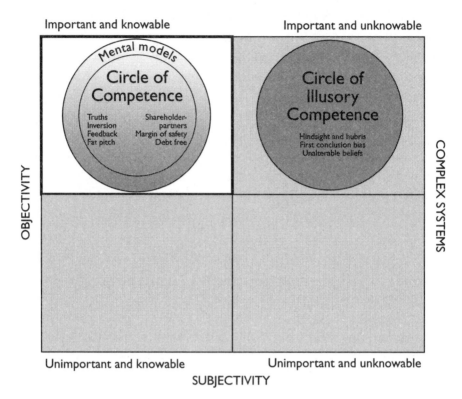

Figure 5 The Circle of Illusory Competence

HINDSIGHT AND HUBRIS

In the business world, unfortunately, the rear-view mirror is always clearer than the windshield: A few years back no one linked to the media business—neither lenders, owners nor financial analysts—saw the economic deterioration that was in store for the industry. (But give me a few years and I'll probably convince myself that I did.)

Warren Buffett[18]

Buffett recognizes that the "foresight" required to persuade ourselves of a Circle of Competence that we do not have comes cheap. All we need is hindsight.

The complex adaptive systems in which the capital allocation function resides may be unpredictable, but they are also explicable. Humans not only tend to view what has happened in the past as inevitable, but also as having been relatively inevitable before it happened. We may even misremember our own predictions so as to exaggerate in hindsight what we knew in foresight.[19] Our memories do not form perfect replicas of the events they are supposed to recall. Instead, we reconstruct our memories by filling in the missing details with plausible material.[20] Therefore, once we know the outcome of a course of events, it is extremely difficult to recreate that state of outcome ignorance that existed before they unfolded, in which situation we *had* to make our forecasts.

In addition to this, humans have an innate talent for spotting patterns, which helps us extract the narratives from history that allow us to explain the previously unknowable. Such narratives are selfish, however. Because alternative scenarios have not been mapped out for us, they discount these and make it difficult for us to envisage a path to them.[21] This is what makes hindsight bias so powerful and such a strong contributor to overconfidence or hubris. Having distilled the complexity of the past, with its confusion of possibilities and contingencies, into a simple version of the truth that eradicates uncertainty, the next step is to overestimate our ability to predict the future. The notion of a surprise-free past is suggestive of a surprise-free future and we can easily persuade ourselves that we know the unknowable.[22]

Warren Buffett is very sensitive to this possibility in his decision making. He says:

When I look at great historic events, nothing I see gives me much of a clue as to which ones would signal major changes in the profitability of American business... Did we foresee thirty years ago what would transpire in the television-manufacturing or computer industries? Of course not.[23]

And, pointing to a failure of the Circle of Illusory Competence, he adds "nor did most of the investors and manufacturers who enthusiastically entered those industries."[24]

FIRST CONCLUSION BIAS

Charles Darwin used to say that whenever he ran into something that contradicted a conclusion he cherished, he was obliged to write the new finding down within 30 minutes. Otherwise his mind would work to reject the discordant information, much as the body rejects transplants.

Warren Buffett[25]

Within his Circle of Competence, Warren Buffett ensures that he knows the important and knowable by inverting his arguments because he is aware that it is in our nature to convince ourselves that we know what we purport to know. This is "an automatic tendency in psychology," says Munger, "often called *first conclusion bias*."[26]

One of the ways we achieve this is by subjecting the hypotheses in our narratives of the past to weak tests. Once we have settled on a version of the past with which we are happy, we tend not to cast around for reasons that we might be wrong. Advises Munger:

You've got to have multiple models, because if you have just one or two that you are using, the nature of human psychology is such that you'll torture reality so that it fits your models, or at least you'll think it does.[27]

In receipt of positive feedback, we attribute our successes to skill and infuse them with foresight. "Man's natural inclination is to cling to his beliefs, particularly if they are reinforced by recent experience," observes Buffett.[28]

When disappointed, we write off failure. We either pinpoint the exact source of error so that it may be corrected next time—unaware that hindsight and hubris are the informants to this process, so that there *will* be a next time—or we declare that bad luck intervened. "In corporate boardrooms," says Buffett, "triumphs are trumpeted, but dumb decisions either get no follow-up or are rationalized."[29]

If we develop decision rules that in reality may be poor, but that our brains convince us work, and if we seek out evidence in their favor, curtailing the search for and/or ignoring evidence that may reveal their inadequacy, we will remain profoundly ignorant of their short-comings.[30] The problem with this complex form of the first conclusion bias is that it abducts allocators of capital away from their Circle of Competence. Buffett observes:

> *About 99% of American management thinks that if they're won-derful at doing one thing they'll be wonderful at doing something else. They're like a duck on a pond when it's raining—they're going up in the world. They start thinking that they are the ones that are causing themselves to rise. So they go over to some place where it isn't raining and they just sit there on the ground. But nothing happens. Then they usually fire their number two in com-mand or hire a consultant. They very seldom see that what really happens is that they have left their circle of competence.[31]*

Buffett notes, for instance, that many corporations have employed a large proportion of their retained earnings on an economically un-attractive or "even disastrous basis." He continues:

> *The managers at fault periodically report on the lesson they have learned from the latest disappointment. They then usually seek out future lessons. (Failure seems to go to their heads.)[32]*

The first conclusion bias can transform a change in behavior into a change in attitude.[33] If CEOs operate within a Circle of Illusory Competence they *will* convince themselves that they know the unknow-able. Lest Buffett fall victim to this, he attests, "If we can't find things within our circle of competence, we won't expand the circle. We'll wait."[34]

"Predicting the long-term economics of companies that operate in fast-changing industries is simply far beyond our perimeter,"[35] says Buffett and he steadfastly maintains:

> *When it comes to Microsoft and Intel, I don't know what that world would look like 10 years from now... I could spend all my*

time thinking about technology for the next year and still not be the 100th, 1,000th or even the 10,000th smartest guy in the country in analyzing those businesses.[36]

That is not to say that Buffett could not make money in technology stocks if he tried—including Microsoft. A close friend of Bill Gates, of course he could. *But Buffett recognizes that the danger lies not necessarily in the one or two stocks that he might misjudge, but in the escalation of participation that he might risk if he gets one or two of them right!*

"Nothing sedates rationality," observes Buffett, "like large doses of effortless money."[37] He notes:

If others claim predictive skill in [fast-changing] industries—and seem to have their claims validated by the behavior of the stock market—we neither envy nor emulate them. Instead, we just stick with what we understand. If we stray, we will have done so inadvertently, not because we got restless and substituted hope for rationality.[38]

UNALTERABLE BELIEFS

Demosthenes said, "What a man wishes that also he will believe."
Well, Demosthenes was right... Individuals vary in how much psychological denial they get. But miscognition from denial overwhelmingly pervades the reality that you're going to have to deal with.

Charlie Munger[39]

Tony Nicely, GEICO's CEO, remains an owner's dream. Everything he does makes sense. He never engages in wishful thinking or otherwise distorts reality, as so many managers do when the unexpected happens.

Warren Buffett[40]

"I've been a director of a lot of companies over the years—and they usually don't spend a lot of time on post-mortems," says Buffett.[41] Within his Circle of Competence, on the other hand, Buffett *checks* that he knows what he purports to know, because it is in the nature of a man who does not do this to live in denial of the negative feedback that should inform him that something is amiss with his model of the world.

On the subject of corporate acquisitions, Buffett says:

I've observed that many acquisition-hungry managers were apparently mesmerized by their childhood reading of the story about the frog-kissing princess. Remembering her success, they pay dearly for the right to kiss corporate toads, expecting wondrous transfigurations.[42]

These managers exist in the Circle of Illusory Competence. Warren Buffett *has* been there. He comments:

In my early days as a manager I, too, dated a few toads. They were cheap dates... but my results matched those of acquirers who courted higher-priced toads. I kissed and they croaked. [Nevertheless,] after several failures of this type... I finally remembered some useful advice I once got from a golf pro... Practice doesn't make perfect; practice makes permanent.[43]

That is the complex form of the first conclusion bias in action. However, Buffett performed postmortems on his early forays into outright acquisitions. Rather than persuading himself that he was using the right rule, he discovered that he was using the wrong rule. He thought he could transfigure a poor business with his own prescient management. His feedback filter told him that he could not. "Thereafter," he says, "I revised my strategy and tried to buy good businesses at fair prices rather than fair businesses at good prices."[44]

Buffett was honest enough in his appraisal of his own performance to escape the Circle of Illusory Competence. Normally, however, our psychological immune systems entrap us there. Humans *need* the illusion of competence because we feed on the illusion of control that comes with it. Our brains have been designed to manufacture the winning arguments justifying the acts our minds induce.[45] We feel compelled to convince the world that we are reasonable, rational, and understanding. We need to convince ourselves of the same. We need answers and sometimes any answer will do. Warren Buffett knows this.

After many years of decrying corporate excesses elsewhere, Buffett lost temporary leave of his senses in 1986 and bought a jet. He told his shareholders, tongue in cheek:

> *Whether Berkshire gets its money's worth from the plane is an open question, but I will work at achieving some business triumph that I can (no matter how dubiously) attribute to it. I'm afraid Ben Franklin had my number. Said he: "So convenient a thing it is to be a reasonable creature, since it enables one to find or make a reason for everything one has a mind to do."* [46]

Once such beliefs have been formed, they tend to become unalterable. "Negotiating with oneself seldom produces a barroom brawl," notes Buffett. [47]

This may be the type of psychology that Buffett is looking for in his franchises: ingrained—wired/behavioral—brand loyalty to a product or service proposition. But it is not the kind of psychology that he wants to see in an allocator of capital. Hence Buffett's most important stipulation to managers of capital: *"What counts for most people... is not how much they know, but rather how realistically they define what they don't know."* [48]

The only way to break the cycle of winning arguments and the formulation of unalterable beliefs is to stop living in denial of incompetence. The person who wants to define a Circle of Competence in the Buffett mold has to admit to his mistakes—in the Buffett mold.

Recounting a story he was told by one of the ex-chairmen of General Re, for instance, Buffett notes:

> *Every year his managers told him that "except for the Florida hurricane" or "except for Midwestern tornadoes," they would have had a terrific year. Finally he called the group together and suggested that they form a new operation—the Except-For Insurance Company—in which they would henceforth place all of the business that they wouldn't want to count... In any business, insurance or otherwise, "except for" should be excised from the lexicon. If you*

are going to play the game, you must count the runs scored against you in all nine innings. Any manager who consistently says "except for" and then reports on the lessons he learned from his mistakes may be missing the only important lesson—namely, that the real mistake is not the act, but the actor *[emphasis added]*.[49]

The strength of Buffett's Circle of Competence is the objectivity it conveys on his cognition and decision making. It is not given to all managers to be so objective. They lack Buffett's insight. Equally, they lack Buffett's design. No matter what their Circle of Competence, some judgments are necessarily subjective. The key for practitioners is to recognize that subjectivity is at its most necessary in the presence of the very uncertainty that Circles of Illusory Competence have evolved to address, which is why such a circle exists to the far right in Figure 5 in the realm of complex systems.

INFORMED SUBJECTIVITY

There is no way for us—or anyone else—to calculate the true odds on super-cat coverages.

Warren Buffett[50]

Just as man working with a tool has to know its limitations, a man working with his cognitive apparatus has to know its limitations.

Charlie Munger[51]

Warren Buffett has made the writing of super-catastrophe insurance policies, which protect against large and nonstandardized risks such as hurricanes and earthquakes, a Berkshire speciality. This should come as some surprise.

What constitutes an appropriate price of a super-cat policy cannot be determined in the way most insurance business can be priced, nor in the way Buffett likes to allocate capital generally. *There are no stable frequencies.* Therefore, Buffett must adopt the alternative frame available for conceptualizing probabilities, that of degrees of belief warranted by the evidence.[52] This is the frame decision makers naturally use when judgments must be made with regard to events that are devoid of the statistical background allowing for the identification of stable frequencies.[53]

In theory, this is inconsequential. Humans are intuitive statisticians. We rationally update our beliefs about probabilities as new variables are added to an equation, or as the relationship between existing variables changes, or as our understanding of existing variables and relationships improves.[54] Based on innumerable observations of how frequently the presence of dark clouds presages rain, for example, or how often a hot and still evening heralds a visit from a mosquito, humans developed a natural feel for probabilistic reasoning.[55] The drawback is, however, that the events on which our instincts evolved were stable frequencies, not single events. When a problem elicits a frame of degrees of belief we can be duped into flouting the basic laws of probability because we defer to the emotions and heuristics that can hijack our cognition.

Three particular heuristics threaten to distort our thinking with regard to probabilistic outcomes when we have to be subjective. We might be inclined to make judgments based on saliency, availability, and representativeness. That is, we might overestimate the frequency of an event because it is currently prominent in our consciousness, because it is easy to bring prior instances of it to mind, or because it resembles others (if it looks like a duck and quacks like a duck...). Thereafter, we run the danger of convincing ourselves of our own sagacity.

Buffett observes that, in the super-cat business, "expectations can be based on little more than subjective judgments."[56] Furthermore, the event risk that he insures against truly is the stuff of those complex systems to the far right of the important and knowable. He notes:

> *Catastrophe insurers can't simply extrapolate past experience. If there is truly "global warming," for example, the odds would shift, since tiny changes in atmospheric conditions can produce momentous changes in weather patterns.*[57]

This means that, in the super-cat business, Buffett is well and truly operating in that part of the financial field where illusory competencies lurk.

Forewarned subjectivity, however, is informed subjectivity. Says Buffett: "No matter what others may do [in the super-cat field], we will not knowingly write business at inadequate rates." In the same breath, however, he makes the following admission:

> We unwittingly did this in the early 1970s and, after more than 20 years, regularly receive significant bills stemming from the mistakes of that era. My guess is that we will still be getting surprises from that business 20 years from now... I actively participated in those early reinsurance decisions, and Berkshire paid a heavy tuition for my education in the business.[58]

As we know, overconfidence is commonplace when feedback from decisions is slow. The illusion of competence is also most in evidence in the presence of true uncertainty. Buffett was victim to both conditions in the super-cat business. Once the feedback came in, however, he recognized enough to change his approach.

As it happens, in the intervening period between underwriting ill-judged risks and learning of the consequences, Buffett also went to school on the workings of his cognitive apparatus. *He got to know its limitations.* By identifying the mechanism of the illusion of competence, he constructed his Circle of Competence. *Now Buffett transports that part of his Circle of Competence that comprehends the way he makes decisions under conditions of uncertainty into judgments that are necessarily subjective.*

Indeed, the super-cat business has grown to prominence at Berkshire because, in Ajit Jain, the man whom Buffett says developed this business from scratch since he joined the company in 1986, Buffett found a person whom he realized was *already* competent in this regard:

> In Ajit, we have an underwriter equipped with the intelligence to properly rate most risks; the realism to forget about those he can't evaluate; the courage to write huge policies when the premium is

appropriate; and the discipline to reject even the smallest risk when the premium is inadequate. It is rare to find a person possessing any one of these talents. For one person to have them all is remarkable.[59]

Buffett's contribution to Berkshire's super-cat business was first to recognize that Jain is the Circle of Competence in bold relief; second to give him the freedom he deserved; and third to be in constant attendance in order to ensure that Jain does not succumb to the insidious traps lying in wait for those who must make subjective judgments, no matter how able they are.

Given Buffett's decentralized management style, he is unusually involved in Jain's management of the super-cat business and the two of them talk on the phone just about every day.[60] Buffett does this in order to provide Jain with the outside view that improves his cognition.

Buffett "has been involved in every piece of business I have done," says Jain. "He has discouraged me from getting too close to the line when it's a close call."[61] Obliquely referring to the process of coming to know the unknowable, he continues: "Every now and then you get sucked into it, and find some rationale why you need to do it. These are very subjective trade-offs, and you may end up on a slippery slope without realizing it."

Managers outside Berkshire Hathaway are rarely so fortunate. Buffett says of the managers who look after the interests of those companies in which Berkshire has large stakes:

We recognize that we are working with experienced CEOs who are very much in command of their own businesses but who nevertheless, at certain moments, appreciate the chance to test their thinking on someone without ties to their industry or to decisions of the past.[62]

So Buffett does furnish these people with the benefits of his perspective. Other managers run the risk of being blinkered by comparison. In order to test their thinking on someone without ties to their industry or to the decisions of the past, they must cock an ear in the direction of the stock market.

BLINKERED CAPITAL MANAGEMENT

Yet investors, mesmerized by soaring stock prices and ignoring all else, piled into these enterprises. It was as if some virus, racing wildly among investment professionals... induced hallucinations in which the values of stocks in certain sectors became decoupled from the values of the businesses that underlay them.

Warren Buffett[63]

Throughout Silicon Valley, makers of PCs, chips, servers, printers and other digital products have admitted to monstrous miscalculations of final demand. Lucent, Corning, Nortel and JDS Uniphase have been devastated by one of the greatest miscalculations of investment capital outside the chronicles of the Soviet Gosplan.

Grant's Interest Rate Observer[64]

Academia's ground-breaking and durable contribution to the investment industry was to formalize the theory of how investors could survive outside a Circle of Competence. Taking the stock-specific risk that Warren Buffett spends so much time and effort trying to reduce, it told investors to diversify it away. As Buffett attests, this is sound advice where subjectivity cannot be avoided. He advises:

If significant risk exists in a single transaction, overall risk should be reduced by making that purchase one of many mutually-independent commitments. Thus, you may consciously purchase a risky investment—one that indeed has a significant possibility of causing loss or injury—if you believe that your gain, weighted for probabilities, considerably exceeds your loss, comparably weighted, and if you can commit to a number of similar, but unrelated opportunities... Paradoxically, when "dumb" money acknowledges its limitations, it ceases to be dumb.[65]

The practical flaw in the implementation of this advice, however, is that diversification often relegates the analysis of specific risk to the back burner. Warren Buffett's filters never allow this to happen. He eliminates risk in the price/value equation. Then he selects the few. Where the quantification of risk is necessarily subjective he diversifies, but only after an analytical process in which he and Jain have set the agenda.

The defining edge of Berkshire's super-cat business is that it operates from a position of extreme competitive strength. "Berkshire is ideally positioned to write super-cat policies," says Buffett.[66] In a risk industry that requires enormous amounts of capital, it has a net worth "ten or twenty" times larger than that of its main competitors. And "the certainty that Berkshire will be both solvent and liquid after a catastrophe of unthinkable proportions is a major competitive advantage for us," adds Buffett. He never *has* to bet in the super-cat casino. In the realm of bounded rationality, this is a must.

In contrast, most investors have their agendas set for them by the benchmarks they are required to outperform. The diversified portfolio of the typical institutional fund manager—normally comprised of 60 or so stocks, drawn from, and replaceable by, as many as 500 stocks, maybe more—means that institutional fund managers have to take on the type of risk that Buffett eschews and place their bets in the casino of subjectivity. But there is a problem with the diversification strategy that this requires: The brain's filters are wide open and it plays straight into the hands of the bounded rationality that Buffett assiduously sidesteps. He observes:

> You might think that institutions, with their large staffs of highly-experienced investment professionals, would be a force for stability and reason in financial markets. They are not: stocks heavily owned and constantly managed by institutions have often been amongst the most inappropriately valued.[67]

"Anybody who tells you they can value... all the stocks in Value Line, and on the board, must have a very inflated idea of their ability because it's not that easy," comments Buffett.[68] Unless they are possessed of Buffett's filtered rationality, portfolio managers will gravitate toward solving the search problem for those stocks that will outperform by deferring to emotions and heuristics. Buffett continues:

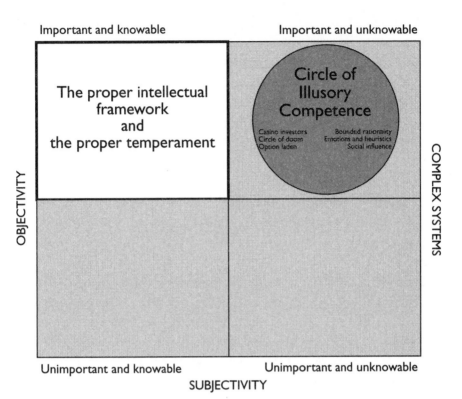

Figure 6 Blinkered management and the misallocation of capital

In my opinion, investment success will not be produced by arcane formulae, computer programs or signals flashed by the price behavior of stocks and markets. Rather an investor will succeed by coupling good business judgment with an ability to insulate his thoughts and behavior from the super-contagious emotions that swirl about the marketplace.[69]

However, basing judgments on signals flashed by prices and informing decisions by deferring to contagious emotion are natural when investors have not set bounds to their Circles of Competence. Both influences speak of the undue role that the social influence of Figure 6 can exert on human behavior, a principle that Buffett illustrates with the following joke:

An oil prospector, moving to his heavenly reward, was met by St. Peter with bad news. "You're qualified for residence," said St. Peter, "but, as you can see, the compound reserved for oil men is packed. There's no way to squeeze you in." After thinking a moment, the prospector asked if he might say just four words to the present occupants. That seemed harmless to St. Peter, so the prospector cupped his hands and yelled, "Oil discovered in hell." Immediately the gate to the compound opened and all of the oil men marched out to head for the nether regions. Impressed, St. Peter invited the prospector to move in... [but] the prospector paused.

"No," he said, "I think I'll go along with the rest of the boys. There might be some truth in that rumor after all."[70]

A scene played out in fiction. A travesty played out in fact.

"For some reason, people take their cues from price action rather than from values," says Buffett.[71] Implicitly psychologists agree, and they have identified a number of factors compelling one person to change their opinion in the presence of others who appear to hold a different view. As Buffett implies with his oil-in-hell joke, all of these exist in the stock market:

1 *Just as they were at the gates of heaven, informational externalities are present.* That is, the behavior of other investors is reflected in the behavior of the stock prices in which they invest and this contains information of which the observer takes note. Furthermore, the efficient market hypothesis observes that there is a fundamental reason for every stock price movement. It contains an authority grounded not only in academic theory but also in empiricism—the market *is* almost impossible to beat—and we all carry a heuristic in our head that tells us to obey authority.[72]

2 *Reputations are at stake.* Underperformance is easily measured, instantaneously available, and highly visible. The ease with which a fund manager can imagine getting sacked for this crime inclines him toward decisions that can be most easily defended after the fact.[73] As ever, failing conventionally is the route to go.

3 *Most importantly, judgments often have to be made in the presence of*

true uncertainty. When investors are making judgments with respect to intangible factors, this materially increases their propensity to key their behavior off the behavior of others. In fact, the greater the ambiguity—as with technology stocks, for instance—the greater the likelihood that social influence will dictate behavior.

Thus, when a group of companies strings together a sequence of strong earnings reports, investors see order and patterns even in data that may be random and/or unsustainable. The heuristic representativeness bias informs them that these companies belong in the sample of companies that can be truly classified as growth stocks and they become valued accordingly. When they are also highly salient and highly available—in the news and in the public domain as the new-economy stocks of the bubble era were, for instance—not merely to fund managers but also to their investment committees and plan sponsors, *and going up*, emotional balance is lost in the strike zone.

Now it's all about possibilities, not probabilities.

We've got fear. The stocks of these companies might be overvalued. *Probably* they will revert to the mean. But *possibly* they won't—and possibly not in the time frame over which my performance is judged. "Instead of focusing on what businesses will do in the years ahead, many prestigious money managers now focus on what they expect other money managers to do in the days ahead," observes Buffett.[74] Besides, the market may actually be right; it is efficient. Perhaps other people know something I don't?

And we've got blue sky dreaming, which psychologists have also found can persuade people to defer to the possible in preference to the probable.[75] Notes Buffett:

> *The propensity to gamble is always increased by a large prize versus a small entry fee, no matter how poor the true odds may be. That's why Las Vegas casinos advertise big jackpots and why state lotteries headline big prizes.*[76]

Thus investors "usually confer the highest price-earnings ratios on exotic-sounding businesses that hold out the promise of feverish change. That prospect lets investors fantasize about future profitability rather than face today's business realities."[77] They lose sight of the odds. They have become the casino investors of Figure 6.

Nevertheless, their excess optimism, another bias of illusory competence, persuades them that they, to the exclusion of all others, will overcome the odds that are stacked against them. Buffett noted in 2000:

> *In companies that have gigantic valuations relative to the cash they are likely to generate in the future, [people] hate to miss a single minute of what is one helluva party. Therefore, the giddy participants all plan to leave just seconds before midnight.*[78]

In light of the effects of social influence on behavior, the advice that Buffett gives investors and by which he lives is that "Mr. Market is there to serve you, not to guide you… [and] it will be disastrous if you fall under his influence."[79] He would also extend this advice to those CEOs who have to test their thinking with regard to the deployment of capital by tapping into the feedback provided by the stock market. When investors lose sight of fundamentals and base their decisions on price signals and supercontagious emotions, the CEO who does this courts trouble because the tail of unrealistic expectations can come to wag the strategic dog.

DISASTROUS INFLUENCE: THE CIRCLE OF DOOM

> *For many years, I've had little confidence in earnings numbers reported by most corporations. I'm not talking about Enron and WorldCom—examples of outright crookedness. Rather, I am referring to the legal, but improper, accounting methods used by chief executives to inflate reported earnings.*
>
> Warren Buffett[80]

> *Over the years, Charlie and I have observed many instances in which CEOs engaged in uneconomic operating maneuvers so that they could meet earnings targets they had announced.*
>
> Warren Buffett[81]

The game of managing to the expectations embedded in an over-priced stock can normally be played successfully in the short term. This illusion of competence emboldens both CEOs and shareholders to longer-term ambition and a mutually supportive embrace. And it pays. Companies that consistently meet investor expectations in their operating results enjoy higher valuations than those that do not; so both parties to the game receive positive feedback.[82] Consequently, management to expectations has become endemic in the CEO community.[83] Far more companies generate linear streams of earnings than can be explained by chance.

However, when stock prices discount the achievement of corporate results that in the circumstance of the marketplace defy incontrovertible truths, capital allocation policies designed to meet these expectations will cease to be dictated by the demands of economic sense. Linear streams of earnings in a nonlinear world, growing at a rate that ignores reversion to the mean, work wonders in the equation for value. They enhance both the forecast and the apparent certainty attached to its production, but this illusion can only be sustained if capital allocation is tailored toward linearity, rather than, paradoxically, the long-term maximization of shareholder value. The longer the bastardization of capital management endures, the greater the chance that intrinsic value will be impaired.

"The problem arising from lofty predictions is not just that they spread unwarranted optimism," says Buffett. "Even more troublesome is the fact that they corrode CEO behavior."[84]

James Kilts, Gillette's recently appointed chief executive (guess why?), is one who has abandoned this game. He correctly identified this type of corporate behavior as being responsible for Gillette's record of capital mismanagement and underachievement prior to his appointment and he came up with a name for it. He called it the *Circle of Doom*, which takes its place in Figure 6 alongside the factors that give it life.

Inside the Circle of Doom, managerial behavior is the inverse of Warren Buffett's:

1 As companies are forced to allocate capital to opportunities that are currently available, return on capital naturally suffers against the alternative of waiting for the best opportunity.

2 As companies attempt to shape themselves to fit expectations, rather than their environments, evolutionary robustness is diminished and survival is put at risk.[85]

3 Attempts to stage-manage operational results often cross the bounds of acceptable, fiduciary behavior.[86]

Buffett concluded in 1998:

> *In recent years, probity has eroded. Many major corporations still play things straight, but a significant and growing number of otherwise high-grade managers—CEOs you would be happy to have as spouses for your children or as trustees under your will— have come to the view that it's okay to manipulate earnings to satisfy what they believe are Wall Street's desires. Indeed, many CEOs think this kind of manipulation is not only okay, but actually their duty.[87]*

It is hardly a surprise that this should be so. "If you use as your test what the stock market is going to do, I think people inherently know they've got a lottery ticket,"[88] says Buffett, maintaining that "a system that produces quixotic payoffs will not only be wasteful for owners but may actually discourage the focused behavior we value in managers."[89]

Stock options reward the wrong behavior. As they present managers with the prospect of outcomes that are not generally available to the owners of the firm, their incorporation into compensation systems encourages managers to lose sight of probabilistic outcomes in the allocation of capital and to focus on the possible. "People would rather be promised a (presumably) winning lottery ticket next week than an opportunity to get rich slowly," observes Buffett.[90]

For his part, Buffett professes:

> *I'll be happy to accept a lottery ticket as a gift—but I'll never buy one… In fact, the business project in which you would wish to have an option frequently is a project in which you would reject ownership.[91]*

And indeed, research suggests that managements who are imbued with options embrace greater risk in their allocation of capital than those who are not.[92] The option-laden CEOs of Figure 6 have a proclivity for transforming the companies they manage into projects they would accept as emotionally imbalanced gamblers, but would reject as emotional balanced owners who receive their rewards in a far more glacial fashion. Incentivized by possibilities, they up the ante in that Circle of Doom, aspiring to meet, or better yet to outdo, the expectations embedded in their stock prices by casino investors. So saying, the story of the blinkered management and the misallocation of capital of Figure 6—standing in stark contrast to Buffett's proper intellectual framework and proper temperament—is complete.

"In the long run," concludes Buffett, "managements stressing accounting appearance over economic substance usually achieve little of either."[93] The honesty and integrity with which Buffett conducts his relationship with shareholders constitute his preferred alternative. "Candor benefits us as managers," says Buffett. "The CEO who misleads others in public may eventually mislead himself in private."[94]

THE UNATTAINABLE VERSUS THE ACHIEVABLE

What a manager must do is handle the basics well and not get diverted. Ralph [Schey] establishes the right goals and never forgets what he set out to do.

Warren Buffett[95]

For years K & W did well but in 1985–86 it stumbled badly, as it pursued the unattainable to the neglect of the achievable.

Warren Buffett[96]

Circles of Illusory Competence are naturally occurring phenomena in the face of uncertainty. They are also perverse.

When the decision rules that worked yesterday cease working today, the sense of control for which a manager strives inside the Circle of Illusory Competence disappears. The source of his error cannot be ascertained. He is lost. And "when a manager of a business feels help-less in asset allocation … you've got a problem," says Buffett.[97] In his vulnerability, such a manager can be easily led by the stock market, by his own biases and emotions, or by advisers who have biases of a different nature. These are the siren songs of corporate shipwrecks.

Buffett's *advice* to a CEO who finds himself in this situation might be to welcome the presence of a strong board:

> *Directors ought to be relatively few in number—say, ten or less— and ought to come mostly from the outside. The outside board members should establish standards for the CEO's performance and should also periodically meet, without his being present, to evaluate his performance against those standards. The requisites for board membership should be business savvy, interest in the job, and owner-orientation.*[98]

The board is there to balance a manager's inside view with one from the outside. "I believe directors should behave as if there is a single absentee owner, whose long-term interest they should try to further in all proper ways," says Buffett. As well as independence, directors must have integrity. "If they lack either… directors can do great violence to shareholders while still claiming to be acting in their long-term interest."[99]

The group decision making that a properly structured and incen-tivized board engages in "may be an adaptive response to bounded rationality," says Stephen Bainbridge at UCLA School of Law, "creat-ing a system for aggregating the inputs of multiple individuals with dif-fering knowledge, interests and skills."[100] If this is the case, then Buffett's *preference* would be for a CEO to transform a Circle of Illusory Competence into a Circle of Competence.

Replete with its filters, Buffett's Circle of Competence is an alter-native, adaptive response to bounded rationality. It delivers the con-trol that humans crave and disarms failure. It allows Buffett to be a one-man capital market, providing the feedback on his own capital management that the stock market is supposed to provide to managers.

Warren Buffett is his own board of directors, possessed of the perennial perspective of one who is detached and which this body is meant to bring to bear on managers.

Buffett's cognition is such that he can do this single-handedly. It's no wonder that he calls this his "happy zone."[101]

Nevertheless, herein lies the challenge to the future of Berkshire Hathaway. When Warren Buffett departs, some other person, or body, will have to fulfill the twin functions of overseeing its capital management and overseeing the capital manager. In rounding off this book, it is to these issues that we now turn.

10

Future Knowable

To find new directors, we will look through our shareholders' list for people who directly, or in their family, have had large Berkshire holdings... Individuals making that cut should automatically meet two of our tests, namely that they are interested in Berkshire and shareholder-oriented. In our third test, we will look for business savvy, a competence that is far from commonplace. Finally, we will continue to have members of the Buffett family on the board. They are not there to run the business after I die, nor will they then receive compensation of any kind. Their purpose is to ensure, for both our shareholders and our managers, that Berkshire's special culture will be nurtured when I'm succeeded by other CEOs.

Warren Buffett[1]

If principles are dated, they're not principles.

Warren Buffett[2]

Normal business was resumed for Berkshire Hathaway in 2002. In what Buffett described as a "banner year,"[3] the book value of the company rose by 10 percent (trouncing the performance of the S&P 500 by over 32 percent), the insurance group increased its float by 16 percent to $41.2 billion, a number approximating 8 percent of the industry's total, and the cost of float fell to 1 percent. At Berkshire's annual meeting Buffett was in his usual form. He lambasted stock options as a "royalty on the passage of time," compared the quick accounting fixes that present corporate earnings in a better light with heroin addiction ("difficult to get off"), advised shareholders not to listen to the projections of management but to look at business economics, and admitted that he had lost the company approximately $8 billion by walking away from the purchase of Wal-Mart shares when the price ran away from him. Most encouragingly, Buffett was able to confirm that General Re had "turned the corner in a big way." Naturally, Berkshire's shareholders were reassured by what they heard. The unanswered question was what the future might hold for them as Buffett advances into his seventies.

Buffett's skill as chairman and chief executive of Berkshire Hathaway lies in combining the twin roles of leadership and capital management with the integrity to act like an owner. This should be the embodiment of any CEO. Current wisdom has it that this embodiment will disappear when Buffett departs the scene. It is commonly believed, for instance, that Lou Simpson, GEICO's chief investment officer, who has overseen that company's equity portfolio since 1979 and whom Buffett says uses the "same conservative, concentrated approach to investments that we do at Berkshire," will take over the capital management role in Buffett's absence. This would leave A.N. Other to become chief executive.

This arrangement looks suspect. Buffett has confirmed Simpson as one of Berkshire's "Hall-of-Famers," and attests that "his presence on the scene assures us that Berkshire would have an extraordinary professional immediately available to handle its investments if something were to happen to Charlie and me."[4] And that's where it stops.

It is not immediately apparent from this inference that Lou Simpson will also be responsible for the capital allocation function, as opposed to the investment function. As CEO, Buffett chooses between an array of capital opportunities available to him, only one of which is to take fractional ownership of other companies via the stock market. Buffett makes no distinction between this exercise and that of buying companies outright, reinvesting in existing subsidiaries, or returning capital to shareholders. The best use of cash gets the cash. It seems imperative, therefore, that whether Simpson manages Berkshire's equity investments or not, one man needs to be in place who can integrate a view on the valuation of equities into a decision incorporating their relative merit against all other possible uses. Current favorites for that post are Rich Santulli of Executive Jet and Ajit Jain.

Beyond this, and in deference to the model presented in this book, I am going to confine my thoughts about Berkshire Hathaway's future to what I consider to be the knowable. In doing so, I will assert that Warren

Buffett will stay inside his Circle of Competence and then address the two elements of the question suggested above, which indeed are suggested by the title of this book: the leadership challenge and the capital management challenge, a subset of which will include some thoughts about the market inefficiencies on which Buffett has relied in the past.

INSIDE THE CIRCLE OF COMPETENCE

Charlie and I not only don't know today what our businesses will earn next year—we don't even know what they will earn next quarter. We are suspicious of those CEOs who regularly claim they do know the future.
Warren Buffett[5]

Numerous Buffett watchers have designated 2003 as the year that he left the confines of his Circle of Competence, deserting capital allocation for politics *and* taking up a new career forecasting the unforecastable. They are mistaken on both counts.

On August 13th the world did indeed wake up to find that Buffett had been named as financial and economic adviser to Arnold Schwarzenegger in the movie star's quest to be elected Governor of California. But this new role should be seen as the latest iteration of a career-long involvement in politics, which Buffett has combined with his role as chairman and chief executive of Berkshire Hathaway. Look no further than previous public statements on taxation, the war in Bosnia, and the Buffett Foundation's contributions to abortion and population control measures to see that this is so, or to his letters to shareholders in which he regularly holds forth on topics of a political (although admittedly self-interested) nature.

Reflecting on Buffett's prognostication in October 2003 on the likely course of the US dollar, some would say he has departed his Circle of Competence in a more serious fashion. "Through the spring of 2002, I had lived nearly 72 years without purchasing a foreign currency," proclaimed Buffett. "Since then Berkshire has made significant investments in—and today holds—several currencies… [and] to hold other currencies is to believe that the dollar will decline."[6] So saying, it looked like Buffett had become what he distrusts: A CEO who claims that he *does* know the future. Casual observation tells us that currency forecasting resides firmly in the quadrant of the important but unknowable and, as such, cannot be deemed to be within Buffett's Circle of Competence. Casual observation is mistaken. Buffett is fond of quoting Herb Stein on the subject of forecasting: "If something cannot go on forever, it will stop."[7] In the same way that Buffett is happy to warn his shareholders that Berkshire cannot possibly grow at 23 percent and more *ad infinitum*, this is the extent of Buffett's forecast of the dollar. It is based on a mathematical and economic truth that sits inside his Circle of Competence: "We were taught in Economics 101 that countries could not for long sustain large, ever-growing trade deficits."[8]

The catalyst that has transformed a forecast into action is the pace at which the US trade deficit has worsened, "to the point," says Buffett, "that our country's 'net worth,' so to speak, is now being transferred abroad at an alarming rate… A perpetuation of this transfer will lead to major trouble… We have entered the world of negative compounding."[9] However, Buffett also has his eye on Berkshire's economics. The purchase of General Re means that Berkshire has considerable foreign currency liabilities. A weak dollar would magnify the cost of a major disaster outside the US and this is a risk that Buffett wants to hedge. "Charlie and I believe Berkshire should be a fortress of financial strength—for the sake of our owners, creditors, policyholders and employees," says Buffett.[10]

Note that timing is not a feature of this forecast. Timing never has been for Buffett. "The course of the stock market," he told his partners in 1966, "will determine, to a great degree, *when* we will be right, but the accuracy of our analysis of the company will largely determine *whether* we will be right. In other words, we tend to concentrate on what should happen, not when it should happen."[11] Over 35 years later, Warren Buffett remains true to those words. He continues to operate inside his Circle of Competence and he will stay there for the remainder of his career.

LEADERSHIP

What happens to this place if you get hit by a truck?
Anonymous and ubiquitous, reported by Warren Buffett[10]

Ten years back, the question that was most often asked about the future of Berkshire Hathaway centered around the possibility of Buffett's accidental death. As Buffett creeps up the mortality tables, that question has morphed into one of a more delicate, more pressing nature and, as far as I know, remains unspoken: "What will happen when you die/lose your mental faculties?"

From a personal perspective, no one is more sensitive to these issues than Buffett himself. From a managerial perspective, therefore, the planning is well in hand. "All in all, we're prepared for 'the truck.'" says Buffett, contemplating the perhaps more polite version of the issue.[12]

Buffett is aware that, when there is separation of ownership from control in an enterprise, it is vital that the board of directors, who represent the interests of its owners, *think* like owners. Berkshire Hathaway's board, post Buffett, most assuredly will think like owners. These people are intimately familiar with and share Buffett's philosophy on this subject. And they will oversee a chief executive who is no less familiar with the principles involved.

Berkshire Hathaway is in safe hands from a corporate governance perspective. Buffett has already identified those who will succeed him in the managerial role. Their names are sealed in an envelope, to be opened at the appropriate time, with a letter that begins: "Yesterday I died. That is unquestionably bad news for me but it is not bad news for our business."[13] (He also jokes that the first thing it says is "Check my pulse again."[14]) When the names in the envelope are read out, nothing at Berkshire Hathaway will change. Warren Buffett has championed a corporate culture second to none. It will survive him. Managers who acted like owners in the past will continue to act like owners in the future. That is in the nature of The Committed.

Important challenges will lie ahead, however. Perhaps the biggest weakness in Buffett's succession plans lies in the secrecy, for want of a better word, surrounding them. The core of Buffett's status as a CEO lies in his personality as a leader: in his high-profile beliefs, integrity, standards, and impeccable honesty. Since Buffett is choosing his own successor, that person will possess similar qualities. While his identity remains a secret, he cannot have the same profile.

The conduct of Jack Welch's succession at General Electric was a public affair, featuring a runoff between three managers, measured over several years. This gave time for GE's shareholders and employees to identify with the next in line. Jeff Immelt was a known quantity when he replaced Jack Welch. Interested parties had already assimilated what he stood for.

At Berkshire Hathaway, Rich Santulli and Ajit Jain, if it is to be one of these two, both have outstanding reputations. Either one of them will benefit enormously from Warren Buffett's endorsement. However, how many of Berkshire Hathaway's shareholders or employees really know these men in the same way that they know Warren Buffett? Some of Berkshire's managers have never even met each other. They certainly have not communicated with its shareholders.

A large element of the commitment Buffett has elicited from his shareholders and employees is personal. It is to Warren Buffett. It is him whom Berkshire shareholders trust. It is Buffett whom Berkshire's managers are eager to please. No one can replace this in an instant. The patina has to be built up over years, of example and of conditioning.

The immediate risk to Berkshire is that this reduces its capacity to attract the right people to the organization. Buffett's acquisition strategy is premised on providing the ideal home to managers who already act like owners or have what it takes to do so. If the allure of Berkshire Hathaway as such dies with Buffett, then so will one of its competitive advantages. A minimum prerequisite of Berkshire's next CEO is that he too is able to take his hands off the reins and give managers their freedom.

A less immediate risk is posed by another succession challenge, which presents itself whether Buffett is CEO or not. Many of Berkshire's subsidiary companies are essentially second-generation family businesses. The risk of failure for such businesses rises with each generation's handover. Certainly by the third generation, if family members of the requisite managerial skill are not available, the intrinsic motivation that drove generations one and two has normally departed.

Buffett has requested that his current managers think long and hard about this issue. He requires each of them periodically to inform him in writing of the names of those who will succeed them, their strengths and weaknesses, and alternative candidates. Buffett says, "I need to have your thoughts in writing rather than try to carry them around in my memory."[15] I doubt this is the reason.

Written commitments, backed up with reasoned argument, take much more deliberation than their mental equivalents.[16] They have a finality about them, suggesting that they are difficult to alter. Knowing that they do not have the escape clause of easily changing their minds, Berkshire's managers will be as diligent in their succession plans as Buffett is in his, and the generational risk attached to the enterprise will be meaningfully reduced.

CAPITAL MANAGEMENT

We find doing nothing the most difficult task of all.

Warren Buffett[17]

If anything is knowable about Berkshire Hathaway's future it is that there is a mathematical limit to the pace at which it can grow once it has reached a certain size. In Chapter 1 I remarked that if Berkshire Hathaway continues to grow at its historical rate, it will become so large that it will absorb the whole of the US economy. An impossibility. At some point between now and 2032, the company's growth rate has got to revert to something more akin to that of the economy and the average of those companies comprising it.

This is an unavoidable fact. And it has to be discounted into any assessment of the company from a shareholder's perspective.

Given Buffett's capital management skills, Berkshire is likely to continue outgrowing the average longer than most mathematically challenged companies would find possible. Indeed, the mother of all mathematical impossibilities threatens to present itself because of Buffett's managerial talent in this regard.

If Warren Buffett is still at the helm when this happens, no problem. He is the first to admit this reality:

Carl Sagan has entertainingly described this phenomenon, musing about the destiny of bacteria that reproduce by dividing into two every 15 minutes... That means four doublings an hour, and 96

doublings a day. Although a bacterium weighs only about a tril-
lionth of a gram, its descendants, after a day of wild asexual aban-
don, will collectively weigh as much as a mountain... in two days,
more than the sun—and before very long, everything in the uni-
verse will be made of bacteria. Not to worry, says Sagan: Some
obstacle always impedes this kind of exponential growth. The bugs
run out of food, or they poison each other, or they are shy about
reproducing in public.[18]

Buffett will not attempt to outgrow Berkshire's potential if it has reached that potential; an attempt that would only destroy value. If he has done his succession planning properly, the next CEO of Berkshire Hathaway will accept reality in like manner. When the limit of Berkshire's ability to reinvest its excess cash at rates that can sustain above-average returns in the long term is reached, stand back. The floodgates are going to open and the cash that normally finds its way to Omaha will be distributed in large amount to all points on the compass.

The challenge in the meantime for Buffett's successor may be more difficult to overcome. The essence of Buffett's Circle of Competence lies in the capacity to do nothing when there is nothing to be done. If anything sits at the heart of illusory competence it is our compulsion to take control, to do something.

In the modern era, mistakes that come from doing something are rarely fatal. In our Stone Age past, they may well have been. In "getting away with it," many of us have lost the most basic survival instinct, intolerance of risk. Warren Buffett has never lost this element of human wiring. He will not risk Berkshire's capital unless he is virtually certain of the outcome. He treats all unquantifiable risks as though they were potentially fatal. In order to emulate the quality of his capital management, Buffett's successor will need to do the same.

MARKET EFFICIENCY

I'd be a bum on the street with a tin cup if the market were efficient.
Warren Buffett[19]

Capitalism is a stripling. The intellectual means by which to tackle uncertainty for gain—capitalism's essence—have only been available to humanity since the Renaissance. We have spent the last 450 years or so refining this ability, only the last 70 or so of which have incorporated understanding of the valuation of the companies that have become the expression of capitalism.[20]

What started as Warren Buffett's playground has grown into a more difficult environment in which to ply his skills. With each successive intellectual advance, markets are becoming increasingly efficient. If I can make any claim for this book, when the Circle of Competence dispels the Circle of Illusory Competence and filtered rationality displaces bounded rationality, the mistakes of capital management will grow still more rare. The fat pitches will be fewer and further between, and the batters awaiting them more numerous. Just as Berkshire will run out of the mathematical opportunity to grow, it seems likely that, unless the human condition remains unchanged, it will also be deprived of the natural—and I use that word advisedly—opportunities on which it relies.

Observing that gambling pre-dated the understanding of probability by centuries, Ian Hacking, a scholar in this field, has conjectured that, traveling back in time several centuries, "someone with only the modest knowledge of probability mathematics could have won himself the whole of Gaul in a week."[21]

A similar thing might be said of Warren Buffett. In that era of capitalism in which we had scaled the intellectual barriers to progress but not yet torn down the walls of psychology and emotion, Buffett will stand out as the man who did. He says:

> I was born at the right time and place, where the ability to allocate capital really counts. I'm adapted to this society. I won the ovarian lottery. I got the ball that said, "capital allocator—United States."[22]

We may never see the like of Warren E. Buffett again. Let's learn from him now.

References

CHAPTER 1

1 *Outstanding Investor Digest (OID)* (1998) vol. XIII, nos 3 & 4, September 24.
2 *OID* (2000) vol. XV, nos 3 & 4, December 18.
3 Janet Lowe (1996) *Benjamin Graham on Value Investing: Lessons from the Dean of Wall Street*, Penguin USA, p30.
4 *OID* (2001) vol. XVI, nos 4 & 5.
5 Letter to the shareholders, Berkshire Hathaway Annual Report, 2000.
6 Andrew Kilpatrick (2001) *Of Permanent Value: The Story of Warren Buffett*, updated and expanded edn, McGraw-Hill, p1087.
7 Letter to the shareholders, Berkshire Hathaway Annual Report, 1985.
8 Letter to the shareholders, Berkshire Hathaway Annual Report, 1986.
9 Berkshire Hathaway Annual Report, 2000.
10 The term "rocket fuel" is used by Roger Lowenstein (1997) *Buffett: The Making of an American Capitalist*, Orion, p135.
11 Email response to material sent to Mr. Buffett for his perusal.
12 Lowe, p86.
13 Lowe, p209.
14 Lowenstein, p46.
15 Letter to the shareholders, Berkshire Hathaway Annual Report, 2000.
16 Inference made by Buffett at Berkshire Hathaway annual meeting, May 1999.
17 Jack Welch with John A. Byrne (2001) *Jack: What I've Learned Leading a Great Company and Great People*, Headline, p54.
18 *Ibid.*, p393.
19 Letter to the shareholders, Berkshire Hathaway Annual Report, 1979.
20 Welch with Byrne, p84.
21 *Ibid.*, p204.
22 Letter to the shareholders, Berkshire Hathaway Annual Report, 1986.
23 Kilpatrick, p1061.
24 Welch with Byrne, p4.
25 *Ibid.*, p225.
26 Janet Lowe (1997) *Warren Buffett Speaks: Wit and Wisdom from the World's Greatest Investor*, Wiley, p106.
27 Letter to the shareholders, Berkshire Hathaway Annual Report, 1988.
28 Letter to the shareholders, Berkshire Hathaway Annual Report, 1985.
29 Letter to the shareholders, Berkshire Hathaway Annual Report, 1988.
30 Letter to the shareholders, Berkshire Hathaway Annual Report, 1988.
31 Letter to the shareholders, Berkshire Hathaway Annual Report, 1993.
32 Testimony of Chairman Alan Greenspan, *Federal Reserve Board's Semiannual Monetary Policy Report to the Congress* before the Committee on Banking, Housing, and Urban Affairs, U.S. Senate, July 16, 2002.

33 Warren E. Buffett (2002) "Who really cooks the books?", *New York Times*, July 25.

CHAPTER 2

1 Adam Smith (1776) An Inquiry into the Nature and Causes of the Wealth of Nations, Modern Library; quoted in Benjamin W. Hermalin and Michael S. Weisbach (forthcoming) "Boards of directors as an endogenously determined institution: A survey of the economic literature," *FRBNY Economic Policy Review*.
2 Brent Schlender (1998) "Gates and Buffett: The Bill and Warren Show," *Fortune*, July 20.
3 Letter to the shareholders, Berkshire Hathaway Annual Report, 1989.
4 Letter to the shareholders, Berkshire Hathaway Annual Report, 1987.
5 Letter to the shareholders, Berkshire Hathaway Annual Report, 1989.
6 Letter to the shareholders, Berkshire Hathaway Annual Report, 1989.
7 Welch with Byrne, p45.
8 Letter to the shareholders, Berkshire Hathaway Annual Report, 1989.
9 Lowe, *Benjamin Graham on Value Investing*, p134.
10 *Ibid*.
11 Lowenstein, pp3 and 24.
12 *Ibid*.
13 *Ibid*., p58.
14 *Ibid*., p49.
15 *Ibid*., p5.
16 Letter to the shareholders, Berkshire Hathaway Annual Report, 1987.
17 Kilpatrick, p1074.
18 *Ibid*., p198.
19 Lowenstein, p128.
20 *Ibid*., p129.
21 Letter to the shareholders, Berkshire Hathaway Annual Report, 1978.
22 Letter to the shareholders, Berkshire Hathaway Annual Report, 1979.
23 Letter to the shareholders, Berkshire Hathaway Annual Report, 1985.
24 Letter to the shareholders, Berkshire Hathaway Annual Report, 1985.
25 Scott Plous (1993) *The Psychology of Judgment and Decision Making*, McGraw-Hill, pp249–50.
26 *OID* (1998) vol. XIII, nos 1 & 2, March 13.
27 Letter to the shareholders, Berkshire Hathaway Annual Report, 1985.
28 Letter to the shareholders, Berkshire Hathaway Annual Report, 1989.
29 Letter to the shareholders, Berkshire Hathaway Annual Report, 1977.
30 Letter to the shareholders: Berkshire Hathaway Annual Report, 1983.
31 Letter to the shareholders, Berkshire Hathaway Annual Report, 1983.
32 Lowenstein, p118.
33 *Ibid*., p106.
34 *Ibid*.
35 *Ibid*.
36 Robert Lenzner and David S. Fondiller (1996) "The not-so-silent partner," *Forbes*, Jan 22.
37 Jim Rasmussen (1999) *Sunday World-Herald*, Omaha, Nebraska, May 2.

38 *Ibid.*
39 Lowenstein, p74.
40 William H. Calvin (1998) "The emergence of intelligence," *Scientific American Presents*, vol. 9, no. 4 (Nov.), pp44–51.
41 Rasmussen.
42 *Ibid.*
43 *OID* (1995) vol. X, nos 1 & 2, May 5.
44 Calvin.
45 Extracts from Munger's lecture at the University of Southern California on "Investment expertise as a subdivision of elementary, worldly wisdom," *OID* (1995) vol. X, nos 1 & 2, May 5.
46 Taken from Lowe, p62.
47 Brent Schlender (1998) "Gates and Buffett: The Bill and Warren Show," *Fortune*, July 20.
48 For a version of rewiring see Robert Hagstrom (2000) *Latticework: The New Investing*, Texere.
49 *OID* (1997) vol. XII, no. 3, December 29.
50 Lowe, p81.
51 Lowe, p135.

CHAPTER 3

1   Letter to the shareholders, Berkshire Hathaway Annual Report, 1994.
2   Taken from Kevin Kelly (1995) *Out of Control: The New Biology of Machines*, Fourth Estate, p163.
3   Letter to the shareholders, Berkshire Hathaway Annual Report, 1995.
4   Letter to the shareholders, Berkshire Hathaway Annual Report, 1995.
5   Stephen Schneider (2001) "Boardroom rejects command and control," *Financial Times*, June 26.
6   Stephen Pinker (1998) *How the Mind Works*, Allen Lane, p377.
7   Letter to the shareholders, Berkshire Hathaway Annual Report, 1993.
8   Letter to the shareholders, Berkshire Hathaway Annual Report, 1989.
9   Robert P. Miles (2002) *The Warren Buffett CEO: Secrets from the Berkshire Hathaway Managers*, Wiley, p262.
10 Letter to the shareholders, Berkshire Hathaway Annual Report, 1984.
11 Lowe, *Wit and Wisdom*, p80.
12 Letter to the shareholders, Berkshire Hathaway Annual Report, 1989.
13 Letter to the shareholders, Berkshire Hathaway Annual Report, 1995.
14 Letter to the shareholders, Berkshire Hathaway Annual Report, 1985.
15 Letter to the shareholders, Berkshire Hathaway Annual Report, 1987.
16 Letter to the shareholders, Berkshire Hathaway Annual Report, 1987.
17 Letter to the shareholders, Berkshire Hathaway Annual Report, 1997.
18 Letter to the shareholders, Berkshire Hathaway Annual Report, 1992.
19 Letter to the shareholders, Berkshire Hathaway Annual Report, 1997.
20 Welch with Byrne, p377.
21 Letter to the shareholders, Berkshire Hathaway Annual Report, 1993.
22 Miles, p192.

23 *OID* (1998) vol. XIII, nos 3 & 4, September 24.

24 Lowenstein, p395.

25 Letter to the shareholders, Berkshire Hathaway Annual Report, 1994.

26 Miles, p278.

27 Donald C. Langevoort (2001) "Monitoring: The Behavior Economics of Inducing Agents' Compliance with Legal Rules," USC Center for Law, Economics & Organization, Research Paper No. C01-7, Georgetown University Law Center Business, Economics, and Regulatory Policy, Law and Economics Research Paper No. 276121, June 26.

28 *Ibid.*

29 Robert B. Cialdini (1993) *Influence: The Psychology of Persuasion*, Quill William Morrow, p92–9.

30 *OID* (1995) vol. X, nos 1 & 2, May 5.

31 *OID* (1999) vol. XIV, nos 2 & 3, December 10.

32 Miles, p260.

33 Letter to the shareholders, Berkshire Hathaway Annual Report, 1995.

34 Letter to the shareholders, Berkshire Hathaway Annual Report, 1999.

35 Letter to the shareholders, Berkshire Hathaway Annual Report, 1999.

36 Memo from Warren Buffett to the Berkshire Hathaway Managers ("The All-Stars"), August 2, 2000, quoted in Miles, p358.

37 Letter to the shareholders, Berkshire Hathaway Annual Report, 1999.

38 Mitchell Resnick (1994) "Changing the centralised mind," *Technology Review*, July.

39 Edgepace.com.

40 Welch with Byrne, pp201–2.

41 Letter to the shareholders, Berkshire Hathaway Annual Report, 1994.

42 Letter to the shareholders, Berkshire Hathaway Annual Report, 1994.

43 Letter to the shareholders, Berkshire Hathaway Annual Report, 1985.

44 Welch with Byrne, p190.

45 *Ibid.*, p190.

46 *Ibid.*, p190.

47 *Ibid.*, p387.

48 Letter to the shareholders, Berkshire Hathaway Annual Report, 1994.

49 Miles, p303.

50 Kilpatrick, p1064.

51 News release, "Berkshire Hathaway Inc. and General Re Corporation to Merge," June 19, 1998, www.berkshirehathaway.com.

52 Alice Schroeder, CIBC Oppenheimer, June 22, 1998.

53 Letter to the shareholders, Berkshire Hathaway Annual Report, 1994.

54 Letter to the shareholders, Berkshire Hathaway Annual Report, 1994.

55 Letter to the shareholders, Berkshire Hathaway Annual Report, 1991.

56 Letter to the shareholders, Berkshire Hathaway Annual Report, 1985.

57 Letter to the shareholders, Berkshire Hathaway Annual Report, 1994.

58 Letter to the shareholders, Berkshire Hathaway Annual Report, 1985.

59 Letter to the shareholders, Berkshire Hathaway Annual Report, 1985.

60 Letter to the shareholders, Berkshire Hathaway Annual Report, 1996.

61 *Berkshire Hathaway Owner's Manual*, 1996.

62 Letter to the shareholders, Berkshire Hathaway Annual Report, 1983.

63 Letter to the shareholders, Berkshire Hathaway Annual Report, 1985.

64 Hersh Shefrin (2000) *Beyond Greed and Fear: Understanding Behavioral Finance and the Psychology of Investing*, Harvard Business School Press, pp24–5.
65 *Ibid.*
66 Letter to the shareholders, Berkshire Hathaway Annual Report, 1994.
67 Letter to the shareholders, Berkshire Hathaway Annual Report, 1990.
68 Richard T. Pascale, Mark Millemann, and Linda Gioje (2000) *Surfing the Edge of Chaos: The New Laws of Nature and the New Laws of Business*, Texere.
69 Letter to the shareholders, Berkshire Hathaway Annual Report, 1995.
70 The principle involved here is articulated in Brune S. Frey and Reto Jegery (2000) "Motivation crowding theory: A survey of empirical evidence," CESifo Working Paper Series no. 245, January.
71 Miles, p111.
72 Letter to Berkshire Shareholders discussing 2001 third quarter earnings results, November 9, 2001.
73 Letter to the shareholders, Berkshire Hathaway Annual Report, 1984.
74 Letter to the shareholders, Berkshire Hathaway Annual Report, 2000.
75 Letter to the shareholders, Berkshire Hathaway Annual Report, 2000.
76 Letter to the shareholders, Berkshire Hathaway Annual Report, 1999.

CHAPTER 4

1 Letter to the shareholders, Berkshire Hathaway Annual Report, 1987.
2 Letter to the shareholders, Berkshire Hathaway Annual Report, 1999.
3 Letter to the shareholders, Berkshire Hathaway Annual Report, 1981.
4 Letter to the shareholders, Berkshire Hathaway Annual Report, 1982.
5 Lowe, *Wit and Wisdom*, p85.
6 Kilpatrick, p1071; *U.S. News & World Report*, June 20, 1994.
7 Letter to the shareholders, Berkshire Hathaway Annual Report, 1982.
8 Kilpatrick, p1069.
9 Letter to the shareholders, Berkshire Hathaway Annual Report, 1987.
10 Memo to Berkshire Hathaway managers ("The All-Stars"), September 26, 2001.
11 Letter to the shareholders, Berkshire Hathaway Annual Report, 1991.
12 Letter to the shareholders, Berkshire Hathaway Annual Report, 1985.
13 Kilpatrick, p1083.
14 Letter to the shareholders, Berkshire Hathaway Annual Report, 1991.
15 Letter to the shareholders, Berkshire Hathaway Annual Report, 1996.
16 Letter to the shareholders, Berkshire Hathaway Annual Report, 1991.
17 Letter to the shareholders, Berkshire Hathaway Annual Report, 2000.
18 Letter to the shareholders, Berkshire Hathaway Annual Report, 1996.
19 Kilpatrick, p287.
20 *Ibid.*, p287.
21 Letter to the shareholders, Berkshire Hathaway Annual Report, 1986.
22 *OID* (2001) vol. XVI, nos 4 & 5, year end edn.
23 *Ibid.*
24 Letter to the shareholders, Berkshire Hathaway Annual Report, 1996.
25 Letter to the shareholders, Berkshire Hathaway Annual Report, 1991.
26 Welch with Byrne, p54.

27 Letter to the shareholders, Berkshire Hathaway Annual Report, 1986.
28 Letter to the shareholders, Berkshire Hathaway Annual Report, 1986.
29 Letter to the shareholders, Berkshire Hathaway Annual Report, 2000.
30 Letter to the shareholders, Berkshire Hathaway Annual Report, 1983.
31 Letter to the shareholders, Berkshire Hathaway Annual Report, 1986.
32 Kilpatrick, p1074.
33 Reported in Ernst Fehr and Klaus M. Schmidt (2000) "Theories of fairness and reciprocity: Evidence and economic applications," CESifo Working Paper Series No. 403; University of Zurich Institute for Empirical Research Working Paper no. 75, December.
34 *Ibid.*
35 Letter to the shareholders, Berkshire Hathaway Annual Report, 1980.
36 Barry Tatelman, Jordan's Furniture, quoted in Miles, p221.
37 Welch with Byrne, p247.
38 Kilpatrick, p499.
39 Letter to the shareholders, Berkshire Hathaway Annual Report, 1991.
40 Letter to the shareholders, Berkshire Hathaway Annual Report, 1988.
41 Letter to the shareholders, Berkshire Hathaway Annual Report, 2000.
42 Richard Brodie (1995) *Virus of the Mind: The New Science of the Meme*, Integral Press, pp88–9.
43 Letter to the shareholders, Berkshire Hathaway Annual Report, 1999.
44 Letter to the shareholders, Berkshire Hathaway Annual Report, 1985.
45 Letter to the shareholders, Berkshire Hathaway Annual Report, 1989.
46 Letter to the shareholders, Berkshire Hathaway Annual Report, 2000.
47 Letter to the shareholders, Berkshire Hathaway Annual Report, 1990.
48 Letter to the shareholders, Berkshire Hathaway Annual Report, 1998.
49 Letter to the shareholders, Berkshire Hathaway Annual Report, 1990.
50 Letter to the shareholders, Berkshire Hathaway Annual Report, 1990.
51 Letter to the shareholders, Berkshire Hathaway Annual Report, 1990.
52 Letter to the shareholders, Berkshire Hathaway Annual Report, 1995.
53 Letter to the shareholders, Berkshire Hathaway Annual Report, 1994.
54 Letter to the shareholders, Berkshire Hathaway Annual Report, 1982.
55 Letter to the shareholders, Berkshire Hathaway Annual Report, 1998.
56 Letter to the shareholders, Berkshire Hathaway Annual Report, 1995.
57 Letter to the shareholders, Berkshire Hathaway Annual Report, 1990.
58 Letter to the shareholders, Berkshire Hathaway Annual Report, 1990.
59 Cialdini, p140.
60 Lowe, *Wit and Wisdom*, pp102–3.
61 Letter to the shareholders, Berkshire Hathaway Annual Report, 1989.
62 Letter to the shareholders, Berkshire Hathaway Annual Report, 1996.
63 Cialdini, pp85–92.
64 Letter to the shareholders, Berkshire Hathaway Annual Report, 1989.
65 Miles, p329.
66 *Ibid.*, p191.
67 Berkshire Hathaway news release, July 2, 2002.
68 Letter to the shareholders, Berkshire Hathaway Annual Report, 1999.
69 Letter to the shareholders, Berkshire Hathaway Annual Report, 1978.
70 Letter to the shareholders, Berkshire Hathaway Annual Report, 1989.
71 Letter to the shareholders, Berkshire Hathaway Annual Report, 1999.

72 Letter to the shareholders, Berkshire Hathaway Annual Report, 1999.
73 Letter to the shareholders, Berkshire Hathaway Annual Report, 1986.
74 *OID* (1998) vol. XIII, nos 3 & 4, September 24.
75 Letter to the shareholders, Berkshire Hathaway Annual Report, 1994.
76 Letter to the shareholders, Berkshire Hathaway Annual Report, 1982.
77 *OID* (1998) vol. XIII, nos 3 & 4, September 24.
78 Letter to the shareholders, Berkshire Hathaway Annual Report, 1982.
79 Stuart Oskamp (1998) "Overconfidence in case-study judgments," in Daniel Kahneman, Paul Slovic, and Amos Tversky (eds), *Judgment under Uncertainty: Heuristics and Biases*, Cambridge University Press, pp287–93.
80 *OID* (1998) vol. XIII, nos 3 & 4, September 24.
81 Letter to the shareholders, Berkshire Hathaway Annual Report, 1982.
82 Letter to the shareholders, Berkshire Hathaway Annual Report, 1997.
83 Letter to the shareholders, Berkshire Hathaway Annual Report, 1982.
84 Letter to the shareholders, Berkshire Hathaway Annual Report, 1982.
85 Cialdini, p244.
86 Miles, p303.
87 Kilpatrick, p1079.
88 Letter to the shareholders, Berkshire Hathaway Annual Report, 2000.
89 Letter to the shareholders, Berkshire Hathaway Annual Report, 2000.
90 Letter to the shareholders, Berkshire Hathaway Annual Report, 2000.
91 Kilpatrick, p1069.
92 Elisabeth Marx (2001) "Shock of the alien can sink a merger," *Financial Times*, April 5.

CHAPTER 5

1 Letter to the shareholders, Berkshire Hathaway Annual Report, 1979.
2 Nigel Nicholson (1998) "How hardwired is human behavior?" *Harvard Business Review*, July–August.
3 Letter to the shareholders, Berkshire Hathaway Annual Report, 1977.
4 1987.
5 Letter to the shareholders, Berkshire Hathaway Annual Report, 1982.
6 Letter to the shareholders, Berkshire Hathaway Annual Report, 1997.
7 Letter to the shareholders, Berkshire Hathaway Annual Report, 1987.
8 Welch with Byrne, p71.
9 Extract from Munger's lecture at the University of Southern California on "Investment expertise as a subdivision of elementary, worldly wisdom," *OID* (1995) vol. X, nos 1 & 2, May 5.
10 Letter to the shareholders, Berkshire Hathaway Annual Report, 1990.
11 Letter to the shareholders, Berkshire Hathaway Annual Report, 1990.
12 Letter to the shareholders, Berkshire Hathaway Annual Report, 1989.
13 Letter to the shareholders, Berkshire Hathaway Annual Report, 1989.
14 Letter to the shareholders, Berkshire Hathaway Annual Report, 1985.
15 1981.
16 Letter to Berkshire Shareholders discussing 2001 third quarter earnings results, November 9, 2001.

17 *Ibid.*
18 Letter to the shareholders, Berkshire Hathaway Annual Report, 1989.
19 Letter to the shareholders, Berkshire Hathaway Annual Report, 1989.
20 Letter to the shareholders, Berkshire Hathaway Annual Report, 1987.
21 Letter to the shareholders, Berkshire Hathaway Annual Report, 1977.
22 *OID* (1998) vol XIII, nos 1 & 2, March 13.
23 Cialdini, p251.
24 *Ibid.*, p262.
25 Principle taken from Pinker, pp393–6.
26 Letter to the shareholders, Berkshire Hathaway Annual Report, 1990.
27 Letter to the shareholders, Berkshire Hathaway Annual Report, 1984.
28 Letter to the shareholders, Berkshire Hathaway Annual Report, 1980.
29 Letter to the shareholders, Berkshire Hathaway Annual Report, 1984.
30 Letter to the shareholders, Berkshire Hathaway Annual Report, 1982.
31 Kilpatrick, p1058.
32 Letter to the shareholders, Berkshire Hathaway Annual Report, 1980.
33 Letter to the shareholders, Berkshire Hathaway Annual Report, 1989.
34 Lowenstein, p72.
35 The Coca-Cola observation is from Lowenstein, p199.
36 Lowenstein, p26, Norma Jean Thrust was the friend; the comment with regard to Mr. Buffett's stocks, p78.
37 *Ibid.*, pp228–9.
38 Letter to the shareholders, Berkshire Hathaway Annual Report, 1979.
39 Letter to the shareholders, Berkshire Hathaway Annual Report, 1979.
40 Lowenstein, p87, reports that when Buffett's wife Susie spent $15,000 on home furnishings he griped to Bill Billig, a golfing friend: "Do you know how much that is if you compound it over twenty years?"
41 Pinker, pp393–6.
42 Lowenstein, p88.
43 Plous, pp248–9.
44 *Ibid.*
45 Letter to the shareholders, Berkshire Hathaway Annual Report, 1984.
46 Kilpatrick, p1064.
47 Letter to the shareholders, Berkshire Hathaway Annual Report, 1998.
48 Letter to the shareholders, Berkshire Hathaway Annual Report, 1980.
49 Michael Jensen and William Meckling (1994) "The nature of man," *Journal of Applied Corporate Finance*, vol. 7, no. 2, Summer, pp4–19 (revd July 1997).
50 Letter to the shareholders, Berkshire Hathaway Annual Report, 1986.
51 Letter to the shareholders, Berkshire Hathaway Annual Report, 1990.
52 Letter to the shareholders, Berkshire Hathaway Annual Report, 1986.
53 Letter to the shareholders, Berkshire Hathaway Annual Report, 1978.
54 *OID* (1998) vol. XIII, nos 1 & 2, March 13.
55 Speech at Miramar Sheraton Hotel, Santa Monica, CA, October 14, 1998, to a meeting of the Foundation of Financial Officers Group, reprinted in *OID* (1998) vol. XIII, no. 7, Patient Subscriber's Edition.
56 Memo to the managers of Berkshire Hathaway, September 26, 2001, www.berskhirehathaway.com.
57 Letter to Berkshire shareholders discussing 2001 third quarter earnings results, November 9, 2001.

58 Cialdini, p257.
59 Letter to the shareholders, Berkshire Hathaway Annual Report, 1984.
60 Letter to the shareholders, Berkshire Hathaway Annual Report, 1985.
61 Letter to the shareholders, Berkshire Hathaway Annual Report, 1985.
62 Letter to the shareholders, Berkshire Hathaway Annual Report, 1985.
63 Lowenstein, pp295–6 (Lowenstein reports $100 million in premium income from this ploy, not the $50 million Buffett reported).
64 Letter to the shareholders, Berkshire Hathaway Annual Report, 1996.
65 Letter to the shareholders, Berkshire Hathaway Annual Report, 1987.

CHAPTER 6

1 *OID* (1998) vol. XIII, nos 1 & 2, March 13.
2 W. James (1890) *The Principles of Psychology* (Vol. 1), Henry Holt, quoted in Carolin Showers, "Self-organization in emotional contexts," in Joseph P. Forgas (ed.) *Feeling and Thinking: The Role of Affect in Social Cognition*, Cambridge University Press, p283.
3 Letter to Berkshire Shareholders discussing 2001 third quarter earnings results, November 9, 2001.
4 *Ibid.*
5 Letter to the shareholders, Berkshire Hathaway Annual Report, 1999.
6 Weston M. Hicks and Christine W. Lai (1998) "General Re and Berkshire Hathaway: In the big leagues," Sanford Bernstein Research, June 26.
7 Letter to the shareholders, Berkshire Hathaway Annual Report, 1982.
8 Letter to the shareholders, Berkshire Hathaway Annual Report, 1982.
9 Letter to the shareholders, Berkshire Hathaway Annual Report, 1982.
10 Berkshire Hathaway Inc. & General Re Corp. Joint Proxy Statement/Prospectus, August 12, 1998.
11 *Ibid.*
12 Gary K. Ransom, Conning & Company, November 22, 1999.
13 Berkshire Hathaway Inc. & General Re Corp. Joint Proxy Statement/Prospectus August 12, 1998.
14 Letter to the shareholders, Berkshire Hathaway Annual Report, 1985.
15 Letter to the shareholders, Berkshire Hathaway Annual Report, 1999.
16 Letter to the shareholders, Berkshire Hathaway Annual Report, 1999.
17 Letter to the shareholders, Berkshire Hathaway Annual Report, 2000.
18 Letter to the shareholders, Berkshire Hathaway Annual Report, 1977.
19 Letter to Berkshire Shareholders discussing 2001 third quarter earnings results, November 9, 2001.
20 *Ibid.*
21 Letter to the shareholders, Berkshire Hathaway Annual Report, 1999.
22 Letter to the shareholders, Berkshire Hathaway Annual Report, 1987.
23 Lowenstein, pp375–9.
24 Welch with Byrne, p225.
25 Letter to the shareholders, Berkshire Hathaway Annual Report, 1990.
26 Letter to the shareholders, Berkshire Hathaway Annual Report, 1984.
27 Letter to the shareholders, Berkshire Hathaway Annual Report, 1980.

28 *OID* (2001) vol. XVI, nos 4 & 5, year end edn.
29 Letter to the shareholders, Berkshire Hathaway Annual Report, 1989.
30 Berkshire Hathaway Inc. & General Re Corp. Joint Proxy Statement/Prospectus August 12, 1998.
31 Letter to the shareholders, Berkshire Hathaway Annual Report, 1997.
32 Letter to the shareholders, Berkshire Hathaway Annual Report, 1998.
33 *Grant's Interest Rate Observer*, vol. 16, no. 15, July 31, 1998, quoting Daniel S. Pecaut, president of Pecaut & Co.
34 Letter to the shareholders, Berkshire Hathaway Annual Report, 2000.
35 Letter to the shareholders, Berkshire Hathaway Annual Report, 2000.
36 Letter to the shareholders, Berkshire Hathaway Annual Report, 1984.
37 *OID* (2001) vol. XVI, nos 4 & 5, year end edn.
38 Letter to the shareholders, Berkshire Hathaway Annual Report, 1987.
39 Letter to the shareholders, Berkshire Hathaway Annual Report, 1987.
40 Welch with Byrne, p126.
41 Lowenstein, p76.
42 *Ibid.*, p216.
43 Letter to the shareholders, Berkshire Hathaway Annual Report, 1987.
44 Carol J. Loomis (2001) "The value machine: Warren Buffett's Berkshire Hathaway is on a buying binge. You were expecting stocks?" *Fortune*, February 19.
45 Letter to the shareholders, Berkshire Hathaway Annual Report, 1977.
46 Letter to the shareholders, Berkshire Hathaway Annual Report, 1978.
47 Miles, pp31–2.
48 Letter to the shareholders, Berkshire Hathaway Annual Report, 1988.
49 *OID* (2000) vol. XV, nos 3 & 4, December 18.
50 Adam Levy (2001) "Where's the fizz?" *Bloomberg Markets*, December, p37.
51 Andrew Hill (2002) "Companies warm to Warren's view," *Financial Times*, July 16.
52 Lowe, *Wit and Wisdom*, p29.
53 Letter to the shareholders, Berkshire Hathaway Annual Report, 1986.

CHAPTER 7

1   Norman Johnson (2000) *What a Developmental View Can Do for You (or The Fall of the House of Experts)*, CSFB Thought Leader Forum.
2   *OID* (1998) vol. XIII, nos 3 & 4, September 24.
3   *OID* (2001) vol. XVI, nos 4 & 5, year end edn.
4   Letter to the shareholders, Berkshire Hathaway Annual Report, 1990.
5   Ed Lamont (1999) "Cherry Coke with the FT: Honcho with a wealth of good fortune," *Financial Times*, May 15.
6   Letter to the shareholders, Berkshire Hathaway Annual Report, 1994.
7   Per Bak (1996) *How Nature Works: The Science of Self-Organized Criticality*, Copernicus, p61.
8   Letter to the shareholders, Berkshire Hathaway Annual Report, 1994.
9   Hagstrom, *The Warren Buffett Portfolio*, pp184–5, makes the same point.
10 Kilpatrick, p1079.
11 *Ibid.*, p1074.
12 Letter to the shareholders, Berkshire Hathaway Annual Report, 1987.

13 *Ibid.*, p1070.

14 Edgar E. Peters (1999) *Patterns in the Dark: Understanding Risk and Financial Crisis with Complexity Theory*, Wiley; concept, not inference, p45.

15 Letter to the shareholders, Berkshire Hathaway Annual Report, 1984.

16 Lowe, *Wit and Wisdom*, p96.

17 Letter to the shareholders, Berkshire Hathaway Annual Report, 1999.

18 Letter to the shareholders, Berkshire Hathaway Annual Report, 1989.

19 *OID* (2001) vol. XVI, nos 4 & 5, year end edn.

20 Speech at Miramar Sheraton Hotel, Santa Monica, CA, October 14, 1998, to a meeting of the Foundation of Financial Officers Group.

21 This school of thought belongs to Baruch Spinoza and is taken from Daniel T. Gilbert, Douglas S. Krull and Patrick S. Malone (1990) "Unbelieving the unbelievable: Some problems in the rejection of false information," *Journal of Personality and Social Psychology*, vol. 59, no. 4, October, pp601–13.

22 *OID* (1998) vol. XIII, nos 1 & 2, March 13.

23 *OID* (1997) vol. XII, no. 3, December 29.

24 *Ibid.*

25 Lowenstein, pp162–3. Lowenstein goes on to say that Munger's "approach to life was to ask what can go wrong. At a high school commencement, Munger gave a sermon not on the qualities that would lead to happiness, but on those that would guarantee a miserable life."

26 *OID* (1998) vol. XIII, nos 1 & 2, March 13.

27 Letter to the shareholders, Berkshire Hathaway Annual Report, 2000.

28 Letter to the shareholders, Berkshire Hathaway Annual Report, 1986.

29 *OID* (2001) vol. XVI, nos 4 & 5, year end edn.

30 Dennis Dittrich, Werner Guth, and Boris Maciejovsky (2001) "Overconfidence in Investment Decision: An Experimental Approach," CESifo Working Papers No. 626, December, www.ssrn.com.

31 Lowe, *Wit and Wisdom*, pp116, 119.

32 Letter to the shareholders, Berkshire Hathaway Annual Report, 1992.

33 Letter to the shareholders, Berkshire Hathaway Annual Report, 1988.

34 Letter to the shareholders, Berkshire Hathaway Annual Report, 1992.

35 2000. In this quote Buffett is extemporizing on his observation that the equation for value is, in fact, over 2,600 years old and can be attributed to Aesop and "his enduring, though somewhat incomplete, investment insight was 'a bird in the hand is worth two in the bush.'"

36 Letter to the shareholders, Berkshire Hathaway Annual Report, 1993.

37 Peters, p166.

38 Hagstrom, *The Warren Buffett Portfolio*, p124, makes a similar point: "With over a hundred years of investment performance data available, Coca-Cola had something very close to a frequency distribution to analyze."

39 Letter to the shareholders, Berkshire Hathaway Annual Report, 1996.

40 Letter to the shareholders, Berkshire Hathaway Annual Report, 1996.

41 Letter to the shareholders, Berkshire Hathaway Annual Report, 1987.

42 *OID* (2001) vol. XVI, nos 2&3, December 24.

43 Letter to the shareholders, Berkshire Hathaway Annual Report, 1997.

44 See Hagstrom, *The Warren Buffett Portfolio*, for an insight into Buffett's facility with numbers.

45 Letter to the shareholders, Berkshire Hathaway Annual Report, 1993.

46 Kilpatrick, pp1066, 1070.
47 *OID* (1998) vol. XIII, nos 3 & 4, September 24.
48 Letter to the shareholders, Berkshire Hathaway Annual Report, 1999.
49 Letter to the shareholders, Berkshire Hathaway Annual Report, 1998.
50 *OID* (1995) vol. X, nos 1 & 2, May 5.
51 Letter to the shareholders, Berkshire Hathaway Annual Report, 1993.
52 *OID* (2001) vol. XVI, nos 4 & 5, year end edn.
53 *Ibid.*
54 Letter to the shareholders, Berkshire Hathaway Annual Report, 1997.
55 Letter to the shareholders, Berkshire Hathaway Annual Report, 1997.
56 Letter to the shareholders, Berkshire Hathaway Annual Report, 1984.
57 Letter to the shareholders, Berkshire Hathaway Annual Report, 1984.
58 Letter to the shareholders, Berkshire Hathaway Annual Report, 1986.
59 Letter to the shareholders, Berkshire Hathaway Annual Report, 1984.
60 George Lowenstein, Elke Weber, Christopher H. See, and Edward Welch (2001) "Risk as feelings," *Psychological Bulletin*, no. 127, pp267–86.
61 Letter to the shareholders, Berkshire Hathaway Annual Report, 2000.
62 Reported in Joseph LeDoux (1998) *The Emotional Brain: The Mysterious Underpinnings of Emotional Life*, Touchstone, pp232–3.
63 Lowe, *Wit and Wisdom*, p116.
64 Lowenstein *et al.*
65 Forgas, p4.
66 Lowenstein *et al.*
67 *Ibid.*
68 Kilpatrick, p1064.
69 Lowenstein *et al.*
70 Lowenstein, p230 and Kilpatrick, p1081.
71 Lowe, *Wit and Wisdom*, p30.
72 Denis J. Hilton (2001) "The psychology of financial decision-making: Applications to trading, dealing, and investment analysis," *Journal of Psychology and Financial Markets*, vol. 2, no. 1, pp37–53.
73 Letter to the shareholders, Berkshire Hathaway Annual Report, 1996.
74 *OID* (2001) vol. XVI, nos 4 & 5, year end edn.
75 Letter to the shareholders, Berkshire Hathaway Annual Report, 1990.
76 Letter to the shareholders, Berkshire Hathaway Annual Report, 1990.
77 Letter to Berkshire shareholders discussing 2001 third quarter earnings results, November 9, 2001.
78 Hagstrom, *The Warren Buffett Portfolio*, p89.
79 Letter to the shareholders, Berkshire Hathaway Annual Report, 1983.
80 *OID* (1998) vol. XIII, nos 1 & 2, March 13.
81 Kilpatrick, p1060.
82 Letter to the shareholders, Berkshire Hathaway Annual Report, 1987.
83 Letter to the shareholders, Berkshire Hathaway Annual Report, 1989.
84 Letter to the shareholders, Berkshire Hathaway Annual Report, 1989.
85 Letter to the shareholders, Berkshire Hathaway Annual Report, 1989.
86 Letter to the shareholders, Berkshire Hathaway Annual Report, 1992.
87 Letter to the shareholders, Berkshire Hathaway Annual Report, 2000.
88 Bernstein, p5.
89 Miles, p247.

CHAPTER 8

1 Letter to the shareholders, Berkshire Hathaway Annual Report, 1994.
2 Letter to the shareholders, Berkshire Hathaway Annual Report, 1984.
3 Kilpatrick, p1068.
4 *OID* (2001) vol. XVI, nos 4 & 5, year end edn.
5 Quoted in John Mayo, deputy chief executive of Marconi (2002) "Exploding some Marconi myths," *Financial Times*, January 18.
6 Letter to the shareholders, Berkshire Hathaway Annual Report, 1982.
7 Letter to the shareholders, Berkshire Hathaway Annual Report, 1982.
8 David Schkade, Cass Sunstein, and Daniel Kahneman, "Deliberating about dollars: The severity shift," John M. Olin Law & Economics Working Paper No. 95 (2nd Series).
9 Letter to the shareholders, Berkshire Hathaway Annual Report, 1984.
10 *OID* (2001) vol. XVI, nos 4 & 5, year end edn.
11 Lowe, *Wit and Wisdom*, p119.
12 Re the following discourse, Fuller and Jensen make essentially the same point; see Joseph Fuller and Michael C. Jensen, "Just say no to Wall Street," Amos Tuck School of Business at Dartmouth College, Working Paper no. 02-01; and Negotiation, Organization and Markets Unit, Harvard Business School, Working Paper no. 02-01, www.ssrn.com.
13 Letter to the shareholders, Berkshire Hathaway Annual Report, 1988.
14 Letter to the shareholders, Berkshire Hathaway Annual Report, 1985.
15 Letter to the shareholders, Berkshire Hathaway Annual Report, 2000.
16 Letter to the shareholders, Berkshire Hathaway Annual Report, 1998.
17 Letter to the shareholders, Berkshire Hathaway Annual Report, 2000.
18 Letter to the shareholders, Berkshire Hathaway Annual Report, 1979.
19 Letter to the shareholders, Berkshire Hathaway Annual Report, 1979.
20 Letter to the shareholders, Berkshire Hathaway Annual Report, 1988.
21 Letter to the shareholders, Berkshire Hathaway Annual Report, 1983.
22 Letter to the shareholders, Berkshire Hathaway Annual Report, 1998.
23 Letter to the shareholders, Berkshire Hathaway Annual Report, 1998.
24 Letter to the shareholders, Berkshire Hathaway Annual Report, 1998.
25 Letter to the shareholders, Berkshire Hathaway Annual Report, 2000.
26 Buffett also illustrates the mistake of anchoring using the following from *Fortune*: "Several times every year a weighty and serious investor looks long and with profound respect at Coca-Cola's record, but comes regretfully to the conclusion that he is looking too late. The specters of saturation and competition rise before him." But Buffett delights in pointing out that this article was written in 1938. "It's worth noting," he continues, "that in 1938 The Coca-Cola Co. sold 207 million cases of soft drinks... and in 1993 it sold about 10.7 billion cases, a 50-fold increase in physical volume from a company that in 1938 was already dominant in its very major industry. Nor was the party over in 1938 for an investor: Though the $40 invested in 1919 in one share had (with dividends reinvested) turned into $3,277 by the end of 1938, a fresh $40 then invested in Coca-Cola stock would have grown to $25,000 by yearend 1993."
27 *OID* (2001) vol. XVI, nos 2 & 3, December 24.
28 Letter to the shareholders, Berkshire Hathaway Annual Report, 1996.

29 Letter to the shareholders, Berkshire Hathaway Annual Report, 1985.

30 Letter to the shareholders, Berkshire Hathaway Annual Report, 1983.

31 Letter to the shareholders, Berkshire Hathaway Annual Report, 1984.

32 *OID* (2000) vol. XV, nos 3 & 4, December 18.

33 Letter to the shareholders, Berkshire Hathaway Annual Report, 1986.

34 Letter to the shareholders, Berkshire Hathaway Annual Report, 1984.

35 *OID* (2000) vol. XV, nos 3 & 4, December 18.

36 Letter to the shareholders, Berkshire Hathaway Annual Report, 1998.

37 Letter to the shareholders, Berkshire Hathaway Annual Report, 1987.

38 Letter to the shareholders, Berkshire Hathaway Annual Report, 1987.

39 *OID* (2001) vol. XVI, nos 4 & 5, year end edn.

40 Letter to the shareholders, Berkshire Hathaway Annual Report, 1987.

41 Letter to the shareholders, Berkshire Hathaway Annual Report, 1990.

42 Letter to the shareholders, Berkshire Hathaway Annual Report, 1987.

43 *OID* (2001) vol. XVI, nos 4 & 5, year end edn.

44 *Ibid*.

45 Letter to the shareholders, Berkshire Hathaway Annual Report, 1985.

46 Letter to the shareholders, Berkshire Hathaway Annual Report, 1985.

47 *OID* (2000) vol XV, nos 3 & 4, December 18.

48 Letter to the shareholders, Berkshire Hathaway Annual Report, 1985.

49 Letter to the shareholders, Berkshire Hathaway Annual Report, 2000.

50 Letter to the shareholders, Berkshire Hathaway Annual Report, 1980.

51 Letter to the shareholders, Berkshire Hathaway Annual Report, 1987.

52 *OID* (1995) vol. X, nos 1 & 2, May 5.

53 Letter to the shareholders, Berkshire Hathaway Annual Report, 2001.

54 Letter to the shareholders, Berkshire Hathaway Annual Report, 1983.

55 Letter to the shareholders, Berkshire Hathaway Annual Report, 2000.

56 Letter to the shareholders, Berkshire Hathaway Annual Report, 1986.

57 Letter to the shareholders, Berkshire Hathaway Annual Report, 1990.

58 Letter to the shareholders, Berkshire Hathaway Annual Report, 1998.

59 Letter to the shareholders, Berkshire Hathaway Annual Report, 1998.

60 Letter to the shareholders, Berkshire Hathaway Annual Report, 1998.

61 Lowe, p111.

62 Letter to the shareholders, Berkshire Hathaway Annual Report, 1987.

63 Letter to the shareholders, Berkshire Hathaway Annual Report, 1987.

64 Berkshire Hathaway Inc. news release, "Berkshire Hathaway issues first ever negative coupon security," May 22, 2002, www.berkshirehathaway.com.

65 *Ibid*.

66 Letter to the shareholders, Berkshire Hathaway Annual Report, 1987.

67 Letter to the shareholders, Berkshire Hathaway Annual Report, 1987.

68 Letter to the shareholders, Berkshire Hathaway Annual Report, 1994.

69 Letter to the shareholders, Berkshire Hathaway Annual Report, 1979.

70 Letter to the shareholders, Berkshire Hathaway Annual Report, 1983.

71 Letter to the shareholders, Berkshire Hathaway Annual Report, 1988.

72 Letter to the shareholders, Berkshire Hathaway Annual Report, 1983.

73 Letter to the shareholders, Berkshire Hathaway Annual Report, 1988.

74 Letter to the shareholders, Berkshire Hathaway Annual Report, 1988.

75 Letter to the shareholders, Berkshire Hathaway Annual Report, 1988.

76 Letter to the shareholders, Berkshire Hathaway Annual Report, 1983.

77 Letter to the shareholders, Berkshire Hathaway Annual Report, 1988.
78 Letter to the shareholders, Berkshire Hathaway Annual Report, 1986.
79 Letter to the shareholders, Berkshire Hathaway Annual Report, 1998.
80 Letter to the shareholders, Berkshire Hathaway Annual Report, 1998.
81 Letter to the shareholders, Berkshire Hathaway Annual Report, 1977.
82 Letter to the shareholders, Berkshire Hathaway Annual Report, 1985.
83 Letter to the shareholders, Berkshire Hathaway Annual Report, 1982.
84 Letter to the shareholders, Berkshire Hathaway Annual Report, 1984.
85 Letter to the shareholders, Berkshire Hathaway Annual Report, 1985.
86 Berkshire's price fall measured from intraday high to intraday low.
87 Letter to the shareholders, Berkshire Hathaway Annual Report, 1999.
88 Andrew Hill (2000) "Buffett deserves D grade," *Financial Times*, March 13.
89 Letter to the shareholders, Berkshire Hathaway Annual Report, 1996.
90 *OID* (2001) vol. XVI, nos 4 & 5, year end edn.
91 *OID* (1997) vol. XII, no. 3, December 29.

CHAPTER 9

1 *OID* (1995) vol. X, nos 1 & 2, May 5.
2 Lowe, p22.
3 Letter to the shareholders, Berkshire Hathaway Annual Report, 1985.
4 Letter to the shareholders, Berkshire Hathaway Annual Report, 1984.
5 Letter to the shareholders, Berkshire Hathaway Annual Report, 1984.
6 Letter to the shareholders, Berkshire Hathaway Annual Report, 1984.
7 Lowenstein, p132.
8 Letter to the shareholders, Berkshire Hathaway Annual Report, 1989.
9 Letter to the shareholders, Berkshire Hathaway Annual Report, 1983.
10 *OID* (1995) vol. X, nos 1 & 2, May 5.
11 Letter to the shareholders, Berkshire Hathaway Annual Report, 1999.
12 Letter to the shareholders, Berkshire Hathaway Annual Report, 1985.
13 Kilpatrick, p1062.
14 Bryan Jones (2001) *Politics and the Architecture of Choice: Bounded Rationality and Governance*, University of Chicago Press.
15 *OID* (1995) vol. X, nos 1 & 2, May 5.
16 *OID* (1998) vol. XIII, nos 3 & 4, September 24.
17 *OID* (1998) vol. XIII, nos 1 & 2, March 13.
18 Letter to the shareholders, Berkshire Hathaway Annual Report, 1991.
19 Baruch Fischoff (1998) "For those condemned to study the past: Heuristics and biases in hindsight," in Daniel Kahneman, Paul Slovic, and Amos Tversky, *Judgment under Uncertainty: Heuristics and Biases*, Cambridge University Press, pp335–54.
20 Plous, pp32–3.
21 Richard A. Crowell, Vice Chairman (1994) "Cognitive bias and quantitative investment management," PanAgora Asset Management, Inc., December.
22 Fischoff.
23 Letter to the shareholders, Berkshire Hathaway Annual Report, 1993.
24 Letter to the shareholders, Berkshire Hathaway Annual Report, 1993.
25 Carol Loomis (2001) "Warren Buffett," *Fortune*, December 10.

26 *OID* (1997) vol. XII, no. 3, December 29.

27 Extracts from Munger's lecture at the University of Southern California on "Investment expertise as a subdivision of elementary, worldly wisdom," *OID* (1995) vol. X, nos 1 & 2, May 5.

28 Loomis.

29 Letter to the shareholders, Berkshire Hathaway Annual Report, 2000.

30 Hillel J. Einhorn (1998) "Learning from experience and suboptimal rules in decision making," in Daniel Kahneman, Paul Slovic, and Amos Tversky (eds), *Judgment under Uncertainty: Heuristics and Biases*, Cambridge University Press, pp268–86.

31 *OID* (1990) vol. V, no. 3, April 18.

32 Letter to the shareholders, Berkshire Hathaway Annual Report, 1984.

33 Plous, pp25–30.

34 Lowe, *Wit and Wisdom*, p119.

35 Letter to the shareholders, Berkshire Hathaway Annual Report, 1999.

36 *OID* (1998) vol. XIII, nos 3 & 4, September 24.

37 Letter to the shareholders, Berkshire Hathaway Annual Report, 2000.

38 Letter to the shareholders, Berkshire Hathaway Annual Report, 1999.

39 *OID* (1998) vol. XIII, nos 1 & 2, March 13.

40 Letter to the shareholders, Berkshire Hathaway Annual Report, 2000.

41 *OID* (1998) vol. XIII, nos 3 & 4, September 24.

42 Letter to the shareholders, Berkshire Hathaway Annual Report, 1992.

43 Letter to the shareholders, Berkshire Hathaway Annual Report, 1992.

44 Letter to the shareholders, Berkshire Hathaway Annual Report, 1992.

45 Robert Wright (1997) *The Moral Animal: Evolutionary Psychology and Everyday Life*, Vintage.

46 Letter to the shareholders, Berkshire Hathaway Annual Report, 1986.

47 Letter to the shareholders, Berkshire Hathaway Annual Report, 1985.

48 Letter to the shareholders, Berkshire Hathaway Annual Report, 1989.

49 Letter to the shareholders, Berkshire Hathaway Annual Report, 1985.

50 Letter to the shareholders, Berkshire Hathaway Annual Report, 1993.

51 *OID* (1995) vol. X, nos 1 & 2, May 5.

52 Ian Hacking (1984) *The Emergence of Probability*, Cambridge University Press, p1.

53 *Ibid.*

54 Robert Hagstrom (1999) *The Warren Buffett Portfolio: Mastering the Power of the Focus Investment Strategy*, Wiley, pp115–19.

55 Pinker, pp345–6.

56 Letter to the shareholders, Berkshire Hathaway Annual Report, 1990.

57 Letter to the shareholders, Berkshire Hathaway Annual Report, 1992.

58 Letter to the shareholders, Berkshire Hathaway Annual Report, 1995.

59 Letter to the shareholders, Berkshire Hathaway Annual Report, 1999.

60 Miles, p76.

61 *Ibid.*, p76.

62 Letter to the shareholders, Berkshire Hathaway Annual Report, 1989.

63 Letter to the shareholders, Berkshire Hathaway Annual Report, 2000.

64 *Grant's Interest Rate Observer* (2001) vol. 19, no. 15, August 3, p2.

65 Letter to the shareholders, Berkshire Hathaway Annual Report, 1993.

66 Letter to the shareholders, Berkshire Hathaway Annual Report, 1993.

67 Letter to the shareholders, Berkshire Hathaway Annual Report, 1985.

68 Lowe, *Wit and Wisdom*, p119.

69 Letter to the shareholders, Berkshire Hathaway Annual Report, 1987.
70 Letter to the shareholders, Berkshire Hathaway Annual Report, 1985.
71 Lowe, *Wit and Wisdom*, p97.
72 Cialdini, p213.
73 Hilton.
74 Letter to the shareholders, Berkshire Hathaway Annual Report, 1987.
75 Lowenstein *et al*.
76 Lowe, *Wit and Wisdom*, p106.
77 Letter to the shareholders, Berkshire Hathaway Annual Report, 1987.
78 Letter to the shareholders, Berkshire Hathaway Annual Report, 2000.
79 Letter to the shareholders, Berkshire Hathaway Annual Report, 1987.
80 Warren E. Buffett (2002) "Who really cooks the books?", *New York Times*, July 25.
81 Letter to the shareholders, Berkshire Hathaway Annual Report, 2000.
82 See Patricia Dechow and Douglas Skinner (2000) "Earnings management: Reconciling the view of accounting academics, practitioners, and regulators," February, www.ssrn.com, for a discussion of this issue.
83 Jeffrey Abarbanell and Reuven LeHavey (1999) "Can stock recommendations predict earnings management and analysts' earning forecast errors?," May, www.ssrn.com.
84 Letter to the shareholders, Berkshire Hathaway Annual Report, 2000.
85 This observation was inspired by John Kay, *Financial Times* columnist and a guest speaker at Merrill Lynch's "Corporate Finance versus Corporate Strategy: What Creates Shareholder Value?," Merrill Lynch Global, 20 May, 2002.
86 This is not to suggest that this is what happened at Gillette.
87 Letter to the shareholders, Berkshire Hathaway Annual Report, 1998.
88 *OID* (2000) vol. XV, nos 3 & 4, December 18.
89 Letter to the shareholders, Berkshire Hathaway Annual Report, 1996.
90 Lowe, p107.
91 Letter to the shareholders, Berkshire Hathaway Annual Report, 1985.
92 Shivaram Rajgopal and Terry J. Sherlin (2001) "Empirical evidence on the relation between stock option compensation and risk taking," October, www.ssrn.com.
93 Letter to the shareholders, Berkshire Hathaway Annual Report, 1981.
94 Letter to the shareholders, Berkshire Hathaway Annual Report, 1983.
95 Letter to the shareholders, Berkshire Hathaway Annual Report, 1994.
96 Letter to the shareholders, Berkshire Hathaway Annual Report, 1987.
97 *OID* (2001) vol. XVI, nos 4 & 5, year end edn.
98 Letter to the shareholders, Berkshire Hathaway Annual Report, 1993.
99 Letter to the shareholders, Berkshire Hathaway Annual Report, 1993.
100 Stephen M. Bainbridge (2001) "Why a Board? Group Decisionmaking in Corporate Governance," UCLA School of Law Research Paper no. 01-3, April; (2002) *Vanderbilt Law Review*, vol. 55, pp1–55.
101 Letter to the shareholders, Berkshire Hathaway Annual Report, 1994.

CHAPTER 10

1 Letter to the shareholders, Berkshire Hathaway Annual Report, 2002.
2 Kilpatrick, p1060; annual meeting 1988.

3 Letter to the shareholders, Berkshire Hathaway Annual Report, 2002.
4 Letter to the shareholders, Berkshire Hathaway Annual Report, 1995.
5 Letter to the shareholders, Berkshire Hathaway Annual Report, 2002.
6 Warren E. Buffett (2003) "America's growing deficit is selling the nation out from under us. Here's a way to fix the problem—And we need to do it now," *Fortune*, October 26.
7 *Ibid.*
8 *Ibid.*
9 *Ibid.*
10 Letter to the shareholders, Berkshire Hathaway Annual Report, 2002.
11 Letter to the partners of The Buffett Partnership, first half, 1966.
12 Letter to the shareholders, Berkshire Hathaway Annual Report, 1993.
13 Devon Spurgeon (2000) "Irreplaceable CEO plans to replace himself with a trio," *Wall Street Journal*, October 17.
14 *Ibid.*
15 Miles, p358.
16 Cialdini, pp82–3 and 85.
17 Letter to the shareholders, Berkshire Hathaway Annual Report, 1984.
18 Letter to the shareholders, Berkshire Hathaway Annual Report, 1989.
19 Kilpatrick, p1073.
20 Bernstein.
21 Hacking, p3.
22 Kilpatrick, p1084.

Index